The Economy as Cultural System

AF663669

The Economy as Cultural System

Theory, Capitalism, Crisis

EDITED BY

TODD DUFRESNE AND CLARA SACCHETTI

BLOOMSBURY

NEW DELHI • LONDON • OXFORD • NEW YORK • SYDNEY

First published in India 2017
First published 2013

© Todd Dufresne and Clara Sacchetti, 2013

Bloomsbury Academic
An imprint of Bloomsbury Publishing Plc
Bloomsbury is a registered trade mark of Bloomsbury Publishing Plc

All rights reserved. No part of this publication may be reproduced or transmitted in any form or by any means, electronic or mechanical, including photocopying, recording, or any information storage or retrieval system, without prior permission in writing from the publishers.

No responsibility for loss caused to any individual or organization acting on or refraining from action as a result of the material in this publication can be accepted by Bloomsbury Academic or the author.

This title published with permission from Bloomsbury Publishing Plc
50 Bedford Square, London, WC1B3DP, UK

Library of Congress Cataloging-in-Publication Data
The economy as cultural system : theory, capitalism, crisis / edited
by Todd Dufresne and Clara Sacchetti.-- 1st ed.
p. cm.
Includes bibliographical references and index.
ISBN 978-1-4411-4003-6 (pbk. : alk. paper)-- ISBN 978-1-4411-7037-8 (hardcover : alk. paper) 1. Capitalism--Social aspects--History--21st century. 2. Global Financial Crisis, 2008- 2009. 3. Economic development. I. Dufresne, Todd, 1966- II. Sacchetti, Clara.
HB501.E286 2012 306.3--dc23

2012025717

ISBN: 978 93 86606 82 2
10 9 8 7 6 5 4 3 2 1
For sale in the Indian subcontinent only

Bloomsbury Publishing India Pvt. Ltd
Second Floor, Building No. 4
DDA Complex LSC, Pocket C – 6 & 7
Vasant Kunj, New Delhi 110070
www.bloomsbury.com

Typeset by Fakenham Prepress Solutions, Fakenham, Norfolk NR21 8NN
Printed and bound in India

Contents

Acknowledgements

We want to thank the contributors to this volume of essays for their intelligence, good sense, and patience, which has made this project a pleasure. Special thanks is owed to Mark Nisenholt for allowing us to use his fabulous drawing for the cover. And, finally, our gratitude to Chris Wood, for editorial assistance, and to the editors at Continuum, most especially Marie-Claire Antoine, who guided us with professionalism and wisdom.

The book was conceived in early 2010, but took its final and decisive shape while we were in Toronto in 2011–12. Dufresne would like to recognize his colleagues and administrative home during this period, The History and Philosophy of Science and Technology at the University of Toronto, where he was a Visiting Professor. Sacchetti would like to recognize the support she received as a Postdoctoral Fellow at the Frank Iacobucci Centre for Italian Canadian Studies at the University of Toronto. Special thanks goes out to Dr. Salvatore Bancheri for his encouragement and sage advice.

This book we dedicate to Chloe, in the hope for a better, kinder, more just tomorrow.

Contributors

Franco Berardi is a Marxist theorist and media-activist who played an important role in the Italian Autonomist movement. He is the author of numerous books, including *The Soul at Work: From Alienation to Autonomy* (Semiotexte 2009b), and *Precarious Rhapsody: Semio-Capitalism and the Pathologies of the Post-Alpha Generation* (Autonomedia 2009a). He presently teaches media history at the Accademia di Brera, Milan.

Todd Dufresne, Professor of Philosophy at Lakehead University, is the author and editor of numerous books, including *Tales from the Freudian Crypt* (Stanford UP), *Killing Freud* (Continuum), *Against Freud* (Stanford UP), and *Beyond the Pleasure Principle* (Broadview). He has been Associated Scholar and Visiting Professor at the History and Philosophy of Science and Technology at the University of Toronto.

Joel Faflak is Associate Professor in Theory and Literature in the Department of English and core member of the Centre for the Study of Theory and Criticism at Western University. Among his many books are *Romantic Psychoanalysis* (SUNY), *Revelation and Knowledge* (University of Toronto Press), an edition of Thomas De Quincey's *Confessions of an English Opium-Eater* (Broadview), and ten edited collections and journal issues. He is currently writing two books on the psychopathology of happiness: one on the American film musical and the other on the rise of psychiatry in late eighteenth-century Romantic culture. He is on the executive of the North American Society for the Study of Romanticism and has lectured widely in North America and Europe.

Max Haiven is a Postdoctoral Fellow in the department of Art and Public Policy at New York University, and an Adjunct Professor of material cultural studies at the Nova Scotia College of Art and Design. Haiven's work on the radical imagination has appeared in *Cultural Critique*, *Affinities*, and *The Review of Education, Pedagogy, and Cultural Studies*. His work on finance has appeared in *Social Text*, *Cultural Studies*, and *Cultural Logic*.

Tim Kaposy is Assistant Professor of Cultural Studies at George Mason University, where he teaches critical theory, theories of globalization, and histories of visual culture. He is co-editor of *Cultural Theory: An Anthology* (Wiley-Blackwell), and author of two forthcoming books: *Documentary in the Age of Global Capitalism* (University of Toronto Press), and *Canada's Quiet Counter-Revolution* (University of Toronto Press).

Thomas M. Kemple is Associate Professor of Sociology at the University of British Columbia, where he teaches and writes on the intersections of classical and contemporary social theory. In addition to *Reading Marx Writing* (Stanford UP), his work has appeared in *Theory, Culture & Society, Journal of Classical Sociology, Telos,* and *Marxism Today*.

Mark Kingwell, Professor of Philosophy at the University of Toronto, is the author of fifteen books in political, cultural, and aesthetic theory, including *A Civil Tongue: Justice, Dialogue, and the Politics of Pluralism* (Penn State UP), *Nearest Thing to Heaven: The Empire State Building and American Dreams* (Yale UP), and *Concrete Reveries: Consciousness and the City* (Viking). He has held visiting posts at Clare Hall, Cambridge, the University of California at Berkeley, and Baruch College, City University of New York, where he was Weismann Distinguished Visiting Professor.

Matthew MacLellan is a PhD candidate in the Department of English and Film Studies at the University of Alberta. His doctoral research examines the shifting morphology of "culture" and "economy" in contemporary discourses on post-industrialism. His work has appeared in *Politics and Culture, The John Hopkins Guide to Literary Theory and Criticism, Reviews in Cultural Theory, Mediations*, and is forthcoming in *Rethinking Marxism*.

Andrew Pendakis is a Postdoctoral Fellow of Contemporary Culture at the University of Alberta. His work has appeared or is forthcoming in *Cultural Studies—Critical Methodologies, Imaginations, Politics and Culture, Essays in Canadian Writing*, and *Mediations*. He is also a contributor to upcoming books on Adorno (Polity Press) and Canadian Cultural Studies (Oxford UP). He is the co-editor of *Contemporary Marxist Theory: An Anthology* (Continuum).

Kezia Picard is a Postdoctoral Fellow at The Advanced Institute for Globalization and Culture at Lakehead University, where she is preparing a monograph on power and environmentalism. She received her PhD in Critical Theory from the University of Nottingham, and teaches philosophy and cultural studies at

Lakehead University. Picard is the co-editor of *Superior Art: Local Art, Global Context* (Definitely Superior Gallery).

Clara Sacchetti is a Postdoctoral Fellow at the Frank Iacobucci Centre for Italian Canadian Studies at the University of Toronto. She received her doctorate in Social Anthropology from York University, where she investigated the discursive and ambivalent nature of Italian-Canadian identity. Sacchetti's work has appeared in *Renegade Bodies* (DCD Press/es), *Italian Canadiana, Migration Letters*, the *Semiotic Review of Books*, and the *Boston Book Review*. She is also the co-editor of *Superior Art: Local Art, Global Context* (Definitely Superior Gallery).

Justin Sully is a Research Fellow in Film and New Media in the University of Alberta's New Media and Visual Culture Research Studio. He completed his PhD in 2011 at McMaster University, with a dissertation on the recent cultural history of population crisis and its mediation through film and visual media. He is the author of recent and forthcoming essays in *Criticism* and *The Johns Hopkins Guide to Literary Theory and Criticism*. He is co-editor of the journal *Reviews in Cultural Theory*.

Preface

Todd Dufresne

Organizing and editing a book is not unlike other forms of entrepreneurial activity. One gathers together academic laborers who contribute expertise, time, and faith in a joint product, a manuscript, that is carefully packaged in a prospectus, which, like a business plan, may convince the right investor, a publisher, to make a calculated bet that it will appeal to libraries, students, and scholars. And so the product is massaged, i.e. subject to a regime of editing and production, marketing and distribution, and delivered to stores. Consumers deliver their verdict, and the book is possibly bought and reviewed, adopted in classrooms and libraries, and debated and cited by scholars. Both the academics and the publisher hope the investment pays off.

True, academics will insist that they rarely do it for the money. Which is fair enough. But academics are still caught up in an economy and are likely to exchange the book for fungible profits that are entirely self-interested. Publishing is not just about satisfaction, prestige, and bragging rights, but about enhanced job prospects, tenure, promotion, merit pay, sabbatical leaves, and, more simply, evidence of research productivity that employers expect. In short, even a book that excoriates capitalism is a part of that economy, and so complicit with it.

Books, like other products, are also subject to the vagaries of fashion and consumer desire. Expectations about length and design change over time, and so too do intellectual styles and ideas. The late 1970s and 1980s were golden years for what was called "high theory," a time when the very best academics produced philosophically sophisticated works about the foundations of knowledge. Things changed in the late 1990s and in the new century. Fashions are reactive; moreover, one chaffs, as Thomas Kuhn (1962) has it, at the increasingly limited room for new insights (and consequently job prospects, tenure, promotion, etc.) within the old paradigm. Hence the rise of "practical" scholarship, which in the extreme is modeled on "participatory action research": one not only walks away from abstract theorizing, but one engages concretely in a community activism where the book becomes (in the ideal) a product of community values and authors. And so the "French genius" has been superseded by social science group-think, just as the book has been superseded by the multi-authored "report."

Of course, the slow shift away from theory to practical, measurable, "real world" outcomes has gone hand in glove with the rise of neoliberalism—even in the university, where everyone is nowadays busy rationalizing efficiencies, quantifying values, measuring outputs, and maximizing utility. It is therefore no longer good enough that academics publish, and so engage in a form of entrepreneurial activity within capitalism. It is rather required (or at least strongly encouraged) that they work collaboratively in groups to achieve the sometimes laughable strategic goals and mission statements of their home universities; work toward measurable and above all socially justified outcomes; "translate" their results in mass publications like newspapers and magazines; and appear in marketing schemes that help sell academe to the masses.

Every thinking person knows that this shift has come at a very high cost to knowledge and what we mean by "academe." One glaring consequence: the humanities have been reduced to a medieval function of preserving the light of philosophy and theory in an age of incredibly uninformed practical research. Today, graduate students are schooled to be willfully ignorant of epistemological questions about the limits of knowledge ("What is the point of that?"); at best, major theorists are acknowledged at the safe remove of a secondary or tertiary source from within their own narrow field ("theory in action"). Ultimately what was once "knowledge transfer" for the benefit of the masses is now spoon-fed to students themselves—who are graduated as quickly as possible to become the next generation of clueless researchers and professors. As a consequence, seemingly practical, pragmatic, socially relevant books are published that presume theoretical foundations that they could not begin to fathom, let alone engage with in an informed and productive way. Instead one churns out one's "findings," at times based on a naïve form of personal experience, and plots the next big multi-authored grant. Neo-positivism is reborn.

The Economy as Cultural System is a return to conjecture, speculation, and interpretation—to *analysis* and *critique*—and as such inaugurates a return to fundamental theoretical questions, not just about "late capitalism" today, but about what it means to think about "the economy" in the context of an academic culture that is complicit with neoliberalism—a big business too often run by functionaries, not visionaries, and stripped of its former glory as a preserve for curiosity-based research and informed debate and criticism about eternal, fundamental questions. This collection is a return, in short, to the theoretical questions that motivate divergence, resistance, hope, thought, chance, freedom, and play.

Arguably, things are different now that capitalism is in such a deep and abiding crisis. It seems timely that we return to issues of foundational significance. And if the results are not subject to the banal regime of measurable outcomes, that doesn't mean they lack calculation and are worthless. On the contrary. Our goal has been to open a space for authors to put the economy to the test of social and cultural theory—and to remind us all, not incidentally, that informed cross-disciplinary scholarship in the arts still has something to teach us about the role of capitalism in our "real," everyday lives. The benefits of this open approach are irreducible, incalculable, but not for all of that incomprehensible. These ten contributions pose questions and at times risk answers, which is the gamble of investments that think capitalism always otherwise. It is what we used to call a good "in and of itself," quite apart from its effects in the "real world." I hope it catches on. And, yes, I hope it sells.

Todd Dufresne
Toronto 2012

Introduction

The economy as cultural system: Theory, capitalism, crisis

Clara Sacchetti

It is difficult to go about our everyday lives without giving serious thought to the way in which we meet our material needs. On a very basic level, human beings require sufficient food, shelter, and a safe social environment in order to subsist. In the few years since the 2008 financial crisis, concerns over basic survival requirements are everywhere discussed, as international agencies, news media, think tanks, and researchers regularly announce that the world economy is still on shaky ground. The United Nations' 2012 World Economic Situation and Prospects (WESP) Report[1] claims, for example, that we are on the cusp of another meltdown. It cites high unemployment, low wage growth, prolonged depressed housing prices, major government and household debt, and a lack of solutions on the part of policymakers to address unemployment and better regulate the financial sector in the developed world. At the same time, the WESP Report claims that the economies of the developing nations, i.e. India and China, will "stroke the engine of the world economy" and low-income and least-developed countries will experience only a mild slowdown. In other words, fears about another global meltdown centre mainly on the economies of North America, Europe, and the UK—in short, the "global North."

Predictably, the WESP Report directs its recommendations for a better economic tomorrow to the global North leaders: use fiscal policy to stimulate employment; invest in infrastructure, green-energy, and food security projects; institutionalize stronger banking and financial sector regulations; ensure sufficient support for developing countries; and co-ordinate national and international fiscal and monetary policies. These recommendations are hardly unique, as numerous experts have already called for the same actions. But all this talk about "the economy," what to do about it and how to avoid another crisis is, in actuality, talk about capitalism. For it is capitalism that profoundly shapes the lives of people on a global scale, even though professional economists, journalists, and pundits regularly refer to it as "the economy" or "the market economy" (see Stanford 2008; Zelizer 2011). Only at the beginning of 2012 have specific sustained, publically articulated conversations about the future of *capitalism as capitalism*, rather than just "the economy," emerged on the world stage among business and political leaders (in contrast to academics, political activists, and public intellectuals).[2] The degree to which they will take hold and effect possibilities for structural and systematic change is yet to be determined (see Pendakis for a discussion of possibilities, chapter 10).

Despite these recent public discussions, capitalism remains a marginal, somewhat subversive, term in the humdrum discourses about the economy. In one way, this is not too surprising given that its almost 300-year existence constitutes a very small part of a 200,000-year human history (Stanford 2008, 33). In another way, however, it is surprising given that capitalism has taken hold in so many parts of the world. Most people live in, or are influenced by, a capitalistic way of making a living, one characterized by the production of stuff for the express purpose of making profit; where input resources, the production process, and its attendant output are not collectively owned or shared but "belong" to particular entities who hold the status of legal "personhood"; where work is mostly defined by groups of people who do not own the means of production and thus have to "rent" out their physical and/or intellectual labors to those who do; and, perhaps most importantly, where the drive for profit overshadows any real consideration for human wellbeing and the environment.

In the post-2008 era, citizens in the global North may be marginally more conscious of the negative consequences occasioned by the competitive drive for revenues, growth, and expansion (i.e. the profit motive), but very little seems to have changed. The (capitalistic) economy is regularly discussed and conceived of as natural, given, and unchangeable, underpinned by a pervasive belief in the effectiveness and efficiency of the profit motive.[3] This is the case at a global level were input resources are extracted in one locale, shipped to multiple locales for partial processing, shipped again to another locale for assembly, and then shipped to consumers everywhere to capture ever more profit. Globalization is presumed to be the extension of the old logic, only grander, and therefore not something altogether new and transformative. Meanwhile, national, regional, and local concerns are eclipsed by an economy run by the dictates of an "invisible hand." And just as the global transfer of commodities is rendered commonplace, goods once strictly regulated by import tariffs, quota restrictions, environmental laws, and safety regulations cross and re-cross nation-states under the sway of our collective commonsense. In short, the minimal friction that encumbers the astonishing processes of the global economy is matched by everyday thinking that is similarly free of friction: well oiled and uncomplicated.

Strangely, this holds equally true for the financial and banking sectors of the economy—what has come to be known as "finance capitalism" or "financialization." On the surface, finance capitalism is characterized by the ubiquitous trading of speculative investment vehicles or products (e.g. Credit Default Swaps, Collateralized Debt Obligations, and Derivatives) that generate high rates of short-term returns. On another level, however, these investment vehicles are nearly beyond comprehension for anyone but experts, and perhaps not even then. Speculation has become the name of the game where, for example, agreements to buy and sell assets in the future are traded and re-traded—all made possible by technologies that allow investment vehicles to move nearly instantaneously across the planet. Yet, the fast, free-flow trading of speculative investment products, combined with current weak national and international regulation, is considered just another iteration of the natural human competitive desire for profit, regardless of the damage it engenders. But, again, conspicuously absent from this explanation is a broader lay understanding of capitalism itself, of how its quest for profit, for rapid growth, bigger markets, better technology, and cheaper resource costs (natural and human), gives rise to deep inequalities between those who own the means of production and those who do not. Missing, too, is a widespread appreciation for how capitalism's underlying logics, whether we consider its production of commodities or its production of financial instruments, is embedded in the cultural system of the global North and parts of the global South.

By contrast, scholars have long engaged with the structural problematics, tacit assumptions, effects of, and normalization of capitalism. Many highlight that capitalism is single-mindedly focused on short-term gain at the expense of concerns for human survival, environmental issues, industrial diseases, and the like. Others point out, as well, that capitalism concentrates power, wealth, and prestige in the hands of a few at the expense of the many, rendering a true, functioning democracy nearly impossible. Still others take issue with how capitalism promotes material over non-material values in its attempt to turn every aspect of human life, e.g. relationships, emotions, curiosity, spirituality, and creativity, into a source of profit (see Picard, chapter 8). While so much has been written about the ills of capitalism, its rapaciousness has only intensified with the fall of the USSR and the rise of China. From this perspective, it is difficult to grasp capitalism's intractable hold over twenty-first century life, spurring scholars to continue their explorations on the topic. This has given birth to a proliferation of new monikers to explain the logic, breezy acquiescence, mindless reproduction, and generalized faith in capitalism. These monikers include, but are by no means exhausted, by the following: postmodern capitalism, contemporary capitalism, recent capitalism, cannibal capitalism, crack capitalism, stakeholder capitalism, natural capitalism, coordinated, state, or free capitalism, flexicurity capitalism, extreme capitalism, global capitalism, informational capitalism, finance capitalism, late capitalism, consumer capitalism, and neoliberal capitalism. The latter three terms are frequently cited in the critical literature on capitalism today, are referenced extensively by the authors in this book, and are further fleshed out below.

Explaining capitalism today

"Late capitalism," arguably the most influential term for humanities-based scholarship and popularized by Fredric Jameson, the influential Marxist, literary, and cultural studies scholar, denotes a particular phase of post-World War II capitalism. As a periodizing term, it is partly informed by Ernest Mandel (1998), who set out, in good positivistic fashion, to demarcate the stages of the capitalistic mode of production on the basis of its structural features. Most relevant for this collection, the structural features of late capitalism, as Harry Targ (2006) nicely summarizes, include an increasing amount of wealth generated by the "FIRE" (Finance, Insurance, and Real Estate) sectors of the economy, as well as the ability of transnational banks to promote financial speculation, lend monies to debt-ridden nations (bringing to mind worries over sovereign debt), and buy and sell equity and bond instruments around the globe. Alongside this, late capitalism is marked by a shift away from Fordist production processes to post-Fordist production whereby factories operating in nations with little regard for decent work, environmental, and/or fair taxation regulations produce commodities in response to mercurial consumer demand.

While the structural features of late capitalism are significant, Jameson's use of the term is more expansive, as it tackles the relationship between capitalism, human consciousness, and the cultural ideas that underpin how people have come to accept and reproduce capitalism. Jameson (1991) stresses that the current stage of capitalism not only includes the rise of multinational corporations, global capitalism, monopolies of banking, corporate power, the incredible influence of the media, and grave inequalities in the distribution of wealth. Late capitalism is just as importantly about the shift from the ideas of parody, the authentic subject, and high culture to the post-world war ideas of pastiche, the fragmented and schizophrenic subject, popular culture, and virtualization. These elements of late capitalism, or what Jameson concomitantly refers to as "postmodernism," are all part and parcel of a broader, systematic way of being in a world marked by a "perpetual present," and, by extension, by a continuous fragmentation in the meanings and practices of our everyday lives (cf. Jameson 1991). Living in so many presents simultaneously, Jameson argues, gives rise to a collective sense of "depthlessness" and an attendant loss of narrative or a lack of caring about the past and its ties to the present, cause and effect thinking, and critical inquiry.

Moreover, late capitalism's erasure of narrative and its postmodern 'presentism' engenders an excessively consumer-oriented ethos whereby the superficiality of life is enacted over and over in the purchase of more and more unnecessary stuff. Scholarly work on the significance of consumption is fairly new, as traditional analyses of capitalism tend to focus on the production processes and social relations established by a particular mode of production. Yet, consumer capitalism pays heed not only to the centrality of consumption but also to the saliency of branding or the meanings, images, and ideas associated with a commodity. Whereas, however, branding was initially employed as a marketing strategy to differentiate similar products from each other, it is now used in much more abstract ways to demarcate a particular lifestyle, identity, and/or community at a global scale, directing attention to the oftentimes vexatious international and transnational consumption of the *meanings*, or signs, of commodities (Featherstone 1991; Haug 1986). At first, analyses centered on how people, aka "the masses," were not aware of their voracious consumption of signs; today, however, scholars interrogate how consumers are cognizant, in varying degrees, of the power of their purchasing patterns (Cerni 2007). Corporations are also aware that the sign of the product, or the image or fantasy associated with a good, is just as important as its functional elements (or its "use-value"). Descriptions of the various spectral, ghostly, simulated, and hyper-abstract meaning of commodities currently abound, as theorists underline the nuances of consumer capitalism. Scholars who are, however, troubled by the rise of exploitative international production lines, the horrible working conditions, and abysmally low wage rates associated with unfettered forms of globalized capitalism want to highlight the avariciousness of capitalistic production rather than turn too quickly to a reductive analysis of consumption (Cerni 2007). The term "neoliberalism" or neoliberal capitalism helps spell out some of these latter concerns.

Sherry Ortner (2011) claims that neoliberalism emerged from the vilification of Keynesian economic ideas and the decline of Fordist production, both of which represented social contracts that protected capitalism from its own excesses. But the term neoliberalism carries a darker undertone to it than late capitalism or consumer capitalism (see Pendakis, chapter 10). The term underscores how nation-states, public institutions (even universities), and social service agencies have all begun to act like global corporations who invest in speculative investment instruments and take advantage of the loosening of laws, rules, and regulations without due regard to the destruction that ensues. Ortner, following David Harvey's (2007) lead, focuses on neoliberalism's accumulation by dispossession whereby the privatization of once public goods and services is widespread and the transformation of just about anything into a financial instrument for the express purpose of making a profit via speculation—a kind of casino capitalism—reigns (see Strange 1997; see Kaposy, chapter 5). The term emphasizes how the state knowingly gives more wealth to the wealthy via tax breaks and loopholes, massively de-regulates rules surrounding working conditions (and hence the troubling discourses about labor union 'concessions' and 'austerity measures' in the global North), encourages an international traffic in assets, liabilities, and financial instruments, and downgrades environmental protection—what capitalists often refer to as "bureaucratic red tape."

It would be convenient here to blame capitalists for such an admittedly awful situation. This does little to explain why neoliberal capitalism is so broadly accepted. What, then, underlines the insidious rise of neoliberalism, especially among those it hurts the most? David Harvey (2007) provides a potential answer: Neoliberalism has become vital in shaping how people act and think in the world. It pervades the media, boardroom, government, World Band, IMF, even university where academics are increasingly called upon to apply their intellectual labors in the service of think tanks for sustainable development, to unleash their creative energies in the development of the next innovative product, service, or idea, and to direct their research and research questions toward policy reports and the like. Neoliberalism is founded on the view that human wellbeing is best achieved by promoting individual freedom and entrepreneurial activity unfettered by any barriers to entry, government involvement, or supposedly "draconian laws." This is the result of an unquestioned trust in the ability of markets to optimize supply and demand, liberated from state power, control, and authority. Putting this logic into practice has led to "business friendly" measures that valorize private property, free markets, free trade, predictable inflation rates for predictable borrowing costs, and investments in military, police, and legal apparatuses for the express purpose of protecting such measures.

Although late capitalism, consumer capitalism, and neoliberal capitalism all attempt to explain the current machinations of our economy and their connections with culture, they, like all concepts, ideas, and abstractions, do not capture the full complexities of our current global economic situation. There are many other terms, cited above, that grapple with such intricacies. Arguably this linguistic proliferation underlines the importance of capitalism in everyday life, highlighting the need for an ongoing dialogue about its effects rather than a triumphal thesis about the "end of history" (cf. Fukuyama 1993). As a major factor in our everyday lives, however, we need to consider why capitalism has become so much a part of a global consciousness, so much a part of the ordinary order of things. One persuasive response is to think about capitalism as a cultural system; to think about it as an interrelated set of constituted practices and ideas that have become an all-encompassing, almost intractable commonsense in the global North.

Capitalism as a cultural system

The Economy as Cultural System makes broad claims about how capitalism is comprised of a set of interrelated ideas and practices that are unproblematically passed along as a natural, universal way of making a living. This claim is repeated in critical writings on the intersections between capitalism and culture. As Billy Williams (2011) points out, capitalism is a key term in a large and growing cultural studies literature. Cultural studies scholars look at how capitalism strips humanity of its true nature, alienates humans from realizing their power to transform the world through their labor, ignores the social relations of production and consumption and, perhaps most importantly, deludes both those who own the means of production and those who do not into thinking that capitalism will set the human race free. Naturally this critical perspective is contested by conservative scholars who argue that capitalism is the optimal way for humans to make a living, as it supports liberal, democratic ideals: for under capitalism, unlike a monarchical or communist state, individuals are free to pursue their self-interest, accumulate wealth, and thus realize a state of maximal happiness (or, alternatively put, "utility"). From this Enlightenment-like perspective, capitalism is the economic system that most effectively increases the general pool of human knowledge, furnishes us with the technologies that make our lives easier, and provides equitable opportunities for all people in a market-economic society.

Critical writings about capitalism challenge its past and continuing grounding on such Enlightenment ideals of human reason, progress, and perfectability, arguing that it is better viewed as an ongoing process rather than the best and final stage of human progress, or what Francis Fukuyama

(1993) calls, following Kojève's reading of Marx's reading of Hegel's *The Phenomenology of Spirit*, the "end of history." As an ongoing process, there is still much to analyze about the operationalization of capitalism. Consider work, for instance, in the field of postcolonial studies that reveal how colonial empires exploited the geographical and human resources in the territories they conquered through cultural discourses of "orientalism." Or consider how the nation and nationalism is imagined and realized in the context of capitalism (Anderson 1983; Gellner 1983). The same holds true for much of the literature on ethnicity, where explanations of primordiality have been discarded in favor of constructivist arguments (Eriksen 2002). This is even more the case in our increasingly transnational, networked, overwhelmingly internet-connected lives as ideas and practices traverse physical place, crossing borders at alarming speeds and generating emergent ethnic, national, and postcolonial identity categories, labels, forms, and associations. There is little in these analyses that signal the end of history.

To suggest that capitalism is dynamically interrelated to culture underlines how it is not fixed, homogenous, bounded, and without friction, as if it is an essential part of our human-ness. Indeed, most academics eschew accounts of capitalism as a natural condition, renewing a debate brought to the forefront decades ago in transnational and cross-cultural investigations about the variety of practices and ideas that surround the machinations of the economy (see Comaroff and Comaroff 2000; Kingfisher and Maskovsky 2008; Peck 2010). A great part of this debate takes issue with the assumptions embedded in the neo-classical economic thinking that informs capitalism. Viviana Zelizer (2011) points out how these assumptions are derived from the overarching idea that capitalism represents the pinnacle stage of human evolution, iterating Fukuyama's premature triumphalist thesis.

In this vein, Zelizer highlights how social scientists and humanities-based academics reject a "rigid concept of 'homo economicus' as a rusty, old-fashioned notion ready for retirement" (2011, ix). This is, she claims, because the assumptions undergirding neo-classical economics—i.e. that resources are scarce; that people make rational rather than emotional choices; that short-term gains are more important than longer-term ones; that humans think and act in self-interested ways without consideration of societal expectations; and that the economic realm is independent from politics, religion, and aesthetics—have been discounted, particularly in the post-2008 world. Zelizer is, of course, not alone in her critical appraisal of "homo economicus," as is evident in the November 2011 edition of the journal *Historically Speaking*, where Joyce Appleby, a well-known specialist in the history of liberalism, political thought, and capitalism, questions the naturalness of many neo-classical economic epistemological and ontological assumptions. While there is certainly nothing new in her remarks, as scholars have long taken apart the idea that humans are single-mindedly motivated by their desire to "buy low and sell high," Appleby does ask why neo-classical economic assumptions have become so dominant given that they were radical, heretical ideas only a few hundred years ago. She notes, as well, how the main tenets of neo-classical economics, e.g. that human greed is natural, that the bundle of resources available in the world is limited, and that the competition to own scarce resources is a result of human self-interest (or greed), have been transformed into truth, even though they are clearly historically–culturally constituted.

Despite challenges to her thesis—as with Eicholz's (2011) suggestion that the constant application of human purposeful behavior (rather than rational, maximizing or greedy behavior) resulted in capitalism—Appleby reminds us that capitalism is not so natural after all. Indeed, these insights have long-shaped the work of social scientists and literary critics who have explored the breezy reproduction of capitalism. Since the inception of anthropology, for example, the economy has figured as one of many other parts of human life (see Comaroff and Comaroff 2000). Literary analysts broach the economy similarly, as the work of Jameson demonstrates. Much past sociological inquiry is likewise grounded on the analyses of capitalism, particularly focused on its rise and effects in the global North (see Kemple, chapter 1). This large and extensive body of scholarship explores how capitalism is culturally and/or historically constituted but is nevertheless popularly understood as "just the way things are." Right across the disciplinary board, save perhaps for the discipline of economics, critical scholars eschew the idea that capitalism is the most efficient, effective, inevitable, and natural way for us to make a living. *The Economy as Cultural System* is therefore an emphatic return to and reinvestment in this venerable tradition, which deserves a wider readership—and that optimistically hopes to alter, even radically, our everyday thinking about the economy.

The economy as a cultural system: Reflections

The authors collected herein take up the notions of visuality, happiness, metaphor, crisis, narrative, work, resistance, and creativity as ways to help illuminate how capitalism is indeed a cultural system. Thomas Kemple's chapter opens up a discussion about the appropriation and commodification of academic knowledge by capitalism. Kemple, an established social theorist, argues that just as the abstract ideas and images surrounding a commodity are as vital as their utilitarian value, both hegemonic and counter-hegemonic intellectual ideas and images are similarly becoming a part of capitalism. The knowledge produced, passed along, and revised by scholars, administrators, researchers, and students is increasingly evaluated for its ability to generate profit, lead to innovation, give birth to new technologies, allow for the development of new drugs and new medical treatments, and so on. Research and creativity for their own sake, coupled with the value of humanities in helping to constitute ethical, thoughtful, and reflexive cosmopolitan citizens, have gone by the wayside—unless, of course, there is some profit to realize (see Picard, chapter 8).

This is not entirely unexpected in contemporary forms of capitalism. What is novel, however, is how such knowledge is caught in a kind of hyperreal consumerism associated with a regime of visual culture (e.g. television, film, photography, advertisements, etc.). This insight extends, rather than departs from, classical theory's work on how culture and capitalism is interconnected. The differences between past and current styles of capitalism is the speed at which such interconnections are forged, as new communications technologies furnish opportunities for ideas, concepts, values, facts, and opinions to travel seamlessly across the global landscape. Furthermore, just as academic knowledge is appropriated by capitalism nowadays, so too are visual cultural materials in that "the gaze itself becomes subject to the appeal of commodification and communication, with product-placement in the movies and on television, or pervasive advertising on the internet and in everyday life" (Kemple, this book, 32).

The implications of Kemple's writing about visuality may at first seem to suggest that analytical engagements with capitalism do not stand outside of capitalism and that critique is always situated. Kemple reminds us that major classical theorists of capitalism have, in differing degrees, understood the conundrum of critiquing a system to which they belong. There is no outside, no objective, disinterested, impartial position from which to critique capitalism, since the terms, concepts, ideas, and practices employed to think about capitalism are ingrained within our cultural system. That does not mean, however, that critique stems from some navel-gazing subjectivism. There is room to acknowledge the situated-ness of critique at the same time that we can acknowledge the existence of a reflexivity—a thinking about thinking—that opens up possibilities for change, transformation, and a better, more just world. Kemple suggests that we turn to a re-consideration of the most classical of classical concepts in the theoretical analysis of the capitalism and culture—i.e. exchange-value, social interactionalism, symbolic institution, and rational action. Such concepts provide the tools to re-think the natural-ness of capitalism and its connections to culture, especially in its current visual, image saturated mode that "distracts us into an "attention deficit," even as it also commands and cajoles us into "paying attention" (this book, 32).

The double-ness of distraction and attraction (paying attention) suggestively highlights the interplay between, and reproduction of, culture and capitalism. That very double-ness helps explain why consumers may be at once seduced by the connotations associated with a given commodity and distracted by the mind-boggling circulation of meanings associated with it. Joel Faflak's chapter on the economics of happiness evokes a similar contradictory simultaneity. Faflak focuses on the emergence of psychiatry, the obsession with being happy, and its relationship with capitalism. Faflak, a theoretically informed specialist of Romantic literature, examines the discourse that surrounds the neoclassical economic (capitalistic) assumption that human beings primordially desire happiness, and that material wellbeing assists in its realization. Yet happiness, according to Faflak, is a state of being that is never fully achievable, as it is "unthinkable without threats to its existence" (this book, 39). The upshot is that happiness is discursively cast as both natural and something to be obtained, leaving us with an endless desire *for the desire* for happiness. The business of psychiatry mediates the tension between wanting happiness and never being able to have it. Furthermore, consumer capitalism is a pivotal hinge of and for the desire for the desire for happiness, grounded as it is on the idea that buying more stuff will temporarily keep "un-happiness" at bay. This is the epitome of therapeutic consumption, which draws attention to how a cultural (rather than natural) expectation of and for happiness is shaped by, and shapes, capitalism.

While Faflak focuses on the discourses of happiness and capitalism, Max Haiven turns his attention to recent discourses of financialization. Haiven begins his chapter with a detailed overview of financial capitalism, which he argues began in the post-colonial, World War II era and is now rooted in the everyday-ness of speculative investment vehicles (e.g. Credit Default Swaps, Collateralized Debt Obligations, and Derivatives). The "world under financialization," Haiven writes, is an "incomprehensibly dense and sickeningly fast world of financial speculation that controls a good deal of our fates" and where "causality and consequentiality are ... virtually impossible to predict or read" (this book, 59–60). Haiven contends that financialization wreaks havoc with our lives, our stories of cause and effect, and our shared sense of the future; or what he refers to as our social (as opposed to personal) narratives, leading him to champion the concept of metaphor as a way of comprehending the interplay between culture and financialization.

The use of metaphor in the field of economics more generally and capitalism more specifically is not without precedent. Haiven, however, challenges its past use, which conflated economic rhetoric with "actually existing, real-world phenomena" (this book, 61). Haiven, a new literary and cultural theorist, has a quite different project in mind. He embraces metaphor to underscore the multiplicities of meaning, a "whole world of associations at play" in human life, culture, and language, where metaphors are constituted by and through other metaphors (this book, 65). He contends that the metaphoric nature of finance exceeds modernist strictures on meaning, thus opening up perspectives on other possible ways of thinking the economy.

Another new literary and cultural critic, Matthew MacLellan, also looks at metaphor in relation to capitalism and the cultural realm. But whereas Haiven provides a broad treatment of metaphor, one useful for rethinking the very frame of finance capitalism, MacLellan takes particular aim at the use of the vampire metaphor in Marxian-inspired investigations of capitalism. MacLellan begins with the claim that all human understanding is metaphoric in nature, as all human understanding is grounded in language. There is no "outside" to this, as metaphors guide our thinking and actions and are, thus, the ways in which humans "know" something about the world, act on that knowledge, and pass that knowhow and its attendant practices on to present and future generations. Like Haiven in this respect, MacLellan reflects upon how the multiple meanings associated with standard, hegemonic, or dominant metaphors may engender alternative knowledges and practices, especially in the cultural, political, and economic realms. This is precisely the case he puts forward in his exploration of the "Marxian vampire."

The hegemonic reading/interpretation of the Marxian vampire illuminates, MacLellan contends, how the economy is propelled by the ever-expanding desire on the part of the greedy, blood thirsty, non-human capitalist for additional profits/blood at the expense of the care of and for human life. This reading, however accurate, is nonetheless worrying as it relies on Marx's humanistic texts, downplays his more economically oriented texts, and results in a static, essentialized, binaristic, and oppositional cultural-political logic—what MacLellan refers to as a populist-ideology—whereby an "antipodal antagonism between the vampire and the human is directly imposed onto the relation between the bourgeoisie and the proletariat" (MacLellan, this book, 86). The standard interpretation of the Marxian vampire closes down the possibility of appreciating the relationship between capitalists and laborers, the cultural relations of production, the fluidity and historicity of capitalism (e.g. how cultural relations of production shift over time), and the possibilities for change. Moreover, this reading runs the risk of ignoring one of the most pivotal foundations of Marxian work: that humans *make their own culture and history* by and through their labor, and that the application of human labor to the world is *continuously transformative of both the world and the human.*

Concerns over the dynamism of culture and capitalism centrally inform the work of Tim Kaposy and Justin Sully as well. Both writers value systematic explanations of capitalism, a somewhat controversial position in our postmodern times. Kaposy, a political and cultural theorist, urges us to re-engage in larger-scale considerations, however much they may smack of modernism's master narratives. He contends that recent scholars of society and the economy downplay universalistic questions of fairness and justice in favor of local, community-based, individualistic narratives (or explanations). The failure to take up these questions makes it too easy to discuss international crises of poverty, warfare, environmental degradation, and human rights abuses as uncontrollable and unexpected events. Framed as chaotic and unpredictable, such events are treated in an ad hoc manner. However, what if crisis (or the rhetoric of crisis) is considered a longstanding issue between culture and capitalism? What is the relationship between capitalism and the hegemonic words and concepts that shape how we think and act in the world? What opportunities exist to rupture such hegemonic words and concepts so as to *resist* and *change* our world for the better? For Kaposy, one answer rests with a shift in thinking about the concept of "crisis" to engaging with the notion of "need."

On the surface, the notion of need is usually thought of as something fundamental for human beings to function and exist in the world (think: food, shelter, and love). On a deeper level—one that Kaposy favors—need is based on the relationships between people and groups, especially between those who meet their own needs by depriving others of their needs. This relational understanding of need is "part of a system of production, circulation, and consumption that is rarely if ever immediate to oneself" (Kaposy, this book, 101). Following Marx, it underscores the unequal social relations of production that eclipse the possibility of human freedom. Interminable talk of crisis, that is, interferes with understanding the connection between need and human freedom, as it masks the systematic exploitation ingrained in today's late-capitalism.

Justin Sully is similarly concerned with crisis. His chapter, however, interrogates the crisis of population aging as a crisis that is tied to capitalism and a linear, progressive concept of time, a topic that is typically missing in academic discussions of globalization, ecological degradation, and financialization. This situation is partly due to the fact that studies in population demographics tend to favor empirical explanation at the expense of theoretical ones. Alternatively, social scientists tend to deal with the problem of aging as either a subjective or sociological condition, keeping its weighty linkages with capitalism at bay. Both are lacking, Sully submits, because both forget about the "temporal form of aging as a mass, demographic process and its uncertain relationship to the still [capitalistic] axiomatic assumption of continuous (population) growth" (Sully, this book, 111).

What is thus required, according to Sully, is a synthetic account of how the assumption of positive population growth informs capitalism's drive for continuous growth, territorial expansion, and the large-scale social transformation that is only really understandable according to a linear, progressive concept of time. The problem of aging does not fit into such a linear scheme, for it delimits both a process of decline (i.e. relative population growth is slowing and aging, and hence capitalism is thus in danger of losing its productive workforce) and of progress (i.e. absolute population is growing). Such simultaneity represents, for Sully, an incommensurability that underpins a "figure of social time that cuts ambiguously across the structuring polarities of growth/decline, expansion/contraction, more/less" (this book, 113). This incommensurability begs the question of aging as a cultural logic, one that is structurally related to how we think about capitalism in a progressivist way and one that is entrenched in the treatment of pensions—an important issue of aging and population demographics—under financialized capitalism.

Mark Kingwell's chapter departs from analyses of the discourses of crisis and the use of metaphors. Yet, not unlike Haiven, MacLellan, and Kaposy, Kingwell critically takes up the associations between language, culture, and capitalism. He begins with a simple but powerful observation: the 2008 economic crisis changed nothing though everyone was cognizant that "[t]he system was bloated and spectral ... borrowing on its borrowing, insuring its insurance, and skimming profit on every transaction" (this book, 128). Kingwell suggests that the continuation of the bloated capitalistic status quo may have something to do with how we approach work, discuss it, and valorize it. Work is not solely required for brute survival, but furnishes us with social position, power, and personal identity—especially when it is tied to the struggle for credentials, merits, just rewards, and recognition. This may help explain why bosses and laborers, blue-, white-, and pink-collar workers, bureaucrats, and politicians are all "slaves to the larger servo-mechanisms of work" (Kingwell, this book, 130). It may also help explain why bureaucracies reproduce themselves without much attention to the need for their existence, why mangers create ever more subordinates, why make-work projects are essential for work, why "the meeting" has become its own end-goal, and why company loyalty is considered a good in its own right. What underpins much of this is the Hegelian Bad Infinite, or working for work's own sake.

Given its dominance, how then does one go about challenging work or, more precisely, what Kingwell refers to as the work idea? How might we begin to engage in the "Good Infinite, where we may begin to see things not as resources, ourselves not as consumers, and the world as a site not of work but of play"? (Kingwell, this book, 138). As a well-known philosopher and cultural critic, Kingwell reflects here upon the relationship between language and the ability to voice opposition to the work idea, advising us that a careful employment of "bullshit," which is indifferent to the articulation of both truth and lies, may prove fruitful. More powerfully, resisting the work idea may rest with, paraphrasing Kingwell, forgetting about work altogether.

Kingwell's suggestion resonates with Kezia Picard's chapter on the problematic of resistance today. She highlights a peculiar notion of resistance that hinges upon the Foucauldian formulation of biopower, stressing that it is part of a discourse of modernity that enables us to become who we are and that shapes our selfhood. The emergence of capitalism is a pivotal element in this regard as it parallels the emergence of a certain kind of biopower that creates a sane, healthy, homogeneous population so needed for a capitalistic economic system that requires disciplined laborers.

Contemporary capitalism differs, Picard argues, from its previous variants because it is based on immaterial labor—a kind of work based on the "brain-labor" of communication, cooperation, and creativity rather than the physical labor of the factory floor. In addition, it is characterized by, as Haiven, Kemple, and Sully emphasize in chapter x, a "massification of stock market investment" whereby ordinary citizens are increasingly vested in financial capitalism, either directly through their participation in self-directed investments or indirectly through their participation in government and/or institutionally managed pension funds (see Sully, chapter 6). Picard makes a case for how the rise of contemporary capitalism or a capitalism based on immaterial labor and financialization has been met with intensification of biopower, as human traits that once more clearly stood outside of capitalism's reach (i.e. communication, cooperation, and creativity), are increasingly absorbed by it. Is there any room, in these circumstances, for people to resist capitalism? Picard, a cultural theorist and feminist philosopher, certainly thinks so. She argues that contemporary capitalism and the current form of biopower gives birth to momentary instabilities, confusions, and uncertainties that may occasion alternative ways of thinking and acting. These alternatives or moments of resistance exist, however, in an in-between space, a space between when they emerge and when they are inevitably absorbed back into capitalism. This in-between space underpins the concept of bio*politics*.

Interrogations of in-between spaces may not always be about resistance but about how such spaces may be utilized in the overt service of capitalism. Todd Dufresne and Clara Sacchetti's chapter on Richard Florida's famous, internationally influential, and much-debated thesis on the locational decisions of the newest group of immaterial laborers—the "creative class"—is a case in point. Florida, a guru of economic development, argues that the economic prosperity of a place is less dependent on Fordist-production and more dependent on the places where "creatives" desire to live, work, and play. Yet, while opponents of Florida's work have criticized his use of statistics, lack of concern for social justice issues, neoliberal bias, repetitive and standard prescription for urban development, and intellectual simplicity, many say little about a central tension in his work about the importance of the "real-ness" of place and the importance of the intangible qualities of place. Dufresne and Sacchetti, both cultural theorists, highlight the slippage in Florida's work between the material and immaterial features of place—one that reflects "the specular or hyperreal version of capitalism that exists today" that is undoubtedly tied to the mind-boggling abstractions of financial capitalism, a situation described decades ago by Jean Baudrillard (1983) and unwittingly employed by Florida in an attempt describe "an economy of pure representation" (Dufresne and Sacchetti, this book, 164 and 162 respectively). How one chooses to engage with this economy is the question they put to both cultural theorists and the proponents of capitalism.

Conclusion: Theory vs. the real

The Economy as Cultural System interrogates the ways in which the fairly abstract notions of spectrality, metaphor, narrative, crisis, resistance, and creativity are part of the interrelationship of capitalism and culture. They help illuminate how the connections between capitalism and the practices and ideas of everyday life are reproduced as a commonsense without giving up hope that it is nevertheless possible to disrupt such commonsense—save for "Bifo," who is clearly much less optimistic about solutions to our current economic woes (see Pendakis, chapter 10). Although not devoid of the concrete or the everyday, chapter x valorizes theoretical work for helping us think through the dynamic, iterative connections between capitalism and culture, or what we are calling the economy as culture system.

We are aware that our emphasis on the theoretical, synthetic, or abstract, may be somewhat controversial in the post-2008 era where people are struggling to meet their basic needs. We are acutely aware, as well, that many scholars have turned away from theory in the name of dealing with the so-called "real world" (cf. Comaroff and Comaroff 2000; Kingfisher and Maskovsky 2008; Peck 2010). What, though, does the recourse to the language of "the real" achieve within the context of downgrading the theoretical?

There are a series of already well-established responses to this question: theoretical work always informs empirical work; theory is always shaped by the real, as the real is always shaped by theory; theory helps simplify everyday life so that we can attempt to grasp some, although admittedly not all, of its systematic logics and meanings; and theory aims to engage in a particular question with an audience of similarly interested conversants who are familiar with the terms involved. Most importantly, though, it seems rather ironic that academic work which prioritizes the everyday by discounting theory may in fact unwittingly play into the logics of late, consumer, or neoliberal capitalism: knowledge, like the goods and services produced under capitalism, ought to be useable to all, like a widget available for purchase in primary colors. Jameson (1976) offers a fine response when he subtly suggests that a historical appreciation for capitalism requires abstract theorization, however much it may be unpalatable to scholars who claim to be interested in the real, the concrete, or the quotidian. Yet it is precisely this sort of deep going understanding that needs to be developed to better grapple with the "nature of the relations between economics, ideology, power, and culture" (Jameson 1976, 39). There are no short cuts in this regard, most especially by valorizing "the real" and concomitantly discounting the theoretical. It is our hope that *The Economy as Cultural System* is useful precisely because it will help develop a more profound appreciation for how capitalism is not an inevitable outgrowth of human nature, but is a highly reproducible commonsense that is culturally–historically constituted and, as such, may be resisted and even transformed. This is both the challenge and the opportunity of thinking the economy differently, and of recollecting theoretical riches for the benefit of everyone.

Notes

1 The WESP Report has been written and developed by the Department of Economic and Social Affairs, the United Nations' Conference on Trade and Development, and the five United Nations regional commissions: see www.un.org/en/development/desa/policy/ wesp/index.shtml

2 See, for example, Barack Obama (2012), Terry Milewski (2012), and Cramer (2012). For popular accounts see Stanford (2008) and Klein (2000).

3 In relation to the economy, globalization refers to flows of money, information about business operations, and labor across the world on a scale and at a speed hitherto unknown. Within this context, scholars interrogate capitalism and its connections to place or locale; the unequal international flow of power and wealth and its effects; and the compression of time and space via new communications and transportation technologies.

1

The I/eye of capital: Classical theoretical perspectives on the spectral economies of late capitalism[1]

Thomas M. Kemple

Social theory today is itself an instance and integral part of contemporary capitalism. As advertising executives learn to use semiotics and industry teaches academia lessons about cultural studies, even the most abstract forms of thought become subject to capitalization and capital finds new ways of absorbing critical modes of thinking. In a recent book, *Knowing Capitalism*, Nigel Thrift makes this point by offering what he calls "a history and geography of the near present" which avoids simply summarizing academic critiques or theoretical analyses of the current state of capitalism, since he finds them to be impotent or unconvincing in view of the system's ability to exploit and co-opt them. Instead, he shows how businesses—including universities and research institutes around the globe—are in the business of selling ideas, marketing innovative knowledges, and promoting novel ways of thinking: "Management theory relies, more than other forms of virtual knowledge, on a conglomeration of performed and book knowledge, and the two are not exclusive but form a part of a chain of production and communication" (Thrift 2005, 91). Managerial ideas and lucrative thought-styles increasingly originate and circulate beyond academic institutions, in the course of which they are communicated not just through formal and traditional media, such as books, tapes, videos, and magazines, but also in informal and less conventional settings, such as email discussion groups, online forums, workshops, retreats, television shows, and speaking tours. As new ways of knowing and doing capitalism emerge through triangulated exchanges between business schools, management consultants, and entrepreneurial gurus, aspiring traders in ideas, information, and other intellectual goods from within and outside the university draw their inspiration from anti-capitalist critics, oppositional social movements, and enterprising academics (Gibson-Graham 2006). In the process, subcultural and intellectual counter-currents become integrated into the cultural and cognitive circuits of capital, and the 'portfolios' of individuals and organizations increasingly include not just material wealth and financial capital but also "stocks" of commercial acumen which incorporate the speculative competence of reflexive institutional and personal knowledge.[2]

Arguably, the classic social theorists of Western capitalism writing in the late nineteenth and early twentieth centuries might be said to have anticipated or even welcomed these developments. They found ways of accommodating themselves to rapidly developing changes in the capitalist world system while also trying to insulate themselves from its most pernicious and damaging effects. When Karl Marx was living in poverty with his wife, daughters, and mistress–maidservant in London's Soho while studying the latest government-issued factory reports and economic texts for his magnum opus *Capital*, he was also drawing a modest income from Engels' family-owned textile industries in Manchester, from local pawn shops, and from his occasional editorials for the *New York Daily Tribune*. A generation later, Georg Simmel struggled to make ends meet in Berlin from his low salary as an adjunct university professor, for the most part by lecturing and writing on a wide variety of cultural and social phenomena emerging out of the rise of the money-economy, the subject of his masterpiece *The Philosophy of Money*. In the same years, Emile Durkheim fought for educational reforms from his academic chair at the Sorbonne in Paris, reforms which he saw as necessary for morally and institutionally regulating the anomic effects of the industrial crisis which he diagnosed in *The Division of Labour in Society*. Finally, around the same time, Max Weber was studying the historical origins of the entrepreneurial ethos in his *Protestant Ethic and the Spirit of Capitalism*, making recommendations about German national economic policy in rural areas and in urban stock exchanges, while also drawing on his wife's inheritance from her family's weaving manufactories. Far from merely formulating canonical concepts for analyzing the capitalist system from outside it, as one might surmise from Anthony Giddens' 1971 textbook *Capitalism and Modern Social Theory* (for years a staple of courses in classical social theory), these early thinkers were deeply implicated in the mechanisms and movements of capitalism. Each acknowledged that social theories of the contemporary financial and industrial order cannot simply project an external view of its *form*; they must also take up a perspective from within its very *substance*—conceived as "exchange-value" in the case of Marx, as "social interaction" for Simmel, as "symbolic institution" in Durkheim's work, and as "rational action" for Weber.

Rather than merely reviewing these founding theories of early capitalism, I want to consider them as starting points for critically rethinking certain features of what I shall call *the spectral economies of late capitalism*, that is, the tendency we are experiencing today toward the financialization, electrification, and virtualization of capital in all its forms. In other words, the basic unit of contemporary capitalism seems to have morphed from the circulation of the *commodity*, defined by its exchange-value (as expressed through price fluctuations, for example), to the communication of *cultural style*, perceived in terms of the differentiation of sign-values (as in can be seen in the competition between brands). Likewise, economic activity now turns as much on the fixed assets and guaranteed securities of privately owned businesses as on high-risk and mobile investments made by institutional shareholders. The very real "spillovers" of economic transactions (or "externalities" in neoliberal jargon) therefore do not just entail environmental damage, poor health, and income inequality. They also include the virtual side effects of financial crises and speculative meltdowns of markets in stocks, bonds, loans, and funds (Lash 2010, 116–25). In what follows, I argue that the acceleration, extension, and intensification of capitalism that we see today does not require us to throw out the baby of classical social theory (Theory 1.0) with the bathwater of corporate thinking (Theory 2.0). Canonical concepts such as commodity-fetishism, rationalization, discipline, and (de)individualization, for example, still afford us some critical perspective on the potential within contemporary capitalism for political transformation and civic regeneration (O'Neill 2004).

Exploiting distraction: Beyond Marx and Simmel

In Marx's draft for a chapter he planned to write on "The Results of the Immediate Process of Production," which he ultimately abandoned but which is often included as an appendix in posthumously published editions of the first volume of *Capital* (*Capital I*), he elaborates on the key theoretical distinction around which most of the main text is organized: between "absolute surplus value" on the one hand—the value added to capital by the extension of the working day or the expansion of markets and manufactories—and "relative surplus value" on the other, which accrues through the acceleration of the work process or by increasing output through technological innovations. In the draft notes, Marx generalizes this argument by contrasting what he calls "the formal subsumption of labour under capital," in which the activity and outcome of the work process remains unaltered as it is appropriated, circulated, and consumed capitalistically (for instance, when traditional handicrafts are sold on the world market), with "the real subsumption of labour under capital," in which the production process itself is fundamentally transformed and reconstituted (such as when subsistence agricultural work is replaced by capitalist industrial labor; see Marx 1977, 1019–38). The historical shift that Marx was already able to identify as a tendency inherent in the dynamics of early capitalism—from absolute to relative surplus value, and from formal to real subsumption—is accelerated and intensified in late capitalism. For example, the proliferation of new design technologies and high-tech marketing campaigns aim at enhancing (relative) surplus value, while expanded outsourcing and lending practices, mergers and acquisitions, tend to foster (real) subsumption. Generally speaking, capital does not just subsume the laboring body by appropriating its intellectual and material capacities (the possessive individual), but also the living body (the possessed individual) whose needs, desires, and thoughts are seized upon and developed by the process of capital itself (Kroker 1992). As Marx expresses this point in the *Grundrisse*, the prosthetic and parasitical potential of capital to absorb the laboring body enhances its human potential while forging new technical and social dependencies, a process which entails "the production of *capital fixe* [fixed capital], this *capital fixe* being man himself" (Kemple 1995, 24–7; Marx 1973, 712). Today this tendency has been intensified insofar as life itself—in its social, human, intellectual, and biological dimensions—is technologically reconstituted and marketed not simply as a fixed and firm *product* of capital but also as a circulating and mobile *medium* of its flux and flow.

In general terms, capital does not increase solely by enhancing instrumental efficiency and extending quantitative homogeneity within the circulation and distribution process, but also by *exploiting distraction* through cultural consumption, above all by promoting qualitative differentiation through the processes of design, production, and marketing. Consider, for example, the corporate brand campaigns of Gap or Nike, or the predatory intellectual property tactics of Google and Microsoft. In each case, trademarking, patenting, and copyrighting entail not just the classic industrial marketing of commodities for commercial profit, but also the postmodern promotion of lifestyle images and the proliferation of bits of cultural information through various media. At the same time as a financial profit is acquired and invested, a *symbolic premium* is productively consumed to achieve a comparative advantage at the level of "sign-value," or "difference-value," in spite (or even because) of occasional outrage over sweatshop labor or copyright infringement at the design and production stage (Klein 2000). At stake in the escalation of these competitive struggles is not just the circulation of goods and money but also the communication of meanings and values, just as the object of capitalist desire is no longer simply the commodity-fetish, which draws on a fantasy of abundance, but also the technology-fetish, which projects a fantasy of participation (Dean 2005). In other words, the production and distribution of material and cultural wealth increasingly comes to rely on *the interpellation of information* and *the call of communication* by transforming (apparently autonomous) individuals into (actually dependent) subjects in the process (Althusser 1971, 182). This capitalist culture of distraction is driven in turn by the imperative of mobility and the compulsion of accelerated adaptability: "Thus there appear to be innumerable relations of exploitation based on *mobility differentials*: financial markets versus countries; financial markets versus firms; multinationals versus countries; large principal versus small subcontractor; world expert versus firm; firm versus casual workforce; consumer versus firm" (Boltanski and Chiapello 2005, 371; italics added). Within the new networks of global capitalism, flows of wealth, power, and information are conveyed through channels which are both local and remote, instantaneous as well as mediated, and which produce simultaneously short-term and far-reaching effects. Simply put, the emerging "knowledge economy" is not just a catchword for the "soft, virtual, and fast capitalism" of the information, communication, and technology (ICT) sectors (Agger 2004; Thrift 2005), but above all a fundamental mutation in the investment, production, accumulation, and consumption processes of capital itself.

With this argument in mind, we need to download and update Marx's "general formula for capital" and his "law of capitalist accumulation" to account for how the processes of production and consumption, accumulation and conversion, are integrated into the socio-technical circuitry of the new media and the flows of speculative finance (see Haiven, chapter 3; Sully, chapter 6). **Figure 1** (below) depicts how the reflexive and reticulated circuits of money (M) and commodities (C) are networked into the ordinary time-space of lived experience and everyday communication in the modern world. As Marx argues in *Capital I* (Marx 1977, 247–80, 762–802), in theory the surplus value of any commodified good may be productively consumed, preserved, destroyed, or accrued at any point along the chain of capital formation, from the points of entry to exit and between the levels of substructure and superstructure (the vertical axis of Figure 1). A surplus (marked here as M-prime and C-prime) is only realized (or valorized in Marx's terms) at the point of sale (for example, when the commodity is converted into cash at the top or end of the cycle, or when some thing or idea is bought and

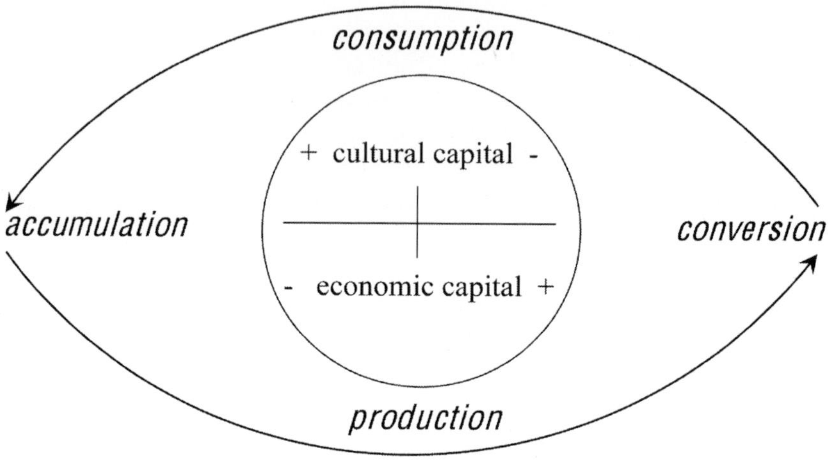

FIGURE 1 *Capital I*
(cf. Marx 1977, 247–80, 762–802)

successfully marketed); or surplus value may be preserved and accumulated insofar as it is stored or reinvested at the bottom or beginning of the cycle (such as when raw materials, labor power, or technologies are acquired, purchased, and productively consumed). By depicting Marx's classic formula in this way, I mean to draw attention to our commonsense understanding of how capital operates by mobilizing "the little things" (Thrift 2000): namely, by integrating mundane objects, activities, texts, images, and words into simple everyday transactions which facilitate the relations of ruling of capital and mediate complex chains of commodification and communication (Smith 1999). In the course of these exchanges, the depths of our 'technological unconscious' tend to become more vast as their material and economic foundations recede from view. As a result, "we may … be witness to a kind of evolution of the commodity which, in turn, is dependent on the evolution of everyday spaces which will endow them with an interactive awareness" (Thrift 2005, 193). As the separation of business enterprise from household activity, which Weber considered to be a defining historical precondition of industrial capitalism, becomes increasingly strained and blurred, the divisions between the private self and its public display seem to erode or collapse altogether.

In a literal sense, then, we might imagine this "Capital I" to trace not just the "dream-work" and "design-ingenuity" to which the macro-processes of capital-innovation are increasingly subject; it also represents the micro-dynamics of *self-formation through social networking* which are the fate of individuals "linked in" to the ubiquitous interfaces of the new social media. Here it is useful to recall Simmel's insights into how the money economy breaks open relatively smaller, more insular, and uniform circles of traditional society both by facilitating social expansion and by intensifying individualization:

> Stimulations of the feelings on which the larger group is dependent for the subjective consciousness of the "I" occur precisely where the very differentiated individual stands amidst other very differentiated individuals, and then comparisons, frictions, specialized relationships precipitate a plethora of reactions that remain latent in the narrower undifferentiated group, but here provoke the feeling of the "I" as what is quintessentially 'proper' to the self through precisely its fullness and diversity. (Simmel 2009, 664; 1992, 848; translation modified)

As Simmel notes specifically with reference to life in the modern city, the escalation of intensified interactions and continuous communications forces the individual to cultivate a kind of "protective organ," in the form of mental discipline or intellectual concentration, for example, or perhaps today with the help of some technological prosthesis such as the automobile or iPhone. Such techniques of distraction and distinction filter the stream of stimuli and control the overload of signifiers while extending the physical and virtual boundaries between the self and its surroundings. "A person," Simmel writes,

> does not end with the limits of his physical body or with the area to which his physical activity is immediately confined but embraces, rather, the totality of meaningful effects which emanates from him temporally and spatially. In the same way the city exists only in the totality of the effects which transcend their immediate sphere (Simmel 1971, 335)

As the modern metropolis morphs into mass media, individual identity becomes subject to the perpetual play of sensation and imagination, and the reality of distance is concealed behind the appearance of immediacy. Ruled by this iconographic logic of speculation, surplus value takes on the form of *tele-value* (TV), at least insofar as culture-at-a-distance is capitalized, with commerce merging with aesthetics and finance being transformed into fantasy (Kemple 1995, 163–4).

With these points in mind, we need to revise Marx's notion of the fetish-character of the commodity (Marx 1977, 163–77) to account for how images and things seduce us into closing the ideological gap between the visible and invisible society: "The commodity fetish is a talking, seeing, feeling god inviting us into the liturgy of consumption to dispel the sorrows of production" (O'Neill 2002, 172). As John O'Neill suggests, capital has learned to operate by de-institutionalizing the self and re-assembling its identities, if not by coercive restraints then through the softer stimulations of *remote-control*, so that the individual comes know itself through the mirror of the media*: televideo ergo sum*. Insofar as the classic disciplinary institutions of modernity—the school, the factory, the hospital, and the factory—no longer function effectively to confine bodies and mold minds into responsible and motivated individuals, technologies of the self must step in to induce desires, inspire ideas, and inform imaginations which can then be packaged and distributed through exploitable networks: "Individuals become 'dividuals' and masses become samples, data, markets, or 'banks'" (Deleuze 1995, 180). As if to extend points made by Marx and Simmel on how processes of commodification and individuation merge with the "Capital I" or divisible self governing the new economies of instant communication and pervasive information, Luc Boltanski and Eve Chiapello have recently sketched a kind of internet profile of what they call the "connexionist man" of the new spirit of capitalism. Such a figure (or "ideal type") is less concerned with accumulating wealth or maximizing work time than with intensifying connections and extending networks: "He prefers to renounce official power in favour of network forms of power, freed of the constraints of supervision, invigilation, management, representation, and respect for the state rules regulating the use of goods and the management of human beings. He leaves that to others, for he prefers autonomy to security" (Boltanski and Chiapello 2005, 124). This new free agent of capital will be "engaged, engaging, mobile, enthusiastic, involved, flexible, adaptable, versatile, employable, in touch, and tolerant" (Boltanski and Chiapello 2005, 112), rather than motivated solely by a civic ethos of entrepreneurialism, a business ethic of individual customization, or a promotional culture of consumerism. In short, the "connexionist dividual" of late capitalism is able to advance a *social critique* of egoism and exploitation along with a *counter-cultural critique* of inauthenticity and alienation, denouncing economic exclusion and deprivation while demanding social integration and self-fulfillment.

Disciplining attention: Beyond Weber and Durkheim

In a passage toward the end of Weber's often-overlooked "Preliminary Remark" to his *Collected Essays on the Sociology of Religion*, he states his preference for the focused insights of specialist experts over the fickle inspirations of casual observers, whose untutored tastes are more like those of the movie-going public:

> Nowadays, fashion or the yearnings of the literati encourage the belief that the specialist can be dispensed with or reduced to the level or subordinate provider for the "viewer". Almost all sciences owe something to the dilettante; they often owe him very valuable insights, [but] those who desire a "show" should go to the cinema [*Lichtspiel*]." (Weber 2002, 368; 1920, 14; translation modified)

Weber's scorn is directed specifically at those who allow themselves to be carried away by the trends of the moment, rather than sustaining a "sense of proportion," *Augenmaß*, with respect to the pressing demands of the day or a disciplined attention to serious matters of intellectual concern. As he suggests earlier on in the "Preliminary Remark," the ascetic work ethic which gave rise to modern Western capitalism has now been secularized and generalized into the dissolute practices of the free market, free labor, and free enterprise, to the point where the "spirit of capitalism" appears to be nowhere in particular and yet everywhere it is considered legitimate or insurmountable (cf. Gibson-Graham 2006; Wilson 2002, 25–42). Marx and Engels' name for this "twisting and inversion" of reality and appearance is *ideology*, which they picture in terms of a famous visual metaphor deriving from one of the proto-photographic and-cinematic devices of their own time: "If in all ideology humans and their relations appear upside-down as in a *camera obscura*, this phenomenon arises just as much from their historical life-process as the inversion of objects in the retina does from their physical life-process" (Marx and Engels 1975, 36; 1983, 26). Far from suggesting that the "historical life-process" runs parallel to and separate from the "physical life process," they argue that "consciousness [*das Bewusstsein*] can never be anything else than conscious being [*das bewusste Sein*]," just as popular visual technologies are the product of particular times and circumstances. A few years earlier Marx had argued that "the forming [*Bildung*] of the five senses is a labor of the entire history of the world down to the present" (Barbour and Kemple 2005; Marx 1964, 141). In other words, the eye, and not just its technological extensions, must be thought of as an agent and object of history.

Human capital theory has developed this general point by observing that not just labor-power but any institutional, objectified, or embodied technique or skill may potentially be cultivated and accumulated as a *resource*: for example, in the form of economic capacities, but also as cultural competence, interpersonal connections, political clout, or symbolic cachet. Pierre Bourdieu has refined and developed this insight into a complex theoretical model for mapping cultural fields or *social spaces* in terms of the relative intervals between agents and the "ratio" or relative volume of "the forms of capital" which they have access to. These distinctions are then used to trace the movement of institutionalized, objectified, and embodied resources through *temporal flows* which can be visualized in terms of the "rates" or relative speed by which the forms of capital are accumulated or converted into one another (Bourdieu 1986, 248, 252–4). By acknowledging the importance of emotional work and immaterial labor in constituting "the economic field" (however abstractly), Bourdieu in effect expands upon Durkheim's insights into the sentimental basis of social solidarity, and into how the common consciousness furnishes the foundation of the industrial division of labor. In short, industrial capital is *incorporated*, not only in the conventional sense that resources and property are concentrated in legally constituted organizations, but also literally as *embodied capital*, that is, when objectified wealth is converted into collective action and internalized into the mind and body of the person (Bourdieu 1986, 244–6). This embodied capital is manifested in what Weber calls "life-conducts," *Lebensführungen*, and what Marx and Engels describe as "ideas, conceptions [or images: *Vorstellungen*], consciousness, [which are] at first directly interwoven with the material activity and the material intercourse [*materiellen Verkehr*] of human beings, the language of actual life" (Marx and Engels 1975, 36; 1983, 26). In Bourdieu's vocabulary, these distinctive modes of conduct, consciousness, and practical sensibility constitute the *habitus*, which he defines as the durable cognitive structures, pragmatic dispositions, classificatory schemes, categories of perception, and "principles of vision and division" which are the distinctive properties of any given field (Bourdieu 1998, 5–8, 25).

Figure 2 (below) is my attempt to depict how the techno-cultural and socio-economic circuits of the flow of money and commodities represented in Figure 1 can also be understood to organize those "categories of perception" or "schemes of vision and division" which embody various forms of capital. As Bourdieu shows us (following Weber, Durkheim, Simmel and—arguably—Marx), the capitalist economy need not be conceived solely as a semi-autonomous field defined by the possession of material wealth (cash and commodities, for instance), but can also be treated as a "total social fact" (to use Marcel Mauss's terms), which has an irreducible cultural dimension, and which must therefore be understood in terms of its social, political, and symbolic aspects. In conventional terms, a certain *ratio* (+/-) of "cultural" to "economic" components makes up the total composition of capital in any given field and for any particular individual, just as the *rate* (-/+) of conversion and accumulation indicates the relative position of individuals or groups in

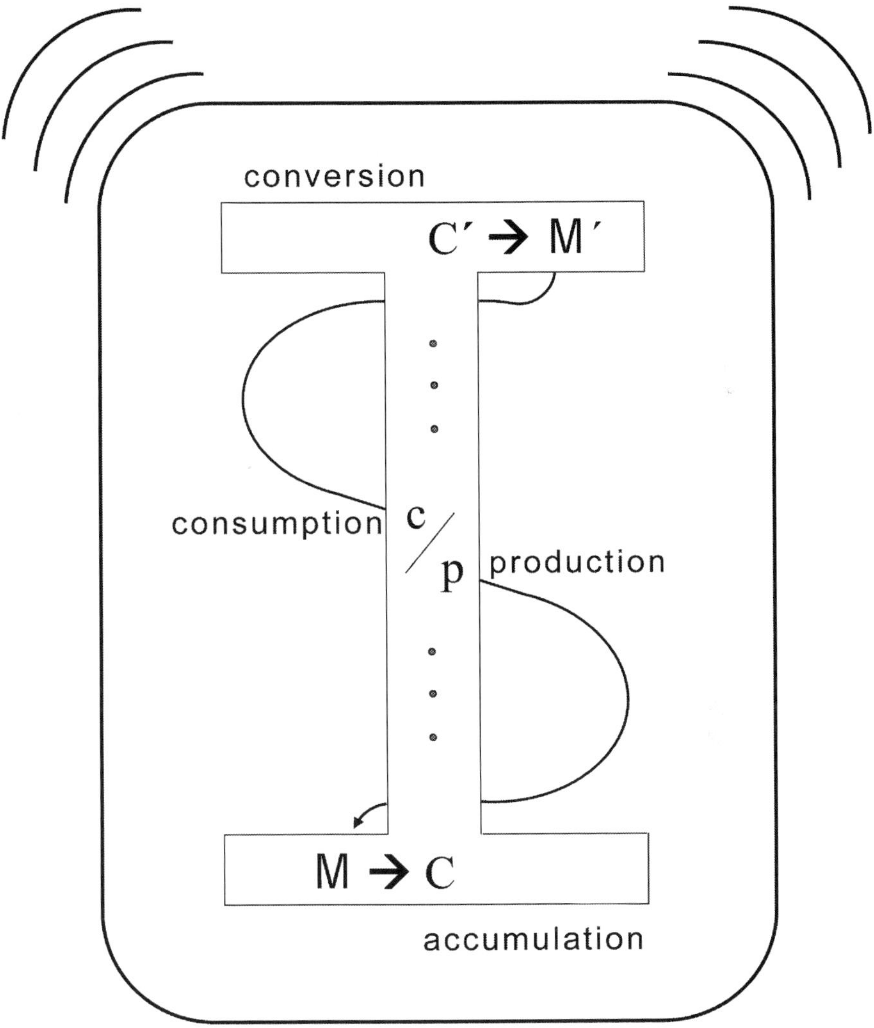

FIGURE 2 *The Eye of Capital (cf. Bourdieu 1986, 244–6; 1998, 8, 25)*

the field at any given time. What this simple configuration is meant to show is that the labor of the senses, and specifically the formation of an *entrepreneurial eye* and its *commodified gaze*, may be both productive of capital and a subject of consumption. Expanding on Erving Goffman's observation that *face-work* can be understood to include images and actions undertaken to maintain the definition of a situation or "expressive order" (Goffman 1967), we can say that the *eye-work* which is manifestly an integral component of both intellectual and manual labor is necessary to sustain the "attention economy" of capitalist culture.

Just as earlier I proposed refining Marx's labor theory of surplus value into a "life theory of tele-value" (to account for the capitalization of culture-at-a-distance), here I want to suggest that his argument can be further developed into a *leisure theory of looking* as a basis for analyzing the structure of the information-entertainment-industrial complex. That is, Marx's emphasis on the relation of surplus to necessary labor in industrial society can be extended and revised in terms of the consumer society to account for the ratio and rate of surplus to necessary *leisure*, understood to include the enforced idleness or voluntary free-time which is one of capital's most valuable, exploitable, and convertible resources. As Jonathan Beller (2006) has argued brilliantly in *The Cinematic Mode of Production: Attention Economy and the Society of the Spectacle*, capitalist production becomes seduction when sensory perception is "remediated" through the technologies of the culture industries, and when the logic of primitive capital accumulation reenters reality in an intensified way by appealing to visual perception and colonizing virtual space. The early theory and practice of cinema, such as the documentary realism and point-of-view camera angles pioneered by Dziga Virtov's "kino-eye" or the more fanciful constructions of Thomas Edison's editing and cutting techniques, do not just imitate the sensory labor of industrial production; they also expand and intensify the disciplinary coordination of bodily work necessary for its design and execution. "Early cinematic montage," writes Beller, "extended the logic of the assembly-line (the sequencing of discreet, programmatic machine-orchestrated human operations) to the sensorium and brought the industrial revolution to the eye" (Beller 2006, 9). Katherine Hayles takes the idea of "the cinematic mode of production" a step further to account for the assemblage of embodied, technological, economic, and social structures that define capital in the information age, that is, as a mode of *informatics* which includes a number of key characteristics:

> the late capitalist mode of flexible accumulation; the hardware and software that have merged telecommunications with computer technology; the patterns of living that emerge from and depend on access to large data banks and instantaneous transmission of messages; and the physical habits—of posture, eye focus, hand motions, and neural connections—that are reconfiguring the human body in conjunction with information technologies (Hayles 1999, 313; quoted in Gane and Beer 2008, 44–5).

This coordination of embodied routines with machinic interfaces should remind us that the logic of "cinema" does not operate simply within the disembodied virtual site of "deterritorialized" production, but also as an audio-visual space and as a programmed habitus wired into the apparatuses of capital itself.

As I suggested above, many of these points were already anticipated in Weber's dismissive remarks on cinema, in casual asides by Marx and Engels on the "camera obscura of ideology," if not also by Durkheim's ideas on the function of "collective representations" in symbolically regulating modern societies. In a more explicit way, they were stated by Simmel in his remarks on "the sociology of the senses," where he emphasizes the historical and cultural variability of sense impressions and perceptions along with the need for a "protective organ" to filter out the hyper-stimuli of metropolitan life. The crush of bodies and buildings in the metropolis, for instance, which forces anonymous city-dwellers to be both physically close and socially distant, simultaneously enhances "the division of labour" and mutual supplementation between the eye, which tends to favor stability and plasticity, and the ear, with its delicacy and fluidity. As Simmel remarks with reference to urban experience in the early years of the twentieth century, "we have become not only near-sighted but altogether near-sensed" (Simmel 2009, 578). Over half a century later, Marshall McLuhan would expand upon this intuition by reflecting on the possibility of recovering or reinventing our primal synaesthetic sense of space from within the apparatuses of the new audio-visual media: "Acoustic space is organic and integral, perceived through the simultaneous interplay of all the senses; whereas 'rational' or pictorial space is uniform, sequential and continuous and creates a closed world with none of the rich resonance of the tribal echoland" (McLuhan 1969, 58). Where Simmel and McLuhan tend to downplay the role of social and political economic structures of capital in configuring these sensory distinctions and combinations, however, Guy Debord stresses how the repositioning of bodies in virtual and social space is necessary for the efficient extraction of value:

> In societies where modern conditions of production prevail, all life presents itself as an immense accumulation of *spectacles*. Everything that was directly lived has moved away into representation. [...] The spectacle presents itself simultaneously as all of society, as part of society, and as *instrument of unification*. As part of society it is specifically the sector which concentrates all gazing and all consciousness. Due to the very fact that this sector is *separate*, it is the common ground of the deceived gaze and of false consciousness, and the unification it achieves is nothing but an official language of generalized separation. [...] The spectacle is *capital* to such a degree of accumulation that it becomes an image. (Debord 1983, Theses 1, 3, 34)

In the emerging "society of the spectacle" or *attention economy*, the gaze itself becomes subject to the appeal of commodification and communication, with product-placement in the movies and on television, or pervasive advertising on the internet and in everyday life, only its most obvious manifestations. It is in this literal sense that the capitalist economy distracts us into an "attention deficit," even as it also commands and cajoles us into "paying attention."

* * *

These notes on what I have called the "spectral economies of late capitalism" are primarily meant to provide a few useful perspectives and initial conceptual distinctions for understanding the everyday experience most of us have of the ebb and flow of working, shopping, watching, and communicating in the modern world. In this respect, my aim here is more descriptive and interpretive than analytical and explanatory. By keeping the examples relatively simple and accessible, I want to highlight how even abstract ideas need not be held apart from the commonsense realities and ordinary experiences they might potentially illuminate. By recovering the metaphorical implications of critical concepts, I am following Friedrich Kittler's (2010) lead in a recent collection of lectures on optical media, where he asks fellow theorists to recall the origins of the "thinking technologies" of communication they presuppose or ignore: "After all, apart from the old ritualistic meaning of 'carnival profession,' the word 'theory'—the primary word of the Greek philosophers—meant nothing other than 'look,' 'observe,' 'a feast for the eyes,' 'a spectacle,' or even 'pageantry,' and it first assumed the meaning of 'scholarly teaching' after or through Plato" (Kittler 2010, 23—4). For classical social theorists such as Marx, Weber, Durkheim, and Simmel, the notion of "theory" as an educative technique of disciplined critique and as a toolkit of concepts for distanced observation could not be easily reconciled with increasingly widespread practices of leisurely spectating or theatrical staging. Instead of analyzing the emerging media of their day in a sustained way, they were more likely to dismiss the stupefying effects of these popular pastimes on the masses, and to denounce their tendency to neutralize critical thought. Today, however, we are compelled to theorize capitalism by thinking both with(in) and against our technologies while recalling how meanings and values from previous eras are incorporated and "remediated" into later forms.

I have placed some emphasis on providing figural displays and visual constructions of the capitalist economy partly in order to draw attention to the non-verbal and often silenced aspects of contemporary manifestations of these processes, and in part to show that our ideas about a self-reproducing "economy" or self-regulating "markets" at least implicitly have an irreducible pictorial dimension. My diagrams are therefore meant to stand within the tradition of techniques of visualization which include the enormous variety of tables, charts, indexes, and columns produced over the past 300 years, in which the flows of material wealth, social transactions, and human ingenuity are displayed across space and time, from the "tableaux économiques" of the eighteenth-century Physiocrats to the graphs and grids of today's economic textbooks. What is needed is a more thorough history and detailed ethnography of these crafts and tricks of visual demonstration, along with a critical account of the reality-effects they are designed to produce (Latour 1983, 13). As Susan Buck-Morss argues in attempting to inaugurate such a project, recovering these subjugated discourses and virtual displays from the historical archive may help us to make aspects of economic thought which tend to be ignored or taken for granted more visible, and therefore more subject to critical scrutiny:

> Because the economy is not found as an empirical object among other worldly things, in order for it to be "seen" by the human perceptual apparatus it has to undergo a process, crucial for science, of representational mapping. This is doubling, but with a difference; the map shifts the point of view so that viewers can see the whole as if from the outside, in a way that allows them, from a specific position inside, to find their bearings. Navigational maps were prototypical; mapping the economy was an outgrowth of this technique. (Buck-Morss 1995, 440)

If the capitalist economy seems to take on a life of its own, this phenomenon may be result of mistaking maps for the territory they represent, or of confusing time-keeping devices for the histories they are intended to track. However imprecise or blurred our images of contemporary capitalism may be, they are often the occasion for our deep ambivalence about the value or survival of this system, so that even representations of it become the object of either hate and horror or of awe and adoration: "Iconophilia and iconophobia only make sense to people who think that images are alive" (Mitchell 2005, 3). To recall the memorable phrase of *The Communist Manifesto*, we may no longer be witnessing the terrifying or benign specter, *Gespenst*, of a new world yet to be born, or of an old one in its death throes, at least insofar as capitalism appears to have triumphed as the only alternative (Kemple 2000, 49–50; Marx and Engels 1968, 461). The new spiritual or "spectral" economy of "late" capitalism therefore seems to confirm the notion that "all that is solid melts into air," or that "everything feudal and fixed evaporates," *alles Ständische und Stehende verdampft* (Marx and Engels 1968, 465), if only into the virtual play of spectacles, sounds, signs, and simulations.

Notes

1 This essay has benefitted enormously from students in my SOCI 350 and 400 classes, who have been tutoring me on the technical and intellectual possibilities of the new media, even as I ban (most) electronic devices from the classroom in an attempt to think through the theoretical and methodological problems they pose. I am also grateful to the Department of Sociology at University of Alberta, where faculty and students responded generously to an earlier version of several ideas discussed here. Rachael Sullivan has again helped get my diagrams into shape with her skillful eye and computer savvy.

2 The case of the charismatic business leader Fernando Flores, discussed by Thrift (2005, 144–7), founder of numerous multi-million dollar management consultant and software design firms based in countries around the world, offers an extreme but instructive illustration of how the otherwise esoteric book culture of academia can be good for business: imprisoned in Chile after serving as former Finance Minister under Allende in the 1970s (that is, after the US's first '9/11' of 1973), Flores later went on to write a dissertation at Berkeley and to publish several popular management texts that trade on a philosophical vocabulary of "care, commitment, and authenticity," and on theories of performative language which express a success ethic of "communicative speech as embodied action and self-creation" (Thrift 2005, 145).

2

Can't buy me love: Psychiatric capitalism and the economics of happiness

Joel Faflak

> Life is only estimable in proportion as it is the means of our perceiving pleasurable sensations—a considerable portion of both our happiness & misery depends on our mutual relations. The laws of our existence order us in our connexion with society to search for our individual pleasure & our private pleasure is wisely connected with that of our fellow creatures. Thus man is impelled to be a social being, is impelled to promote the happiness of his fellow creatures on account of its connexion with his own happiness. He is obliged to be benevolent. Humphry Davy (ca. 1800)

Happiness in right

When Humphry Davy wrote the above notebook entry, the Western world was (arguably) on its way to becoming a happier place. Happiness historian Darrin McMahon (2006) notes that ancient notions of virtue, the ground for Christian training in a felicitous afterlife, laid the groundwork for the Enlightenment idea of a natural right to happiness. Medical historian Roy Porter puts the shift this way: the Enlightenment "translated the ultimate question, 'How can I be saved' into the pragmatic 'How can I be happy?'" (Porter 2001, 22). One immediate answer was the birth of a psychiatry designed to alleviate individuals' mental and emotional suffering but also to improve society's welfare and wellbeing, a broader psychiatric imperative tied to eighteenth-century moral philosophy, political economy, and economics. Psychiatry's pragmatism thus reflects not only moral and ethical vision but also sociopolitical efficiency. In short, from early on psychiatry was about good business as well as good intentions. The increasingly global triumph of psychiatric pharmacology in the later twentieth century suggests that the good business of psychiatry has become the big business of happiness. This chapter thus reads back to the future of psychiatry in neoclassical socioeconomic thought as an allegory of our contemporary obsession with happiness. I locate this obsession partly in the advent of what is called "happiness economics," the merger of economic theory and recent advances in psychological, sociological, and cognitive research to produce an economics *of* happiness. Like early psychiatry, this economics is non-materialistic and altruistic in its pursuit of solutions to complex global crises. But its "obligation to be benevolent" has an ideological fallout in the development of later capitalism, which increasingly appears to triumph because of, as much as in spite of, crisis—a global economy that thrives on debt, addiction, ruin.

As if to parody Humphry Davy, Slavoj Žižek (2008), marking the uncanny connection between happiness and torture, says that happiness has become our "supreme duty" (Žižek 2008, 44). Žižek speaks of the discipline of "happiness studies" from which happiness economics derives as a "combination of cognitive science and Buddhism," but with an "ethical twist": "what is offered in the guise of scientific research is a new morality that one is tempted to call *biomorality*—the true counterpart to today's biopolitics. And indeed, was it not the Dalai Lama himself who wrote: 'The purpose of life is to be happy'" (Žižek 2008, 45). To this Žižek adds the following riposte: "This is *not true* of psychoanalysis" (Žižek 2008, 45). Here Žižek alludes to Breuer and Freud's *Studies on Hysteria* (1895), in which Freud, asked by a patient how he intended to proceed with her treatment, replied that only "fate" could answer mental illness. "But," he continued, "you will be able to convince yourself that much will be gained if we succeed in transforming your hysterical misery into common unhappiness. With a mental life that has been restored to health you will be better armed against that unhappiness" (Breuer and Freud 2000, 305). With such friends, one might say ...

By the time of his 1930 text *Civilization and its Discontents* (an early title for which was "Unhappiness in Civilization") Freud had enshrined common unhappiness as culture's "convincing" defense against its own illusions, the pleasurable instinct of which was always destined to wreck itself on the shoals of its own death-driven nature. Todd Dufresne (2000) speaks powerfully for how this unavoidable Freudian insight protects psychoanalysis against its own blindness in order to shore up the field's institutional and cultural authority.

I paraphrase Dufresne's argument for my current purposes thus: Freud, confronted by psychiatry's confidence in a scientific and empirical validation to which psychoanalysis could only aspire, instead ensures the survival of psychoanalysis on the ruins of a traumatic suffering it knew it couldn't heal. Since then psychoanalysis, especially the American appropriation of Freudian practice as ego psychology, has often labored cynically on behalf of a broader psychotherapeutic industry driven by an economics of happiness in turn fuelled by the unbridled assurance of its own success at getting populations in the habit of wanting to be happy, thus increasingly linking and conflating the embodied feelings of our neurological chemistry and the immaterial yearnings of our souls. Yet I want to offer Freudian unhappiness as a mode of powerful speculation and critique that offers an antidote to the crisis-driven economics of psychiatric capitalism.

Before getting to this psychoanalytical "end," this chapter explores how early psychiatry's attack on psychopathology, already working in the spirit of democratic capitalism, constitutes a public education that yokes mental transformation to civic duty. This imaginary classroom binds self-empowered subjects in the labor of managing wayward thoughts and feelings as a way of internalizing and thus naturalizing one's obligation to the state. This enlightened examination of feeling produces the evangelical imperative to feel well, to not worry, and to be or get happy (to paraphrase Judy Garland's final number for MGM in 1950, ironically at the height of America's love affair with psychoanalysis) in the name of a "natural" empathy between individuals, a 'naturally' benevolent attention toward others. Indeed, Porter's shift to rehabilitation encrypts an ethos of salvation that psychiatry never quite leaves behind, yet one that counts on (indeed thrives on) the breakdown of minds. In short, the cynical traffic in crisis between psychiatry and capitalism is that it *addicts individuals to the right to be happy*. Happiness doesn't repair the break but instead attunes subjects to a compulsively repetitive psychopathological crisis that requires the constant pursuit *of* happiness. This (limitless) desire—bearing in mind George Bush Jr's injunction to get shopping after 9/11 and its now irrevocable alertness to sociopolitical crisis and terror—only capitalism can (temporarily) fulfill. But to beg a question to which I shall return at the end of this chapter: Can Freudian unhappiness act as a mode of powerful speculation and critique that offers an antidote to the crisis-driven economics of psychiatric capitalism?

Finding happiness

Psychiatry develops during a time of unprecedented and volatile socio-political and economic revolution and reformation, a sense of imminent emergency that invoked in individuals a sense of immanent crisis of which psychiatry's emergence is one of the time's most telling symptoms. Thomas Pfau (2006) argues that what we have come to understand as a Romantic attention to one's interior life develops (through) three moods: Revolutionary paranoia, post-Revolutionary trauma, and post-Napoleonic melancholy. These states, by signifying how feelings constitute subjects' "[capacity] for agency per se," thus offer in turn an "affective template for social praxis" (Pfau 2006, 35).[1] Yet such abject or anxious states also speak to a broader theorization of happiness as the linchpin of social organization and civil cohesion. The eighteenth century's increasingly sympathetic disposal toward the world informs moral philosophy (in the work of David Hume and Adam Smith, for instance) and aesthetics (Edmund Burke or Immanuel Kant), which in turn suggests a national training in how to overcome adversity, especially in the wake of Revolutionary crises that required among populations broad emotional re-adjustments. Key models here are Rousseau's *Emile* (1762), Goethe's *The Sorrows of Young Werther* (1774), Schiller's *On the Aesthetic Education of Man* (1794), and Godwin's *Political Justice* (1792), which together constellate in later eighteenth-century thought an emergent pan-European public education that simultaneously critiques the happiness of progress and the progress of happiness. Yet as we shall see, the Enlightenment inducement and imperative to seek happiness secures itself via a vicarious pleasure in the suffering of others, a tendency toward self-actualization masked by a greater promise of social amelioration. The roots of this rampant individualism produced on one hand a florid psychological exploration. On the other hand, by confronting an increasingly complex understanding of how the psyche and human desire work, this individualism also marshaled anxieties about the modern self. Deciding the self's permanence was less crucial than ratifying, and thus making pleasurable, the labor of an individual will trained to confront, surmount, and make coherent its own internal contradictions.

This pleasure principle, seeking to alleviate excessive agitation at any cost, compromises the modern liberal democratic project from the outset. The industrial, economic, and cultural interconnections bringing the world inexorably closer to its inhabitants made progress at once apparent and elusive. Managing this necessary and unavoidable social dimension of human nature was crucial to civic and cultural progress. Put another way, progress appeared part of humankind's natural evolution insofar as progress seemed *natural*, which is to say *desirable*. Naturalizing happiness as the immediate benefit and driving effect of social advance and amelioration thus became essential to this process. Hence, the eighteenth century's "felicific calculus" (McMahon 2006, 213) that found its optimal solution in Jeremy Bentham's utilitarian principle, expressed in *A Fragment on Government* (1776): "it is the greatest happiness of the greater number that is the measure of right and wrong" (Bentham 1988, 3)—a kind of Happiness Advisory Alert of a society's secure moral register. That Bentham uses the superlative "greatest" to characterize the ineffable state of happiness, but the comparative "greater" to correspond to its implementation in practice, should alert us to ghosts in the machine. Bentham's faith in the progressive nature of civil society had been epitomized in Locke's earlier reformist egalitarianism, which argued for the right to life, liberty, and property against poverty, injustice, and slavery. Stated in his second of *Two Treatises of Government* (1689), Locke thus speaks of natural rights deriving from the "State all Men are natural in, and that is, a *State of perfect Freedom* to order their Actions, and dispose of their Possessions, and Persons as they think fit, within the bounds of the Law of Nature, without asking leave, or depending upon the Will of any other Man" (Locke 1988, 269). Natural rights are those we expect government to ensure.

Guaranteeing these rights' inalienability, however, necessitated the social contract and its network of legal rights, to whose impartial jurisdiction men would cede the right of natural law in order to protect this law from abuse. Again, protecting an individual's natural rights required naturalizing in individuals the idea that rights *were* natural. So, for happiness to be man's natural property, he had to learn to acquire and thus deserve happiness, to discern true from illusory forms of happiness, to manage pain in order to foment pleasure. McMahon reminds us of one of Locke's fundamental paradoxes: attaining the goal of happiness is secondary to our desire for the goal in the first place. Locke names happiness as the prime mover of human desire only insofar as it counters the "uneasiness" of the will as an autonomous spur to action. Uneasiness arises in "the absence of anything, whose present enjoyment carries the idea of delight" (Locke 1975, 217). Locke sees uneasiness as the productive drive of human desire, the check ensuring that humankind kept its eyes trained on the goal of its own amelioration. Happiness only counts once "our desire ... makes us uneasy in the want of it" (Locke 1975, 234). Locke at once enshrines the pain of potential loss as essential to the attainment of happiness and encrypts the impossibility of happiness. Producing no clear equation, this felicific calculus leaves unresolved and unresolvable a desire for happiness that makes the equation possible to begin with, happiness, like utopia, being unthinkable without threats to its existence.

Locke's ambivalence evokes thereafter the struggle to account for the intangible quality of happiness. That Locke discusses happiness, not in *Two Treatises of Government*, but in *Essay Concerning Human Understanding* (1690), thus rooting the socio-political aim of happiness in the cognition and epistemology of desire, makes uneasiness symptomatic of broader anxieties about minds exceeding their own grasp. Inventing the term "*Psychiaterie*" in 1808, German physician and physiologist Johann Christian Reil wrote of psychiatry's promise of happiness: "A bold race of men dares to take on this gigantic idea, an idea that dizzies the normal burgher, of wiping from the face of the earth one of the most devastating pestilences" (cited in Shorter 1997, 8). Emerging from an eighteenth-century medical science that sought to eliminate madness's threat to civic and social progress, early psychiatry was balanced between transformation and reformation, the former rehabilitating madness as a sign of psychic potentiality, the latter suggesting a "calculated management of life" whose "will to knowledge" mobilizes the "technology of power" (Foucault 1990, 140; 12; see Picard, chapter 7).[2] In 1794, Philippe Pinel famously unchained the inmates of the Bicêtre asylum in Paris. Instead of confinement, restraint, and exclusion, Pinel advocated *traitement moral* ("moral" also meaning "psychological" or "emotional"), which stressed rehabilitation and became psychiatry's driving characteristic thereafter. An alternate early name for psychiatry, however, was "moral management," and between the two terms we see a symptomatic split that has also defined the field ever since: between psychological and physiological cure, between therapy and biology (Shorter 1997, 34), and thus between helping minds and training the mind in the body, and thus managing the body politic.

Further tensions between rehabilitation and maintenance, therapy and bureaucracy, emerged as institutions assumed custodianship of the insane from family and community. Early therapeutic communities like the Tuke family's 1792 York Quaker retreat rescued the mentally afflicted from an increasingly frenzied and complex social environment that only exacerbated their maladies. A society whose increasingly hegemonic sense of family values framed domesticity as a sentimentalized "picture of bliss" (Shorter 1997, 50) had no place for psychopathology, making its diagnosis and cure that much more urgent. This begs a further question: Did therapy teach the mentally ill how to fit into society or release them from its normative pressures? Such confusions indicate the complexities of social, political, and economic exchange confronting eighteenth-century moral philosophy and political economy. Discussing Adam Smith's dictum that we can only imagine, not share, the other's suffering, David Marshall argues that Smith, unable to see "fellow-feeling [as] automatic or even natural," explores "what it is like to want to believe in the fiction of sympathy, and what it's like to live in a world where sympathy is perhaps impossible" (Marshall 1988, 180–1). In other words, sympathy's spectacle of witnessing is an empathic mask hiding the more individualist and egoist concern for self-mastery, self-concern, and self-interest. Not being able to experience the other's suffering gets us off the hook for having to take ultimate responsibility for others.

Vivavsan Soni argues that Smith's *Theory of Moral Sentiments* (1759) "becomes a conduct manual, teaching those who suffer how to manage their behavior so that the spectator can sustain the fiction of sentimental communion; it is less interested in sentimental concern for suffering than the regulation of sentiments" (Soni 2010, 310).[3] Aestheticizing sympathy as participation in others' tragedy, Smith makes us vicarious witnesses who experience self-satisfaction rather than pathos, a sentimental veneer of ethical concern that masks a sadistic narcissism: "all men for others" is really "every man for himself." Soni's account suggests a different spin on psychiatry's implicit assumption of benevolence and a natural right to happiness. In his classic text of future political economy, *The Wealth of Nations* (1776), Smith's feeling subject is also a yeoman, whose self-commanding moral sentiment licenses taking charge within the body politic. Smith's view reflects Thomas Reid's Scottish Enlightenment notion of common sense as "that degree of judgment which is common to men with whom we can converse and transact business" (Soni 2010, 421). Edinburgh also being the epicenter of modern medicine in the eighteenth century, one sees an implicit connection between market leader and psychiatrist, both at once self-developed, empathic, and self-interested individuals disciplined in the efficient deployment of healthy feelings. In short, psychiatry is good business: keeping bad feelings at bay ensures a healthy citizen who ensures a healthy marketplace.

This equation makes little sense given that, as Andrew Scull (1991) notes, by the Victorian period psychiatry had "failed most abjectly." But its "insidious and worrying capacity to suppress non-conformity in the name of mental health," he continues, ". . . proved highly efficacious as a repressive instrument for controlling large numbers of people" (Scull 1991, 155–6). Where psychiatry failed medically and scientifically, its emergence between capitalist expansion and social regulation assured a different kind of socio-political and cultural profit that accrues from mobilizing the anxious *desire* for moral management by getting society compulsively attuned to its psychopathological life.[4] The anxiety is ironic given the Empire's profitable trade in habituates, but in light of this uncanny traffic between intemperance and sobriety, one can rephrase early psychiatry's aborted excursions into psychopathology as success by another route. The failure itself instilled the *idea* of its success—what one might call the psychiatric consciousness of a desire to domesticate the perils of looking inward for the collective payoff of getting people oriented toward the habit of wanting to be better people. To re-phrase my earlier equation: The ethical exercise staged by Smith's theatre of sympathy becomes the desire for the desire *for* happiness.

Guaranteeing happiness

Early psychiatry redounded on American shores in the early nineteenth century at the Philadelphia Hospital and Benjamin Rush, founder of American psychiatry and, ironically, prison reform. In many ways psychiatry's egalitarianism had its perfect home in the United States Declaration of Independence, which named "life, liberty & the pursuit of happiness" as the "inalienable rights" of the American people (Wills 1978, 374). Yet as Christopher Castiglia (2008) argues, the early psychopathology of American democracy's everyday institutional life (profoundly indebted to European models) works by a nervous economy whose politics of feeling is constitutive of modern liberalism itself.[5] As Soni notes, when "confronted with the opportunity to write their visionary politics into law," by enshrining these rights in the United States Constitution, "the period's revolutionary thinkers [in both America and France] balked" (Soni 2010, 2), although their constitutional documents address society's general welfare. At the precise moment that "secular happiness as a political project" (Soni 2010, 1) emerged with particular socio-historical force, it goes missing in this project's discursive forms. By way of explaining this "obsolescence," Soni argues that the eighteenth-century obsession with happiness "is better understood as the pathological symptom of an insoluble problem than as evidence of a viable political concern" (Soni 2010, 4). Eighteenth-century moral and political philosophy "balked" at happiness, not as a repression of its impossible realization, but precisely in order to think through this impossibility as part of what Soni calls "mourning happiness." Such a pursuit of happiness accepts the necessarily indeterminate and limited but nonetheless profoundly cognate nature of happiness, a melancholy embedded in the classical, Solonian judgment of happiness as a "somber event always coloured by the grief that pervades mourning" (Soni 2010, 83). The political modernity born of eighteenth-century post-Enlightenment thought has, Soni argues further, forgotten how this melancholy might be politically productive. In place of a fundamentally tragic understanding of happiness as an inevitably fraught process of ethical and political struggle and engagement we have moved to an essentially dehistoricized metaphysics of happiness embodied solely in the individual as he finds solace in "the realm of the family and marriage" (Soni 2010, 21) and in the "affective conception of happiness" (Soni 2010, 19) that turns it into "an ordinary concept with no particular privilege" (Soni 2010, 22).

Stating that "[h]appiness names the realm of privacy itself" (Soni 2010, 21), Soni thus reminds us how an eighteenth-century ideal of felicity has turned from an ethical or political to an ideological concern—or rather, to a politics aspiring to a purely ideological dimension of the subtle yet persuasive discipline of subjects within supposedly liberal society.[6] In short, is the fact that we are "obliged to be benevolent," to cite Davy, symptomatic of a more obsessive compulsion to seek out happiness at all costs which masks more insidious passions? Addressing another affect, Karyn Ball (2006) argues that modern civil society uses guilt to excuse the excessive governmentality that is the symptom of democracy's unconsciously sadomasochistic nature. For Ball, borrowing Freud's notion of how guilt "transforms sadism into masochism" (Ball 2006, 53), masochism internalizes guilt in order to economize a broader, more destabilizing, and ultimately ideologically effective sadism. Liberal democracy's crisis of conscience encrypts an intrepid avidity by which capitalism ultimately profits: "liberal criticism not only seeks to regulate this excess but also acts it out masochistically at the level of a wounded and guilt-ridden identification with democratic state ideals" (Ball 2006, 57). Put another way, liberal democracy makes a spectacle of confessing its guilty part in perpetrating global socio-economic imbalances in order to mask and thus alleviate its guilt for the pleasures it gains from such inequities.

Perhaps our current obsession with happiness is the Janus face of a liberal guilt driving happiness as an intangible ideal rendered utopian precisely by the metaphysics of its own impossibility. In the face of problems that threaten happiness and thus require a confrontation with real unhappiness—natural disasters, economic volatility, political instability, all impacting an increasingly broader and interconnected geopolitical terrain—happiness becomes the default position to which we recur in the mode of what Slavoj Žižek calls "interpassivity" (Žižek 2007, 22–7). Like prayer wheels that do the work of faith for us, or pornography that fornicates for us, the pursuit of happiness in contemporary society works by a "bourgeois humanism" (Eagleton 2003, 205) that substitutes for the real work of living, for the ethical and political complexities and engagements necessary to undertake the forward movement of surviving on the planet. Accepting happiness as our "supreme duty," to paraphrase Žižek, allows us to avoid its darker responsibility.

Žižek might also be thinking of "happiness economics," exemplified in the socio-economic theories of Richard Layard (2005) and Bruno Frey (2008). Layard's and Frey's theories are indebted to the more general phenomenon of happiness studies Žižek mentioned earlier, the academically more "legitimate" progeny of the earlier development of self-help manuals, pop psychology, and what is broadly (and usually disparagingly) called New Age philosophy. Unsurprisingly, this history goes back to Bentham. For Layard, founder of the Centre for Economic Performance at the London School of Economics and a member of the House of Lords, Bentham, "one of the greatest thinkers of the Enlightenment," epitomizes a spirit of egalitarianism that, in the face of the twentieth-century diminishment of religious belief and the "secular religion of socialism," produced the "non-philosophy of rampant individualism" and its "ideal of 'self-realization'" that has left us yearning for an earlier Enlightenment "concept of the common good" (Layard 2005, 5). To this yearning, Layard concludes, we are finally, again, paying serious attention. Layard sees in the advances in cognitive and behavioral psychology since the mid twentieth-century, which in turn sparked the current revolution in pharmacology, a theoretical elixir offering practical solutions. This "new psychology of happiness," coupled with neuroscience, sociology, economics and philosophy, will allow us to "produce a new vision of how we can live better, both as social beings and in terms of our inner spirit" (Layard 2005, 4).

Lest we stall at the implicit New Age-iness of this last statement, Layard qualifies that "the Enlightenment philosophy can now at last be applied using evidence instead of speculation" (Layard 2005, 6). This focus on the empirical is key to the research of another guru of happiness economics, Swiss academic Bruno Frey, who also proclaims the productive cross-fertilization between standard economics and the new psychology of happiness. Introducing the three main innovations this new psychology presents for economics—measurement, new insights, and policy consequences—Frey argues that "[h]appiness research enables us not only to acknowledge these behavioral features [of humans attempting to distinguish and judge between material vs. immaterial liabilities and assets of personal and social satisfaction] but also to analyze them empirically" (Frey 2008, x). Key to both Layard's and Frey's approaches is thus the desire to put a human face on the otherwise statistical and conceptual inhumanity of standard economic practice, and to offer this as a model governments might follow in rethinking future economic policy.[7] This anthropomorphization gives specular form to the psychopathology of an economy's everyday life, as if Bentham's philosophy was simply waiting for the embodied form of contemporary psychology in order to psychoanalyze and thus cure what might (and did) go implicitly wrong within this philosophy's otherwise altruistic form. Yet we have already seen within Bentham's dictum the viral form of its own political economy. In short, one notes in happiness economics a desire to make one of the most elusive of human endeavors empirically verifiable in order to allay our deepest fears. The human desire to avoid "mourning happiness" is perfectly understandable; fomenting the illusion that this melancholy *can* be avoided is rather more problematic. That happiness economics exists largely as a spur to government economic policy reform betrays a rather conservative bias against tampering with the illusions of happiness of which the recent Occupy movement and its attention to the realities of economic crisis is a potent reminder.

Buying happiness

A recent cover story for *Harper's* puts the socio-political aims of an economics of happiness in mediating our current mode of global crisis in rather stark and disturbing relief. In "The War on Unhappiness: Goodbye Freud, Hello Positive Thinking," (2010) Gary Greenberg, practicing psychotherapist, depression patient, and author of *Manufacturing Depression: The Secret History of a Disease* (2010), documents his experience of attending the Evolution of Psychotherapy Conference at the Anaheim Convention Centre. The conference's message was clear: psychoanalysis has failed and psychotherapy needs to move on, especially in a country at once constitutionally predisposed to avoid unhappiness at all costs. In the 1950s, America's post-World War II psyche, haunted by triumph, embraced psychoanalysis largely by championing the ego's ability to surmount threats within and beyond its defenses (the ego psychology that infuriated Jacques Lacan). But post-9/11 political and economic volatility has in turn rallied a patriotism impatient with the idea of examining the nation's psychopathological life, what Greenberg calls "[Freud's] notion of an unseen other—the mysterious unconscious self who bedevils our every decision, who eludes us yet must be sought—... [that] courses through the white noise of our lives" (Greenberg 2010, 29).

For psychoanalysis, the resistance to introspection indicates a repression and evasion the understanding of which is one of talk therapy's primary goals. Yet dealing with psychic indeterminacy, and thus risking lingering with failure, no longer fits our increasingly socialized mode of ceaseless action, which explains why psychoanalysis has been eclipsed by cognitive behavioral therapy (CBT): "Identify and repair the glitches in our operating system—*dysfunctional thoughts* that arise automatically from our unduly negative *core beliefs*—and we will find no adversity we cannot meet with resilience. We will be programmed for success" (Greenberg 2010, 31). Whereas psychoanalysis tarries with the complex and often regressive nature of human relations, CBT, avoiding such delays and detours, believes in sympathy's illusions. Martin Seligman, one of CBT's heirs and inventor of positive psychology, stresses the individual desire for happiness as a capacity for "human flourishing" (cited in Greenberg 2010, 32). Cultures flourish because they fit their individuals for success. In the 1960s Seligman, one of Layard's and Frey's tutelary spirits, subjected dogs to electric shocks, many of whom "simply whined and curled up in a ball" after "the first jolt." Applied to humans, this "learned helplessness" confirmed a key cause of depression. By thus learning to identify and avoid the sources of trauma, Seligman held, one could be a happier person. Most recently, the American military (to the tune of $10–15 billion annually) has deployed positive psychology "to create an Army that is just as psychologically fit as it is physically fit ... [S]oldiers who learn optimism will heal faster when they are wounded on the battlefield" (Greenberg 2010, 34). Positive psychology offers a rather ironic twist on the orientalist stereotype of the threat posed to Christian civilization by insensate Muslim hordes steeled by opium: a happy army is an invincible army. As Greenberg notes, it should come as no surprise "that a country dedicated in its infancy to the pursuit of happiness would grow up to make it a compulsion" (Greenberg 2010, 35). One might say "addiction."

I return to Žižek's both profoundly and hilariously morose addendum, "This is *not true* of psychoanalysis," which names psychoanalysis' default position of disillusioned unhappiness, an irrefutable skepticism that Dufresne, as we saw earlier, addresses as the endgame of psychoanalytic theory. By *Beyond the Pleasure Principle* (1920), Freud and the science on which he pinned his personal and professional hopes were embattled, a psychodrama that plays out with Freud's death in 1939 as a Jew exiled by National Socialism. This narrative's pathos masks the false consciousness of Freud's theory, which traps us in the repetition compulsion of its irrefutably tragic nature. For Dufresne the death drive is the crux of a "metapsychology [that] became the delicate inner space of psychoanalysis, a theater or cave from which everything began and will return again and against which nothing truly critical can be said" (Dufresne 2000, 182).[8] The death drive and repetition compulsion name how we are doomed, like Oedipus, to avoid our own insight. Yet they also constitute the discipline's theoretical alibi: psychoanalysis explains why we avoid psychoanalysis. Such an alibi guarantees psychoanalysis' potently spectral half-life in the cultural unconscious. Hence every decade or so *Time* or *Newsweek* declares Freud dead—a melancholic resuscitation that perpetually forestalls any attempt to move past psychoanalysis.

Dufresne's analysis, somewhat counter-intuitively to that of Greenberg, also speaks implicitly to the cynical economy of psychiatric capitalism we have explored to this point—to the uncanny relationship between Freud's ordinary unhappiness and CBT's extraordinary happiness. Yet Greenberg, like Žižek, also reminds us of psychoanalysis' haunting as a profoundly necessary theoretical rem(a)inder. As much as the various discursive, institutional, and therapeutic practices of psychoanalysis, like those of psychiatry, constitute a form of ideological manipulation, psychoanalysis also unmasks this ideology's fantasy structure as being at once mobilized and haunted by a desire that always exceeds ideology. In an article in the *London Review of Books* several years ago, Žižek states that "reality is for those who can't sustain the [perversity of the] dream" (Žižek 2006b, 34). Žižek revises the implicitly idealist notion that dreams fulfill our repressed wishes, the over-arching point of Freud's *Interpretation of Dreams*, by reminding us that the dream speaks to the fundamental crux of our desire, the location of which Lacan calls the real. We disavow this desire through the substitutive structure of a reality by which we presume to live. That is to say, in place of our desire—and, paradoxically, in order to deal with our desires—we substitute ordinary reality as a both ineluctable and necessary fantasy structure that sustains desire's otherwise excoriating nature. The point is not to exterminate ordinary reality—as if we could, though history keeps trying—but rather compulsively to redress our attention to reality *as* fantasy.

Reading happiness economics *avec* psychoanalysis means mourning rather than realizing happiness as perhaps our ultimate fantasy version of reality. Psychiatry's utopian, benevolent drive from early on also produced one of the earliest and indeed most radical forms of a later psychoanalysis whose epistemology takes as its constitutive nature the mind's resistance to enlightenment, what Jacques Derrida calls psychoanalysis' "greatest speculative power" (Derrida 1998, 118).[9] The point of such speculation is of the utmost political and ethical consequence: to remind us that desire itself is always beyond our grasp. One might answer Layard or Frey, who work in the implicitly psychiatric spirit of Bentham's dictum, with an ethos of a happiness always attentive to its own impossibility, a knowledge that never mistakes reality for the desire by which it is sustained, for the achievement of this reality signals the most devastating idealism of all: the end of human desire itself. Put another way, the point is not that desire *can* be claimed, for *to* claim desire ultimately signals the end of the *desiring* subject—which is to say, the end of the subject.

I am also thus suggesting one dangerous pitfall of this approach, however, for it is precisely on this impossibility that late-capitalist myths of progress feed by training us to desire what it knows we can never have. Indeed, in the more than apparent, ever-growing rift between the ever-richer super-rich and an expanding underclass one sees in the death-driven perpetuation of the pursuit of happiness its rather more cynical drive and necessity. To say that higher incomes are not and should not be the only source of happiness, one of Layard's and Frey's corrections to standard economic theory, is also implicitly to get people accustomed to a world that offers them rather more of less than a politics and ethics of selflessness, empathy, and self-restraint might suggest. Žižek deploys Lacan as part of a post-Marxism that explains how society disavows desire *on our behalf.* Holding out the promise of happiness to individuals is society's way of disavowing happiness on our behalf, which in turn holds out the illusion of a possible attainment *of* happiness that precludes our mourning its impossibility, our getting on with the business of living. Most disturbing about the broader psychiatric capitalism and its economics of happiness is the extent to which it sustains this disavowal via a kind of crisis management. The repetition compulsion of the desire for the desire for happiness exploits the vicissitudes and volatilities of human nature as an inevitable response to socio-economic change. Perpetrating the very global instabilities to which it can then be seen to respond, this economics puts happiness itself in a perpetual state of crisis, continually threatened by its lack of attainment as an unhappiness that ensures the endless play upon an inevitably anxious human response for which it offers the tantalizing tangibility of cures. The new economics of happiness that I am suggesting holds out the promise of real solutions, but it also teaches us how to be happy with the very crises it produces. Put simply: it teaches us how to be happy with, rather than to live with, death. One eventuality of the felicific calculus that generated the modern science of psychiatry has been the spectacular growth of pharmacology and the pharmaceutical industry, which bypasses thought altogether by putting good feelings directly into the population's veins. While one would never dispute such prescriptions in the case of profound psychological suffering, let's hope they haven't become our only emotional currency.

Notes

1 See also Favret (2010).

2 The study of psychiatry's history veers between the pioneering medical history of Porter and the poststructuralism of Michel Foucault, the godfather of anti-psychiatry, which finds its most vocal advocate in Thomas Szasz. Between Porter and Foucault one can read a tension between psychiatric *history*, in which slamming psychiatry takes a back seat to assessing the facts, and psychiatric *historiography*, which interprets historical evidence as symptomatic of a broader cultural imaginary with ideological designs on individuals and populations. My work is inspired by Foucault's methodology, but is increasingly mindful of the productive objectivity of Porter's ironic detachment.

3 Soni continues: "In this perverse shift, *The Theory of Moral Sentiments* turns into very nearly its opposite: it places responsibility not with the spectators, but with those who are afflicted, enjoining them to regulate their conduct in such a way as to occasion as little disturbance as possible in the equanimity of spectators" (Soni 2010, 310).

4 Texts like Thomas Trotter's 1807 *A View of the Nervous Temperament* (Trotter also wrote one of the first tracts against drunkenness) sounded the call for sobriety: "the temperate man is observed to bear sickness with more patience and resignation, than those accustomed to indulgence" (Trotter 1976, 137). Moderation restores bodily vitality to the body politic by managing its habits, which, Trotter claims, "if not restrained soon, must inevitably sap our physical strength of constitution; make us an easy conquest to our invaders; and ultimately convert us into a nation of slaves and ideots [sic]" (Trotter 1976, xi).

5 Critics such as Evan Gottlieb, in *Feeling British: Sympathy and National Identity in Scottish and English Writing, 1707–1832* (2007), and Jon Mee, in *Romanticism, Enthusiasm, And Regulation: Poetics and the Policing of Culture in the Romantic Period* (2003), make a similar if methodologically different pitch for the formation of British Romantic thought, culture, and politics.

6 This is Soni's fundamental revision of McMahon's comprehensive history of happiness: "whereas McMahon finds the emergence of a political concept of happiness in the eighteenth century, I find the emergence of a crisis that will render happiness obsolete as a political concept" (Soni 2010, 3n).

7 A recent publication refuting the general premise of happiness economics that benign government intervention in the name of non-material gains can produce successful social outcomes is the volume of essays *... and the Pursuit of Happiness: Wellbeing and the Role of Government* (2012), edited by Philip Booth. As Mark Littlewood, Director General and Ralph Harris Fellow of the Institute of Economic Affairs, writes in his Foreword, the "arguments and conclusion" of "those 'happiness economists' who believe in deliberate government action and planning to increase measured wellbeing" are "either trivial or wrong" (Booth 2012, 17). The implicit tension addresses here is between government intervention and the free will of the marketplace.

8 Dufresne argues that Lacan's perpetuation of the Father's legacy is crucial to this half-life, for "having found the place of Truth empty in light of the deaths of God and Man, [he] nonetheless continued to play the role of resurrected father; like Freud, Lacan occupied a privileged reference point in the transmission of psychoanalytic knowledge" (Dufresne 2000, 11).

9 One study that examines how psychoanalysis emerges in tandem with psychiatry in the late eighteenth and early nineteenth centuries: see my *Romantic Psychoanalysis* (2007).

3

Metaphoric wealth: Finance, financialization, and the end of narrative

Max Haiven

Introduction

This chapter asks us to understand finance as a *cultural* system. The past forty years have seen the rise of "financialization": the growing influence of financial speculation on the global economy, and the deep imbrications of financial "logics" into everyday life the world over. Throughout this period, finance has come both to influence culture (as a realm of shared understandings, representations, and human relationships) and to be increasingly "cultural" in that it both influences and relies upon social action and meaning, shared belief, and linguistic participation. I argue that financialization is *both a cause and a consequence* of a broad shift away from narrative and towards metaphor (see MacLellan, chapter 4). Financialization forces us to contend with a fragmentary world where narratives no longer seem to hold and where our shared understandings of social and economic processes are increasingly disjunctive and chaotic. But while finance may be a metaphoric system, where abstractions of money and risk create a hyper-complex interwoven system of representations, it is not merely an elite hallucination of "imaginary money." On the contrary, finance expresses the phenomenal power and obscene perversion of the collective imagination under an incredibly dangerous form of global capitalism.

Financialization and the foreclosure of the future: An overview

The past forty years have been marked by the rise of neoliberal globalization: the toxic cocktail of social forces organized around free market fundamentalism and the systematic destruction of the Keynesian welfare state (where it existed) and its associated forms of collective wealth and insurance (McNally 2011; Giroux 2008). The role that financial speculation played in this massive global transformation is only now becoming unavoidably apparent, at least in the global North. But in the "third world" the neocolonial politics of debt and credit have been widely acknowledged for several generations (Bello, Bullard, and Malhotra 2000; Nkrumah 1980). The predatory and disastrous agendas of international lending institutions like the World Bank and International Monetary Fund came to shape the economic (and, subsequently, social and political) lives of the vast majority of the world's inhabitants through the latter half of the twentieth-century, subverting much of the revolutionary hope and imagination that animated anti-colonial movements (Benjamin 2007; Prashad 2008). Conversely, with the advances in transportation and communication technology after World War II, "first world" capital was able to "globalize" production as never before, taking advantage of Southern nation states "softened up" by predatory lending (and direct or indirect political subversion) in order to move the bulk of manufacturing "off-shore" (De Angelis 2007; McNally 2011). The neoliberal attack on public services and industrial and corporate regulation, as well as the insistence on the liberalization of trade through organizations like the World Trade Organization (and through subsequent nation-to-nation trade agreements), led to a condition of unprecedented capital mobility, with "foreign direct investment" rushing in and out of economies around the world, typically with disastrous effects (LiPuma and Lee 2004; Strange 1997). In addition, nations now operating under huge deficits (due to neoliberal tax-cuts and inflation) were dependent as never before on the sale of bonds and the stability of their currencies, both of which were traded with terrifying alacrity on an increasingly interconnected network of global exchanges. The millennium opened on to a global scene where anonymous, fickle, and unpredictable financial markets held a sword over the head of most countries around the world. Craven governments and leaders around the world generally responded by seeking to anticipate the dictates of neoliberalism and competed to obey them so as to prove their countries worthy of "investment" from increasingly mobile multi-national corporations and the mercurial flows of financial forces (Albo, Ginden, and Panich 2010).

This "race to the bottom" to eliminate any "barriers to trade"—workers' rights, environmental protections, taxes, tariffs—was not only the fate of poor, indebted countries but also large, Northern "developed" nations. The flight of industry from these economies for the greener pastures of Export Processing Zones and low-bidding Third World subcontractors, along with the decay of the power and will of organized labour and a systematic attack on the welfare state, left the Northern middle classes shadows of their former selves (Aronowitz and DiFazio 2010). By 2008, household debt had come to vastly outpace household assets in the United States and other Northern countries (Foster and Magdoff 2009, 28–32; Sauvé 2011). Declining real wages, increasing user fees (for health and education), and ever-rising housing, food, and fuel prices meant that people were borrowing in order to maintain the middle-class lifestyles they had come to associate with meaningful social belonging and security, all while corporations and financiers devoured the share of social wealth that once made that "class" a possibility. Meanwhile, the commodification of practically everything—child- and elder-care, social security, pensions, etc.—meant that Northern post-citizens were expected to borrow, save, and invest as individuals, rather than as collectives (Martin 2002).

As a result of all this, by the 2008 financial crisis something profound had happened. Finance was no longer the playground of elites, a realm of idle speculation by bankers and high rollers. It was a fact of everyday life for almost everyone around the world. By finance here I am referring to a shifting category, one that begins with the so called "FIRE" (finance, insurance, and real-estate) segment of the economy and broadens out to include the inter-related system of saving and lending that increasingly intersect our lives at multiple levels (Langley 2008; Martin 2007). From the "beneficiaries" of micro-finance loans in the Third World (Bateman 2010) to the debt-burdened and mortgaged post-middle-class of the global North, few could say their lives and fates were not bound up with the abstractions of financial markets. As Randy Martin (2007, 3–7) has pointed out, neoliberalism saw the rise of (and contributed to) a cultural idiom of "risk management." As the welfare state and other forms of collective social good retreated under the neoliberal barrage, a new set of "practices of the self" advanced which advocated that individuals see themselves less as a part of a broader society and more as individualized "risk-takers," solely responsible for their fate in a world where they should expect no help from the state or society if they "failed" (Martin 2007, 2002). The ideological promotion of "good debt," the proliferation of credit cards, the sub-prime mortgage balloon, and the privatization of pensions and social security all implied the emergence of a neoliberal subject who gleefully embraced globalization as the liberation of Economic Man from the stifling nursery of the Nanny State (Brown 2005; Perelman 2011).

Meanwhile, however, the financial economy has become more invested in everyday life than ever before. For one, as the sub-prime crisis revealed, everyday finance (like mortgages and consumer debt) is today deeply integrated into the global speculative market in ways that cannot be untangled. So too do indicators like "consumer confidence," housing starts, and the average default rates on student loans and credit card debt influence the global economy in ways that are as complex as they are dramatic (Akerlof and Schiller 2009). Further, just as multinational corporations have come to control more and more aspects of daily life, so too do the financial markets come to control (in abstract ways) the actions of these corporations, imposing a universal discipline on firms to increase profitability by cornering new markets, reducing labour costs, globalizing production, and "externalizing" the social and environmental costs of business (De Angelis 2007). As new computing and networking technology enabled a hyper-accelerated spectrum of investment opportunities and a financial empire of round-the-clock trading, new "investment vehicles" were developed for the dissection and reassembly of financial securities that defy the imagination. Credit Default Swaps, Collateralized Debt Obligations, and other products of financial alchemy became household names in the wake of the financial crisis, but they represent only the tip of an iceberg of forms of speculation based on the trade in "derivatives": not actual real-world assets but abstract agreements to buy and sell financial assets at a future date, agreements which themselves become tradable objects for further speculation (LiPuma and Lee 2004, 33–66). Wall Street bundles, breaks up, and rebundles assets from all over the world in complex, shifting ways as assets pass back and forth between banks and major financial institutions in ways that boggle the imagination (Henwood 2003, 187–225). These securities—which include or refer to consumer debt, household debt, student debt, the debt of third world countries, the debt of major corporations, and first world treasuries—all met, collided, and fragmented thousands if not millions of time per day as massive financial players capitalized on speculation (Foster and Magdoff 2009, 67–88). In this way, as much as finance has entered everyday life in unprecedented ways, so too has everyday life entered finance.

A number of scholars have encouraged us to understand this as a moment of "financialization": both the domination of the "real economy" by finance and the deep integration and dependence of finance on everyday life (Langley 2008; Martin 2007). The term financialization auspiciously forces us to acknowledge that finance is no longer a *thing* existing separate from the "real economy," but a heading for a wide variety of complimentary *processes*: the way corporations are increasingly disciplined by abstract international markets; the way nation states increasingly function to seduce and solicit those markets; the way individuals (must) embrace debt and credit to make do; and the way a logic of speculation, risk-management, and the asthmatic constriction of futurity has come to characterize popular culture and lived experience.

For critics like Ernst Bloch (1995) and Robin D. G. Kelley (2002), the future is not merely "what comes next," nor is it an individualized relationship to causality and social life. Instead, *futurity is the way we share an anticipatory idiom*, the means by which social life is always negotiated within shared frameworks of expectation. We are able to cooperate—fairly or unfairly, equally or exploitatively—because we share an understanding of the likely future outcomes of our actions. In this sense, futurity has less to do with the actual future and more to do with how shared ideas of the future (based on narratives of the past and present) come to "work" on the "now." From this approach, social power is always invested in influencing or shaping how subjects imagine the future, on controlling or constraining the sense of the possible and the inevitable. While this may be easiest to imagine in the case of a totalitarian theocracy, which cites supernatural forces to justify the eternal validity of its rule, it is equally true of the (neo)liberal system of today, albeit in complicated ways.

The dramatic effect of finance on our social sense of futurity stems, to a large extent, from its pre-emptive capacity. The flows of financial wealth respond less to real-world circumstances and more to a spectrum of possible outcomes. Increasingly complicated financial logics and technologies for calculating "risk"—a quantitative explanation or numerical "metaphor" for the likelihood of profitable returns—effective pre-maps the world, transforming the inherent possibility and uncertainty of human action into a tradable commodity (see LiPuma and Lee 2004, 119–25; Martin 2007, 3–4). Conversely, however, finance's *disciplinary* power, the way it shapes the behaviors of individuals, corporations, nation states, and other economic actors, is based less on actual actions (e.g. defaulting on a loan, caving to workers' demands, or curtailing corporate freedoms) and more on the *risk* of these actions. Hence finance allows the system as a whole to anticipate and pre-emptively intervene in the flows of social, economic, and political life. For this reason I have elsewhere suggested that we understand finance as the "imagination" of the economic system as a whole: it offers global capital a synthetic "sense" of global totality and futurity (Haiven 2011).

Financialization in many ways defines the new paradigm of struggle. Even as revolutionary movements, such as those in Egypt and elsewhere, struggle for meaningful democratic autonomy, they do so in the shadow of transnational financial markets that preventively divest themselves of national assets if they suspect the national economy might become less "business friendly" (Hanieh 2011). Similarly, today seemingly stable Northern governments have yet to discover a means by which, in the face of global financial mobility and the globalization of the manufacturing sector (and now a good deal of technological and intellectual labor), they can sustain the carrot of a "middle-class lifestyle" for a sufficient portion of their population. Consequently, they too are under the incessant blackmail of the market.

The collapse of narrative

As capital and finance expand both intensively (into the social fabric of reproduction) and extensively (to every corner of the globe), we have witnessed the regrettable retreat of radical visions of a different world (Haiven and Khasnabish 2011). As Jean and John Comaroff (2001) note, neoliberal "millennial" capitalism is marked by cultures of fatalism and despair wrought of a world without guarantees, where (ironically) the future at once seems increasingly unpredictable *and* stagnantly inevitable. The "end of history" that Francis Fukuyama (1993) announced shortly after the fall of the Berlin Wall was a masthead for neoliberalism as a cultural narrative that insisted that all of human history had led to the current moment of global capitalist supremacy. Henceforth, all struggles would be small corrections to political systems to enable the magic of the free market. The eternal struggle of humans for Hegelian "recognition" by their peers would no longer take the form of big ideas, but of personal goals and rewards within the universal capitalist economy. But as social visions eroded under the cultural idiom of "risk management" and the privatization of futurity, so too did much of the context for people's misery and dislocation. Fatalism, cynicism, and resignation have become cultural norms, at least where they haven't been countered by rising forms of nationalist or religious fundamentalism that desperately seeks to protect older modes of life (real or imagined) from the market. For our purposes here, it is important to note another key aspect of this cultural problem. As globalization advanced, the means people had of explaining their existential conditions to themselves became disjunctive. As Arjun Appadurai (1996, 27–46) has noted, globalization both undermines previous worldviews and allows for new, hybrid narratives—pastiches—of many elements of an increasingly global cultural landscape. The problem is that the whole system is far too complex for even the most arrogant worldview to fully comprehend. Frederic Jameson (1984), for one, has noted the increasing difficulty we have in "mapping causality" under globalization: the narratives we once used to explain our lives, where we fit and what we can achieve, no longer seem reliable or particularly useful in explaining the massive complexity of the global system and its subtle and not-so-subtle impacts on all our localized lives.

Indeed, even neoliberal ideologies and free-market fundamentalists find themselves largely unable to explain or predict global outcomes. While the hubristic pronouncements of the End of History have been somewhat chastened by the 2008 financial crisis, there were signs of narrative crisis long before this moment. While neoliberal demagogues insisted that cutting corporate taxes and dismantling state regulatory regimes would lead to broad prosperity, there were very few reliable narratives about when, where, and how this would work. And while answers were proffered about why it *didn't* work in the Asian Tigers, in the post-Soviet states, and in many countries in Africa and Latin America, the truth was that neoliberalism could only offer faith in free markets, not a reliable narrative of how those free-markets actually *worked*. Setting aside the (valid) arguments that neoliberal rationalizations of finance were merely theoretical obfuscation by political and economic elites, the flows of international finance are simply too volatile and complicated to spin into a reliable narrative outside the confines of theoretical abstraction and circumstantial examples.

Similarly, fundamentalist religious and ethnic-nationalist narratives have also encountered crisis. Both are generally based on the elevation of certain "intrinsic" values over all others. But under financialized neoliberalism, where the future seems ever more volatile and where all social values must subordinate themselves to the "almighty dollar," the capacity for reworking fundamentalist or nationalist values is diminished. For instance, fervent patriotism has not led to the revivification of the American golden age, nor have "religious family values" led to the salvation of normative family units from the ravages of neoliberal austerity, job loss, and economic precarity. Sadly this has not led to the rejection of these proto-fascistic narratives—quite the opposite. But it does indicate that their power to map social causality increasingly relies on faith, rather than a real ability to predict or offer meaningful agency over the future.

Arguably this failure of narrative has a good deal to do with finance and financialization. For one, our capacity for social narrative, for "mapping causality" through stories, depends on our ability to chart our relatively linear futures: the consequences of certain present tendencies and trajectories. When we do so, however, we are in conflict with another part of ourselves: the financialized elements of our subjectivity that, by necessity, have come to interpret the world and its possible futures in the mode of "risk management." As Randy Martin (2007, 32–7) explains, this mode is based less on long-term vision or even coherent prediction but the reduction of the future to a matrix of risks and profitability. For instance, education has largely ceased to be seen as a pursuit offered and undertaken for the public good, i.e. to produce competent and responsible citizens cognizant of their rights and responsibilities and prepared to take up roles in civil society. Instead, education is marketed as a site of personal and financial investment: students are encouraged to take out loans in order to build their "human capital" in order to make more money in the future (Williams 2009). Education is seen as a vector of risk to be embraced and leveraged into private prosperity.

In this sense, in an era of financialization—where we have all been taught to manage our lives like individual risk portfolios—any collective social or political vision comes to be seen as an alien intrusion. What is slowly eroded here is any narrative of *shared* futurity or possibility. Indeed, even private narratives are filled with contingencies and the unforeseen. Youth are encouraged to understand a narrative of one's life as untrustworthy and to embrace moment-by-moment risk management as a means to succeed in a world without guarantees (McRobbie 2002; Ross 2009).

As a result, we are left largely bereft of any shared language to make narrative sense of world events. This was especially evident in the wake of the 2008 financial crisis where pundits, politicians, commentators, and other figures were at a loss to explain how and why the system had failed. In the end, the crisis was generally blamed on greed, avarice, and deceit—seemingly eternal and irascible human traits that poisoned an otherwise rational system. While some off-handed references were made to past financial crises and many alarming allusions were drawn to the Great Depression, what emerged in the aftermath of the Crisis was no tangible narrative of how or why the crisis came to pass.

While this may have a good deal to do with the way corporate and profit-oriented media, education, and entertainment industries have dramatically delimited the possibilities for the sophisticated discussion of critical social issues, the financialization of society has a lot to do with the failure of narrative itself. Finance encourages us to see the future as a landscape of risks, rather than a horizon of sociopolitical opportunity, and as it systematically breaks down any experience or possibility of collective agency, it leaves our culture barren of the resources for constructing or sustaining shared narratives (Reinsborough 2011). More profoundly, financialization participates in a dramatic "end of temporality," the collapsing of the past and the future into the present (Jameson 2003). When all past moments are held to have led to the current neoliberal bliss and the future is understood as merely the continuation of the same, the possibilities for telling stories about how we came to be in this situation and where we may go diminish dramatically. Importantly, this one-dimensional temporality is not merely an "ideological" imposition imposed upon us by propaganda. It is part of the fabric of our financialized existence. A good example of this cultural tendency is the recent Oliver Stone film *Wall Street: Money Never Sleeps*, a sequel to his 1984 classic starring

Michael Douglas as the high-rolling scumbag Gordon Gekko. This film is a good-faith attempt to spin a compelling and critical narrative out of the 2008 financial crisis, one that mobilizes all of the considerable talent and Hollywood resources the director can bring to bear. While often simplistic, melodramatic, and kitsch, it is hard to deny that Hollywood is the most compelling forge of narrative commodities the world has ever seen, producing scores of spell-binding films each year that dazzle and seduce audiences around the world with their near-narcotic mix of honed visual and narrative technique, appealing and beautiful (if typically one-dimensional) characters, and easily digestible plot and motive concepts.

Yet despite this, the film failed in Stone's objective: where the realities behind the financial crisis are not buried under simplistic interpersonal melodrama they severely test audience attention spans. Ultimately, the film reinforces the idea that the crisis was the result of greed and profligacy, rather than deep systemic contradictions. This has a lot to do with the necessity (in a Hollywood film that espouses social criticism) of focusing on sympathetic characters and their interpersonal tensions, and their inevitable resolution. As such, Stone casts a variety of characters that unfortunately do not do justice to the complexity and magnitude of the issue. The reason, however, has more to do with the film's form than with its contents. While Stone is among the most critical film-makers left in Hollywood, his attempt to tell the story of the financial crisis with the rather blunt and die-cast building blocks of commercial cinema has a difficult time accounting for the forms of abstract collective agency that led to the speculative fever and the ensuing crisis. Indeed, there seems to be no means of representing the crisis as a *social* problem except as it figures through symbolic characters.

My argument is that, under neoliberal financialization, there is no longer any reliable logic of consequentiality undergirding our lives. The flows of global power and the causes and consequences of economic success and failure have been rendered so chaotic and volatile, and our lens has become so deeply individualized, that the social order of causality is more than sublime—it is often absurd. True, the winds of fate have always been beyond our comprehension. As Jameson (1981) suggests, our inability to fully grasp our social totality and know, with certainty, what is to come is the structural root of narrative. But the world under financialization is different. It is not merely the sublime magnitude of the entropic universe and the dense totality of human interaction that escapes our comprehension. It is the incomprehensibly dense and sickeningly fast world of financial speculation that controls a good deal of our fates. As Brian Holmes (2009) puts it, financialization is a hall of mirrors where economic and social value is reflected back upon itself in ways that make the original image impossible to trace. Like a hall of mirrors, causality and consequentiality are, under financialization, virtually impossible to predict or read. For this reason, our shared logic of consequentiality, on which narrative depends, is utterly fragmentary and disjointed. Jameson (1997) has linked this tendency to the term "postmodernism" and suggests that culture, in an age of finance capital, is animated by disjunction. Nowhere is this clearer than cultural approaches to finance itself.

In other words: financialization creates the cultural conditions of its own incomprehensibility. Like the ego of some demented being, it creates a world and a logic of sense and reason from which its own full operations are occluded. Financialization murders narrative because it renders social causality incoherent, seemingly agentless, and largely non-linear. In these circumstances, social narrative loses its animating claim to universality—its ability to narrate cause and effect, action and reaction. Obviously narratives persist, woven as they are into the fibre of human sociality. But explanatory narratives, "grand narratives," have become shadows of their former selves, or they have become incredibly violent.

Metaphoric wealth: Global capitalism with a *différance*

Arguably, with the decline of narrative a concept of metaphor can help us better understand finance and financialization. While narrative affords us the ability to chart changes over time and to develop a complex and multi-layered explanation of causal relations, metaphor allows for an eerie simultaneity in comparison. Unlike simile, which interrupts the comparison with "like" or "as," metaphor offers a shocking immediacy, a sense that two aspects of the world are overlapping. Importantly, there is no necessary or causal relationship between two aspects of a metaphor: one merely signifies the other. For instance, if I write that the 2008 financial crisis was a "perfect storm" I am not implying any direct connection between storms and the global money markets, despite that speculation on weather futures does indeed play a considerable role in contemporary finance. Rather, by bringing these two unconnected ideas into confluence we (me the writer, you the reader) create a new network of meanings, no less so because the term "perfect storm" is already quasi-metaphoric and rests on a whole network of other associations. I suggest we understand metaphor as the dominant mode of financial understanding because metaphor speaks to the way finance itself offers speculative value as a metaphor for real world values. So, for instance, finance represents 10,000,000 barrels of oil as a derivative "options" contract between two parties. This options contract effectively "stands in" for the oil, acts as a metaphor within the milieu of the financial economy.

A number of scholars have taken up the thematic of metaphor in economics, although few have done so with explicit attention to finance. Notably, Deirdre McCloskey has been a preeminent proponent of understanding the "dismal science" as a linguistic culture. In her influential 1995 article "Metaphors Economists Live By," she insists that we understand economic theories, measures, and constructs as metaphors for actually existing, real-world phenomena. While McCloskey is celebratory of economic science and the capitalist system that gave birth to it, her life's work has been dedicated to challenging the hubris of economics' claims to "scientific" infallibility and reminding her broad readership that economics, like any other discipline, is in part the product of social and cultural pressures and forces. For McCloskey, metaphor is an inevitable part of the rational, scientific process, and acknowledging it as such is an essential part of perfecting economic instruments to afford greater leverage over the real-world phenomena they seek to describe.

McCloskey's work has been followed by a great deal of debate as to the objectivity and reliability of economic claims, and has contributed to a wider debate about the objectivity of science in general.[1] Much like the so-called "culture wars" in the 1980s and 1990s, debates within economics (and the study of economics itself as a discipline) have tended to be caught between two, largely imaginary, poles. On the one hand is the vastly dominant one: economic terms and figures are taken to be the immediate linguistic signification of real-world phenomena. This approach sees terms like "supply" or "gross domestic product" as accurate linguistic signifiers of what is actually happening "out there" in the "real economy" and sees the numbers associated with these terms as accurate quantifications of reality. On the other side, there is a school of thought (to which I am clearly more sympathetic) that stresses the way economic discourse is the accumulation of "dead metaphors," metaphors whose very metaphoricity has been forgotten (see McGoun 2003; Phillips 2010). These critics argue that economics can only provide a very limited view of the world because of the assumptions inherent to its linguistic and cultural idiom. Some have argued that economics is purely ideological: that it merely serves to facilitate and legitimate exploitation by sanitizing oppression and cruelty in elitist numerical jargon. Perhaps more importantly, many critics have sought to historicize and contextualize the cultures of economic knowledge and power through their birth within, and contribution to, the rise of European imperialism, colonialism, capitalism, and patriarchy. Mary Poovey (2009), for one, has sought to show the complicated relationship between money and text in eighteenth- and nineteenth-century Western Europe, noting that paper money, and the imaginative and collective "leap of faith" its value requires (as pieces of paper are, ultimately, "worthless"), depends on a textual community and shared assumptions about the truth of claims to meaning and value. Similarly, Ian Baucom (2005) has sought to show how the rhetoric and practices of financial economics, risk management, credit, and insurance were developed within and facilitated by the transatlantic slave trade where individuals were not merely reduced to commodities, but became objects of speculative investment.

Recently, critics like Donald MacKenzie and others (Callon, Millo, and Muniesa 2007; MacKenzie 2006; MacKenzie, Muniesa, and Siu 2007) have suggested that we transcend this debate by understanding economics and economic markets as "performative." Mackenzie and others have encouraged us to understand economic discourse and economic markets as inseparable. Economic discourse makes the manipulation of "real" economic objects possible, the effects of which are, in turn, measured and reflected in economic discourse. From these authors' perspectives, knowledge and action in economics and especially in finance are in a *reflexive* relationship: economic statements may be metaphors, but they have real-world effects on the economies they seek to describe. So, for instance, a bond-rater's decision to downgrade a country's credit rating represents a *cultural* act, a means by which a metaphor (an "AAA rating") comes to stand-in for a whole array of "real world" processes (e.g. the ability of a government to keep workers' demands unmet, the willingness of the country to loosen trade regulations, the potential effect of rising fuel prices on the national economy, the recent appointment of a business-friendly central bank chief, etc.). But, in turn, this metaphor fundamentally reshapes the way global markets will respond to the country's economy. Indeed, financial "instruments" and metaphors, because they are typically based in speculation, have a way of creating the conditions they seek to describe: the downgrading of a country's credit score will help create the conditions (slackening economic growth, poor investment returns, etc.) about which the bond-raters were speculatively concerned (LiPuma and Lee 2004, 141–89). Of course, there are a great many pressures that impinge on a bond-rater's decision and their actions are not the sole determinant of the value of a financial asset: we should not succumb to the temptation to imagine a shadow-world of financial masterminds running the planet by prefigurative fiat. But analyses such as Mackenzie's do give us the sense that the system as a whole is not merely the product of an automatic and autonomous process, as neoliberal pundits would have us believe. Economics and finance pass through a linguistic, metaphorical dimension.

Christian Marazzi (2008, 22–9) argues that finance, or at least the upper echelons of the financial economy, is facilitated by the consolidation of a "linguistic community." The value of financial assets is only vaguely related to the social wealth they ostensibly represent. For instance, the price of an options contract to purchase oil at a certain point at some point in the future may trade for a price that is only tangentially related to the current supply and demand of crude, or reflects the whole market. Instead, Marazzi suggests we understand the value of speculative assets as derived, in part, by competing *claims* to value and the relative "credibility" of those claims. When I offer to sell 1,000,000 barrels of oil to you at a certain price in a year's time, we are entering into a linguistic relationship where you must be credulous to my claims to actually have (or be able to afford) that oil at that time—otherwise the contract I offer would be worthless. Of course, you intend to turn around and sell this contract to another financier, or break it apart and rebundle it with other contracts, or use it as collateral for a loan or against another investment. As Marazzi argues, as the distance between financial speculation and the real world grows, the financial economy becomes more and more like a web of inter-referential claims suspended higher and higher above the "real" economy. This web of claims grows ever wider as financiers may make many speculative investments on the basis of a single asset (i.e. promising it to many people at once), reasoning that, short of systemic collapse, not all debts will come due at once.

While there have been successive waves of regulatory efforts to mitigate this sort of speculative fever, the recent advances in computing and networking technology (which allows for much more complex and rapid "over the counter" derivative exchanges) and the increasing complexity of the financial economy has meant that such groundless speculation is (especially before the 2008 crash) not only virtually uncontrollable, but functionally unintelligible to any single human imagination. The problem is that, while the speculative web of inter-referential claims to value grows wider and wider, the strands become weaker and more brittle. While it might be fine if a few strands break—such as Enron, or Long Term Capital Management, or even most of the Asian Tigers—what cannot be admitted is that the entire system is largely cultural: were investors, *en masse*, to recognize that the entire system is based on linguistic games, and were they all to seek to call in their debts and transform their investments into hard cash, the system would collapse.

Marazzi (2008, 129–33) speaks of this situation as "panic": namely, a failure of language, an animalistic terror and vertigo that sets in as the awful truth dawns. "Runs on the bank" are the material manifestation of investors desperate efforts to transform cultural or "linguistic" claims into hard and fast material wealth. But, of course, because the speculative economy has run away with itself, there isn't enough real wealth to go around. While by no means a perfect indicator, consider the Bank of International Settlements (BIS), a global body that seeks to offer some grounding to the planet's trade in futures, options, and derivatives: The BIS estimated that, just prior to the 2008 financial crisis, the global trade in derivatives contracts outweighed the Gross Domestic Product of the entire globe by a factor of at least fourteen.[2] As panic sets in, communication breaks down and the "liquidity" of the market (the convertibility of claims to "real world" value into "real world" assets) seizes up. Credit and credibility evaporate.

For Marazzi, the key to understanding finance's failures is to return to questions of value. Financial assets seek to render the world in speculative monetary terms. They seek to quantify and commodify real world possibilities as present-day risks. But the reality of social cooperation they seek to measure and predict is inherently and ontologically immeasurable and unpredictable. In an age of "cognitive capitalism," where the system as a whole is increasingly invested in lived culture, in people's subjectivities, relationships, and cultural life—what he terms the "biopolitical" fabric of language (see Picard, chapter 8)—there is a critical *excess of meaning* that renders any financial asset an unreliable claim to real world value (Marazzi 2008, 48–50). For instance, in the dot.com bubble that "popped" in 2001, financiers rushed to pump liquidity into a market for overheated digital properties. They did so because the financial markets were unable to capture and measure the sorts of energies and "cognitive" labours being invested by workers in these ventures, or the value of those ventures to eventual consumers (Marazzi 2008, 126–9). As capital enters social and cultural life in new ways, and as the world is increasingly embraced and composed by high-tech forms of communication and cultural interface, finance's ability to "read" society is increasingly volatile and uncertain.

In this context I want to draw on Marazzi's work to argue for a better, more explicit recognition of finance as a metaphorical system. A financial asset, like shares in an oil field, is a metaphor: a stock certificate implies or signifies ownership, despite the fact that the holder of a certificate may never set foot on the land or actually possess the physical oil it produces. The strength of the "metaphor"/asset depends on many factors (see Harvey 2006). But most notably it depends on the strength of property law and the willingness of the officials in the country where that oil field is located to enforce its ownership by some absentee financier. It also depends on the credibility of banks and the banking system, as well as the robustness of the central back and securities commissions in that country. If it seems like the local banks will fail, or the state might repossess the oil-field, or there may be some other dispute over ownership, the certificate will not be worth much. Already we can see that the value of the stock certificate in question is not merely a matter of the current supply and demand for oil. The amount I can get for the stock certificate, if I wanted to sell it, would depend on the speculative price of oil in the future, and the credibility of the certificate that it can actually entitle the possessor to that oil at that time. In this sense, the certificate is not merely a metaphor for oil; it is a metaphor for the future of oil, and the future of the economy, local, and global of which that oil is a part. The certificate is, in effect, a metaphor for the entire global economic sublime: there is a critical excess of meaning within it. Indeed, it is this excess which defies narrative, which is, ironically, the source of finance's utility to the capitalist economy: were the value of financial assets transparent and their relation to the real economy fixed, it would not serve as a realm of competitive speculation which is critical to the circulation of capital in the global economy and the expansion of the economic system in general (Harvey 2006, 239–324).

Theorists of the metaphor like Jacques Derrida (2007; 1982) have observed that a metaphor is never only a direct one-to-one equivalence between two things. When I speak of a "financial tsunami" the linguistic play relies upon a world of associations. Finance itself is a metaphor for a massive range of speculative economic activities. And for the metaphor to work, I need to know what a "tsunami" is, a process that itself relies on a world of significations and other metaphors. Metaphor, because it is rooted in this dense world of associations, always possesses "excess" meaning. When I say "financial tsunami" I am clearly implying the disastrous effects of financial crises, as well as its immediacy and destructiveness. But again it relies upon a whole world of associations at play in our vernacular. Crucial here is that the significations on both sides of the metaphor depend on other metaphors. And my metaphor of "financial tsunami" comes to participate in the language of which it is a part. We can no longer understand "finance" or "tsunamis" as we once did as they have been brought into metaphoric association. The metaphor "financial tsunami" resonated differently before the global economic crisis in 2008 and before the disastrous tsumani in Japan in 2011.

Importantly, for Derrida and others, all of language is an interwoven, dynamic webbing of mutually suspending metaphors. In "Truth and Lie in an Extra-Moral Sense" of 1873, Nietzsche was among the first to note that all words are, in effect, "dead metaphors": metaphors that we have forgotten are metaphorical (1977, 42–7). This would become a key tenet of Western thought throughout the twentieth century. Sociologists, philosophers, psychoanalysts, and linguists questioned the "necessary" relation between signifier (words) and signified (that to which they referred), with structuralist thinkers seeking to find the overall root or pattern to language and meaning and later post-structuralists investigating the infinite and self-referential play of language itself. They reasoned that if all words were metaphors, surely there must be some words that are not entirely arbitrary, some ultimate referent. Or, alternatively, there must be some underlying syntactic structure that allows language to operate.

Unlike Saussure and other structuralists, more recent thinkers like Derrida and Ricoeur do not believe that this infinite play of inter-referentiality has any general or inherent structure. Rather, it is the product and medium of everyday action and interaction. We are always in the process of relying on, interpreting, and coining metaphors. Metaphors succeed or fail in the messy intertext of daily life. Some fail to provide an accurate picture of life and fall flat: they are not *credible* linguistic strategies—they do not find their mark and create linguistic "value" in terms of durable or shared meaning or significance. Others are so successful they sediment into the vernacular as "dead metaphors," figures of speech no longer recognized as metaphors at all (such as "to coin a phrase"). As a hermeneut, Ricoeur (1978) argued that the invention (and, conversely, the reception and interpretation) of new "living" metaphors represented the dynamic key to human meaning and imagination: dialogical and cooperative. As a deconstructionist, Derrida (2007) complicated this notion, suggesting that all "living" metaphors are in the process of "dying," being folded back within language as dead metaphor. For Derrida metaphor is constantly "retreating"[3] into language, yet language itself is ever more metaphoric as new layers of metaphor (metaphor upon metaphor upon metaphor) animate our shared linguistic world. For Derrida, metaphors are "always already" in excess of themselves: they do not merely refer to another thing; they inherently refer to that other thing's play within language as a whole.

It is the notion of "metaphoric wealth," where assets acquire value within the interwoven "language games" of the financial system, that helps us better comprehend financial speculation. For while the original "referent" of a financial option (like our oil field, above) may seem to ground the asset in the real world, the poetry of the speculative market soon sees that referent disappear. Already, as we have seen, the financial asset refers not merely to the real-world thing, but to speculation on that thing's future as it intersects the state, banks, the rest of the market, and so on. Like metaphor, there is a critical excess of meaning in the financial asset—it is not merely a one-to-one relationship between signifier and signified. And like the Derridean notion of metaphor, financial assets refer to a whole world of meaning. The price of the stock certificate in an oil field will depend on the rest of the world's oil-fields, on the situation in the Middle East, on the sale of cars that year, on weather conditions around the world (in terms of the demand for oil in home heating or the supply of plant-derived ethanol), and on an infinite number of other factors. Further, the idea that someone would speculate on a single oilfield is charmingly anachronistic: today that asset would be a fragment within hundreds, possibly thousands of securities, broken apart and re-aggregated, speculated upon dozens, scores, or hundreds of times, buried in possibly millions of contracts, holdings, and speculative puts.

Indeed, like metaphor, there is also the *retrait* of finance. New assets are constantly being "coined" and created: new forms of speculation (on weather, on art, on terrorism) are constantly being invented to offer financial markets ever more ways of digesting the world in economic data. New "instruments" for assessing, measuring, and evaluating "risk" are always being developed, sold, and bought, used as collateral, hedged, decomposed, recomposed, and securitized. Yet at the same time all these novel assets are "retreating" back into a overall financial economy of which they are a part and become part of the global economic fabric that not only determines the relative value of financial assets (new and old alike), but increasingly the global "real" economy and the lives, societies, and cultures on which that "real" economy is based.

There are implications here that go beyond marvelling at the terrifying height of the house of cards that is the global financial sector, where metaphors lean against metaphors atop metaphors atop metaphors. The problem with metaphors is that they can be extremely violent: they can reduce the singularity and difference of the world by naming a slew of processes as one thing. "Slave" is a metaphor for a human being held in bondage and exploited by an entire system of injustice and oppression. "Man" is a metaphor for a collection of traits associated with a socially constructed understanding of "masculinity" which, when ascribed to a body, give the bearer phenomenal rights and "privileges" denied to others. In both cases, and so many others, the metaphors allow us to forget the dense social work and collaboration that goes into constantly reproducing systems of unjust power relations. This is no less true of financial assets. As Brian LiPuma and Benjamin Lee (2004, 168–85) note, financial derivatives and their attendant logic of "risk management" has allowed seemingly abstract and authorless global flows of speculative capital to enact singularly terrifying violence the world over. Ecological destruction, sweat-shop exploitation, collapsing standards of living, and mass unhappiness all disappear into financial assets to such an extent it is incredibly difficult to assign responsibility for the terrible consequences of "globalization." Worse still, as we all become "investors," imbricated in the financialization of daily life (pension savings, investments, loans, debt, etc.), we all become part of this violence; violence that is often directed back against us in terms of government austerity measures, public and private sector layoffs, and deepening ecological crises (at the behest or in the name of "the markets"). Financial assets as a metaphor for the real world both depend on and facilitate tremendous violence because they detach economic motives from human reason and consequence. The most powerful financial and corporate CEOs feel (rightly or wrongly) helpless in the face of "shareholder" or "market pressure."[4]

Yet at the same time, one implication of metaphoric wealth is the colossal power of shared imaginaries. We cooperating human subjects have created and are perpetuating, out of the force of belief and action, a social construct that is a marvel of our shared ability to imagine and create. There is something perversely inspiring in the sick celestial clockwork that is the financial market and its ability to influence and shape the way we live together. It is the diametric inverse of the potential for a global moment of peace, understanding, justice, and compassion based on common horizons of hopes, dreams, passions, desires, and reason. It is the twisted manifestation of the common imagination. If we can create such a thing as finance, what else/ other might we create?

Conclusion

But here's the rub: there is no real separation between finance and the real economy. Those who believe that the capitalist system works (or works with government regulation) have recently sought to frame the economic crisis as one created by the separation of financial speculation from the "real economy"—of Wall Street from Main Street, as the saying goes. From this perspective, the crisis was the result of unscrupulous bankers and investors whose zeal for accumulating literally uncountable riches led them to forget themselves and engage in an incestuous group hallucination of ever more financial wealth. When things operate "as they should," finance remains relatively aligned to the real economy, allowing firms, governments, and individuals to manipulate money over time and distance (Harvey 2006, 239–82). From this perspective, finance, when it is in its "proper place," operates as a sort of reflection of the "real economy," of people making and doing stuff. In still other terms, the problem with finance, we are told, is that this "imaginary money" has too far exceeded the "reality" of cold, hard cash. But there has never been a time when finance and the real economy have enjoyed the sort of harmonious distinctness these critics wish for. Finance, in terms of promissory notes, credit, and insurance actually predates capitalist economies and is the basis of the monetary units on which "real economies" run (Ferguson 2008). A coin is, in reality, a token that (once upon a time) entitled the bearer to a certain quantity of other materials (gold, grain, salt, etc.) from a state treasury or an issuing bank or firm. In this sense, money has always already been metaphoric. After all, most coins are worth less than their stated value if melted down into ore. So posing the financial economy as an abstraction and the "real" (monetary) economy as "real" is already false (see Dufresne and Sacchetti, chapter 9). Further, there has never been a moment in the history of capitalism where the value of money (and labour, and goods and services) has *not* been deeply and inexorably implied in and by financial speculation. While certainly the recent tendencies of globalization and deregulation have led to a much deeper and murkier relationship between speculation and "real money," in actuality the "real economy" *has always already been financialized.* Financial speculation has long influenced the price of base commodities like grain and fuel. It has never *not* been the driving force behind ground rent and property prices. And it has never been absent from the business of transportation or manufacturing. It has underwritten slavery and colonialism. The British Empire ran, in large part, on debt-bondage and promissory notes. In short, finance and the real economy have something of a metaphoric relationship. In Derridean or deconstructive terms, there is no "original" of which the other is a derivative representation; they are always already implicated in one another.

In this sense, the recent financial crisis is not merely the collapse of metaphor. Here the web of meanings is stretched too thin and as one key strand breaks—most recently, in the sub-prime mortgage market—the web gives way, assets hurtling downwards. It is also the case that the financial crisis is a metaphor for other, deeper crises occluded within the speculative field. The global ecological crisis. The impending global food crisis. The (coming) water crisis. The crisis of the middle class. The crisis of housing and social welfare in the United States and elsewhere. The global humanitarian crisis. The political crisis that seethes beneath a world of inequality until it rears its "surprising" head in Egypt, Greece, Ireland, Korea, Chiapas, and Wall Street. All these overlapping crises have been both intensified and covered over by the rise of finance over the past forty years, which has, nearly everywhere, forced nation states and other levels of government to accede to neoliberal doctrine at the expense of the people. It is a system that stood behind the neocolonial project that recolonized the "third world" with debt and financial terror. It was the motor of globalization that allowed for the formation of a global archipelago of temporary sweatshops and intensified the exploitation of natural resources (and this dispossession of those who had the misfortune to make their lives on top of them) for the production of ever-more consumer and electronic goods.

As Brian LiPuma and Benjamin Lee point out (2004), finance does read and interpret these crises and they do factor in to the price of financial assets. But what finance cannot see is the big picture. Like Walter Benjamin's angel of history, it flies backwards into a future of its own creation, speculating on the ruins it flies past. This is no accident: in many ways finance is the culmination of the "irrational rationality" Benjamin and other Frankfurt School theorists saw germinating throughout the twentieth century: a system that exists on the basis of individualized acts of hyper-rational speculation (based on cost/benefit/risk analyses) that, on a systemic level, have produced a system of monetary flows so powerful that no "rational" force on earth can stop it. Financial power has grown to such an extent that it has effectively vetoed any and all attempts to reign it in through policy. The recent caps on speculative investment imposed by "first world" countries will do little to prevent another cycle of speculative fever from rising (McNally 2011). The disastrous failures of the Copenhagen and Cancun climate summits were a terrifying testament to the ability of transnational capital to veto even a congress of the world's leaders and insist that billions of people be consigned to climate-induced death and misery so as not to frighten or jar "global markets." But more severely, as austerity emerges as the answer to the financial crisis we will see only an intensification of what Henry Giroux (2008) calls "the terror of neoliberalism" and the systematic attack on social life that has always accompanied financialization. And as the final nail is hammered in the coffin of any institutional basis for the redistribution of social wealth and the control of capital, all of the social problems that underwrote this financial crisis will get worse and worse.

Notes

1 Are all scientific terms of reference merely metaphor and, if so, what are the epistemological consequences? (See Boehm et al. 2002.)

2 There are no adequate statistics on the total value of financial wealth. In June of 2008, just preceding the recent credit crisis, the Bank of International Settlements estimated the annual circulation of over-the-counter derivatives contracts at $684,814 billion (US) (see http://www.bis.org/statistics/derstats.htm; accessed 14 November 2012), although this represents only a fraction of the total value of speculative capital. This figure dwarfs, by a factor of eleven, the 2008 Gross Domestic Product of the entire globe, estimated by the World Bank at $60,587 billion (US) (http://go.worldbank.org/B5PYF93QF0; accessed 4 December 2012).

3 Derrida uses the French term *retrait* because of its multiple valences: it implies not only the retreating or receding of a thing but also the washing back over—he uses the metaphor of waves both pulling back from and crashing again upon a shore. Re-treat also has the meaning of "treating" something again, which in French implies to return or revisit a subject, to look again at a debate. Finally, the words "treat" and "trait" do not enjoy the same distinction in French as they do in English, offering yet other layer of possibility for this rich metaphorics. To re-trait is to give-meaning, to (re) inscribe a trait or feature (again).

4 Of course, the difference is that, as Derrida makes clear, we can't live without metaphors as linguistic tools for reproducing a living language. We can live without finance. Perhaps more accurately, we can live a life that is not dominated by a metaphorical system by which we control our collective behaviour via the speculative quantification of risk.

4

The burden of metaphor: Marx's vampires, populist politics, and the dialectics of capitalist abstraction

Matthew MacLellan

Cognitive linguistics has long rejected the "substitution theory" of metaphor—according to which metaphor is considered secondary or epiphenomenal in relation to literal meaning—and has come to the more profound consensus that cognition itself is at a deep level metaphoric. In their influential *Metaphors We Live By* (1980), for instance, George Lakoff and Mark Johnson contend that metaphor cannot be considered solely the property of the "poetic imagination and the rhetorical flourish," since "most of our ordinary conceptual system, in terms of which we both think and act, is fundamentally metaphorical in nature" (Lakoff and Johnson 1980, 4; see Haiven, chapter 3). Yet where theoretical linguistics tends to celebrate the metaphoric structure of human cognition as manifestation of the brain's innate capacity for complex, non-literal thought, commensurate philosophical criticism more often foregrounds metaphor's problematic tendency toward hypostasis. Considered a ubiquitous effect of the absolute distance between subject and object posited by Western empiricism, the unavoidable metaphoricity of language is, in this philosophical view, an object of critique for simultaneously obfuscating the very problematic that the metaphoric discourse was designed to illuminate. "Philosophers who wrote about the mind were searching for the best metaphors to illustrate it," as Colin Turbayne explains in *The Myth of Metaphor* (1962), "but few were aware of what they were doing. Most were the dupes of metaphors previously made or of those of their own devising. For example, it seems that Locke mistook his model of the mind, at least in part, for the thing modeled: an empty room at birth which was slowly filled with ideas" (Turbayne 1962, 98).

Given metaphor's double-bound character,[1] particularly within theoretical discourses, this chapter examines one such metaphorical trope in the works of Karl Marx—the vampire metaphor—in order to better elucidate the pitfalls involved in an uncritical acceptance of metaphor, particularly a metaphor as powerful as the vampire. Within the scholarly literature on Marx's vampires, there is a general consensus that the metaphor is an especially apt rhetorical device for illustrating the excessive and predatory nature of capitalist economics. Yet these positive appraisals rarely consider the diverse cultural narratives that orbit the figure of the vampire and inflect a wider range of meaning on to the Marxian metaphor than is generally considered. Without being able to exhaust the theme—the hermeneutics of the vampire is a vast and diverse field in its own right—this chapter reconsiders the vampire's significance as an economic metaphor through an analytical framework that not only considers the specific occasions in which Marx had recourse to vampirism, but which also interrogates the politics of vampire fiction and the political fictions that are sustained by recourse to vampires. Beginning with a description of the vampire metaphor in Marx's works, preceded by a brief exegesis of the secondary scholarship on the topic, I demonstrate that the Marxian vampire is not a singular or monolithic metaphor but manifests a definite duality: at times standing in for capitalists or the bourgeoisie, at times standing in for capital itself. After marking this duality within the Marxian vampire, I argue that the traditional reading of the metaphor—in which the capitalist plays the role of the bloodthirsty vampires while the working class rounds out the drama as the vampire's imperiled victims—masks the historicity of capitalism, which is to say its status as a transient economic system, by aligning the class conflict inherent to the capitalist mode of production with the conventions of vampire fiction. By stressing the subtleties of Marx's later, more economically oriented version of vampire metaphor, I offer a modified interpretation of Marx's vampire that conceives of the metaphor not as a straightforward denunciation of the evils of capitalism but as a commentary on the overdetermined processes of social and cultural abstraction that invariably accompany widespread and systematic capitalist accumulation.

Marx's vampires

The dominant, indeed almost uniform, interpretation of Marx's vampire metaphor within contemporary scholarship reads the rhetorical figure as a poignant and dramatic means of articulating the excessive nature of nineteenth-century industrial capitalism. In *Reading the Vampire* (1994), for instance, Ken Gelder asserts that "the representation of capital or the capitalist as a vampire was [intended by Marx] to produce a striking figure *defined* by excess and unrestrained appetite" (Gelder 1994, 22). This same conclusion is also drawn by Franco Moretti (1983) who, through reference to Stoker's novel, contends that "like capital, [the vampire] is impelled towards a continuous growth, an unlimited expansion of his domain: accumulation is inherent in his nature" (Moretti 1983, 90). Showing more interest in the metaphor's textual environs, Terrell Carver's *The Postmodern Marx* (1998) argues a similar point by marking the connection between the vampire metaphor and the capitalist's imperative to extend the working day as far as possible:

> Vampires are well-known creatures of the night, an attribute Marx exploited when he wrote that the "prolongation of the working day beyond the limits of the natural day, into night, only acts as a palliative." "It only slightly quenches the vampire thirst for the living blood of labour." Capitalist production, he concluded, has an inherent drive "toward the appropriation of labour throughout the whole of the 24 hours in a day." The vampire will not let go "while there remains a single muscle, sinew or drop of blood to be exploited." (Carver 1998, 15)

While it would be overstating the matter to describe these interpretations of Marx's vampire metaphor as inaccurate, the homogeneous literature on Marx's vampires nevertheless paints a picture of the metaphor with a broad brush: vampires are rendered synonymous with capitalism, capitalists, and capital without distinction and these readings always speak generally of Marx's ethical distaste for the excessive character of capitalist economics. What this general appraisal consistently overlooks, however, is that the Marxian vampire is not a metaphoric monolith, but appears in a markedly dual fashion: at times the vampire is used to characterize (or rather demonize) capitalists or the bourgeoisie, while in other instances the vampire stands in for capital itself. What makes the absence of this distinction in the secondary literature especially aberrant is that this dual[2] usage of the metaphor is not manifest randomly across Marx's corpus, but rather tends to correlate with content. In his political or—to borrow Althusser's (2009) epistemological distinction[3]—humanist works, one finds that the vampire metaphor is used almost exclusively to describe capitalists, the bourgeoisie, and the various superstructural institutions they are said to dominate. In *The Eighteenth Brumaire of Louis Bonaparte* (1852), for instance, Marx writes that "the bourgeois order ... has become a vampire that sucks out [the peasantry's] blood and marrow and throws them into the alchemistic cauldron of capital" (Marx 1978d, 611). In *The Class Struggles in France* (1850), Marx describes the French National Assembly as "a vampire living off the blood of the June insurgency" (Marx 1978a, 88), while in the *Inaugural Address of the Working Men's International Association* (1864) Marx described British industry as an entity that is "vampyre like," and which "could but live by sucking blood" (1978c, 517). In these politico-historical tracts, the metaphorical function of the vampire is straightforward and uncomplicated: the vampire is used to demonize capitalists and the bourgeoisie while defining their class relationship as parasitic rather than symbiotic, as was otherwise asserted by the mainstays of nineteenth-century liberalism.

When one turns to Marx's more economically oriented or, in Althusser's (2009) phraseology, anti-humanist texts, one finds a striking modification to the metaphor's function: no longer a descriptor of a villainous bourgeoisie and ravenous capitalist class, the vampire metaphor is re-purposed as a means of articulating capital's strange fluidity and duality. In what is far and away the most oft-cited instance of Marx's vampirism, the tenth chapter of *Capital* titled "The Working Day," one observes that Marx now uses the metaphor to combine a sense of the transformative ontology of capital alongside the exploitative significance generally associated with the vampire metaphor. As this passage demonstrates, it is not only clear that it is now the indeterminate object "capital," rather than the more determinate notion of the "bourgeoisie," that has been vampirized, but that capital's transformative character now also marks the vampire's significance as an economic metaphor:

> As a capitalist, he is only capital personified. His soul is the soul of capital. But capital has one sole driving force, the drive to valorize itself, to create surplus-value, to make its constant part, the means of production, absorb the greatest possible amount of surplus labour. Capital is dead labour which, vampire-like, lives only by sucking living labour, and lives the more, the more labour it sucks. (Marx 1977, 342)

This same shift is manifest even more clearly in the *Grundrisse* (1858), as Marx comments on nineteenth-century British economist David Ricardo's failure to recognize the dual nature of capital as both *fixed* and *circulatory*, wherein, as Marx puts it, "the same capital appears in the same business in the two different forms, the particular modes of existence of fixed and circulating, hence [existing] doubly" (Marx 1973, 645). And again, it is capital's capacity for appearing in multiple forms simultaneously that warrants the invocation of the vampire metaphor:

> Capital posits the permanence of value ... by incarnating itself in fleeting commodities and taking their form, but at the same time changing them just as constantly; [capital] alternates between its eternal form in money and its passing form in commodities; permanence is posited as the only thing it can be, a passing passage—process—life. But capital obtains this ability only by constantly sucking in living labour as its soul, vampire-like. The permanence—the duration of value in its form as capital—is posited only through reproduction, which is itself double, reproduction as commodity, reproduction as money, and unity of both these reproductive processes. (Marx 1973, 646)

While the metaphor still clearly speaks to the antagonistic structure of industrial capitalism, this element no longer dominates the totality of the metaphor's significance. Rather, it is now combined with Marx's conception of the strange morphology of value within a system of production that not only splits exchange-value from use-value but also subordinates the latter to the former. This distinction *internal* to Marx's vampire opens up the possible interpretations of the metaphor beyond the obvious connotations of excess and exploitation that have typically been associated with the rhetorical device. Prior to engaging with any alternative readings of the metaphor, however, it is important to outline why the standard reading of Marx's vampires is both epistemologically and politically problematic. To this end, I offer a culturally oriented framework that maps the politics of vampire fiction and considers how the various generic forms of vampire narratives can be thought to align with different forms of political disposition or attitudes. In this way, I aim to show how the very form of vampire fiction is itself pre-disposed to a particular modality of political ideology and that an alternative reading of Marx's vampire metaphor is not only possible but also desirable.

Normativity in the vampire genre

Sue-Ellen Case's essay "Tracking the Vampire" (2009) provides a useful starting point for mapping the political structure of vampire fiction insofar as its conception of the relationship between the literary vampire and modes of social taxonomy is both sociologically and genealogically rudimentary. According to Case, the literary vampire owes its significance to a pernicious philosophical dualism that she refers to as the "Platonic parameters of Being," according to which a particular conception of the "good" is aligned and identified with a paralleling notion of the "natural" (Case 2009, 63). Of course, the virtue of this type of binaristic criterion, from the perspective of power, is that it permits a broad and malleable classificatory logic through which social groups, whatever their content (class, sex, race, etc.), can be carved out of a generalized communal existence and organized hierarchically in a manner that renders this arrangement as non-contingent or ontologically pre-determined. As Case asserts,

> the category of the unnatural was one of an aggregate of notions aimed at securing the right to life for a small minority of the world's population. The right to life was formulated through a legal, literary, and scientific discourse on blood, which stabilized privilege by affirming the right for those who could claim blood and further, pure blood, and the consequent death sentence of those who could not. (Case 2009, 68–9)

Echoing Michel Foucault's thesis that ancient and medieval power was organized primarily through a "symbolics of blood" (Foucault 1990, 148), Case traces a literary genealogy arching from the poetry of John of the Cross through writers such as Rimbaud and Wilde in which European literature continually sought to affect a "break with a dominant discourse that legislated the right to life through pure blood" (Case 2009, 71). For Case, again reflecting Foucault's thesis that power always generates its own forms of opposition or resistance, the appearance of the vampire in European literature, which she describes as "the one who waits, strikes, and soils the living, pure blood," can be understood as a counter-discourse designed to rob the elite of their claim to privilege while muddying the waters of social distinction more generally (Case 2009, 72).

While Case's essay insightfully elucidates the genesis of Western literary vampire as intertwined with the strictures of feudal society in which "power spoke through blood," it is important to recognize that the normative function of the vampire is not constant or universal but rather shifts valence through historical and generic development (Foucault 1990, 147). In considering the significance of the Marxian vampire metaphor, then, the more pertinent question concerns how the vampire's relation to normativity is modified as the scene of vampire fiction moves from an aristocratic setting to a more industrial–capitalist milieu. The first and perhaps most important distinction in recognizing this temporal shift is the *inversion* of the logic of normativity as European societies transitioned from a feudal-agrarian order to a modern-industrial system of production. As Foucault's analysis of the birth of the modern era observes, while feudal societies may have applied a logic of normativity which granted only a small minority the right to life, this relation was dramatically reordered in the modern period, wherein, particularly after Malthus, the population came to be viewed as the principle source of wealth for the nation-state. Thus, instead of exercising a negative or punitive modality of power based on the what Foucault called the spectacle of the scaffold (Foucault 1977, 3–73), modern capitalist societies were compelled (for various reasons that cannot be explicated here) to re-organize their method of governmentality in favor of an increasingly, though only formally, democratic system designed to enhance the life of the population:

> The old power of death that symbolized sovereign power was now carefully supplanted by the administration of bodies and the calculated management of life ... The "right" to life, to one's body, to health, to happiness, to the satisfaction of needs, and beyond all the oppressions or "alienations," the right to re-discover what one is and all that one can be, this "right" —which the classical juridical system was utterly incapable of comprehending—was the political response to all these new procedures of power which did not derive ... from the traditional right of sovereignty. (Foucault 1990, 139–45)

Thus whereas conceptions of the "natural" and the "normative" were previously deployed to grant special privilege to an aristocratic minority, its modern application is inverted as interlinked conceptions of the "natural" and the "good" became the dual mechanisms for constructing the binding norms that valorize the sexually disciplined and economically productive majority; for if Foucault stresses anything in regards to the transition from the feudal to the modern epoch, it is "the growing importance assumed by the action of the norm, at the expense of the juridical system of the law" (Foucault 1990, 144). Against this historical transformation, the subsequent development of the vampire genre, beginning in the late nineteenth century, can be read in a somewhat different fashion: rather than a destabilizing counter-discourse challenging aristocratic privilege, the vampire figure can also be read as narrative device which, within the crisis format of the genre, unifies a hegemonic majority against a parasitic minority. Thus while it may very well be that a good measure of the significance of Marx's vampire metaphor is drawn from its ability to express "the horror of a property-owning class that appears to be vampire-like in its desire and ability to suck the life out of the working class" (Neocleous 2003, 668), the easy metaphoric imposition of the vampire/human dyad on to the relationship between the property-owning class and the working class under a capitalist system of production also risks hypostasizing what is, in Marx, a thoroughly historical relation. Put differently, the vampire metaphor implicitly endorses an essential, or non-dialectical, conception of the relation between the bourgeoisie and the proletariat in which the latter aims to continually re-constitute itself by annihilating what is perceived as an exogenous or alien threat.

But before further explicating the problematic nature of this relational dynamic in the context of contemporary Marxist theory, it is worth considering more fully how these dialectical nuances are played out within vampire fiction itself, particularly as the genre shifted from a feudal to an industrial setting. In this regard, Franco Moretti's essay "The Dialectic of Fear" (1983) provides a number of insights as to why the standard reading of the late nineteenth-century vampire as a feudal aristocrat proves insufficient as a hermeneutical framework. According to Moretti, "Dracula is an aristocrat only in a manner of speaking [because] Dracula lacks precisely what makes a man 'noble'" (Moretti 1983, 90). Specifically, Moretti observes that Dracula employs not servants ("The Count has read Adam Smith: he knows servants are unproductive workers" [Moretti 1983, 90]) and lacks the aristocrat's conspicuous consumption. Nor does Dracula spill blood like his namesake, Vlad the Impaler, but rather he meticulously consumes it: "Dracula," Moretti concludes, "is a saver, an ascetic, an upholder of the Protestant Ethic" (Moretti 1983, 91). While identifying those behaviors or traits that suggest that Dracula is more accurately interpreted as a capitalist than aristocrat, however, Moretti also observes how Dracula strangely functions within the narrative as an exogenous threat to the prosperous bourgeoisie of Victorian England; that is, as a threat to modern capitalism itself. "Dracula is a true monopolist," writes Moretti, "[and] like monopoly capital, his ambition is to subjugate the last vestiges of the liberal era and destroy all forms of economic independence ... hence the horror for the bourgeois mind" (Moretti 1983, 92). In this respect, Dracula appears as something of a feudalistic "return of the repressed" given the economic and political sensibilities of the novel's geopolitical setting. As Moretti continues, "the nineteenth-century bourgeois is able to imagine monopoly only in the form of Count Dracula, the aristocrat, the figure of the past, the relic of distant lands and dark ages" (Moretti 1983, 93).

The vampire in Stoker's novel is thus, according to Moretti, a paradoxical figure. From one perspective, Dracula indeed appears as an anachronistic threat to the liberal-capitalist system driving Victorian England further into the industrial age. From another view, however, the Dracula character constitutes a rupture marking the passage from England's aristocratic and its capitalist future.[4] While appearing to conform to the conventions of the nineteenth-century genre whereby the vampire appeared as a solitary aristocratic figure, the vampire in Stoker's novel displays what we might call the *functional* convention more characteristic of the genre in the twentieth century: specifically, the vampire's role within the narrative as a catalyst for uniting his potential slayers in a common bond. Consider the following excerpt from Jonathan Harker's journal wherein the novel's protagonist begins to realize it is a vampire that he is "helping to transfer to London, where, perhaps for centuries to come, he might, amongst its teeming millions, satiate his lust for blood, and create a new and ever widening circle of semi-demons to batten on the helpless" (quoted in Moretti 1983, 91–2). While the nineteenth-century vampire was typically solitary and aristocratic, and thus constituted a discrete threat that preyed on discrete individuals, Count Dracula's expansion beyond this limitation can be understood as based in his capitalistic, rather than aristocratic, venture—namely, his drive to accumulate real estate in London. Hence, Dracula is fundamentally an overdetermined character, "the final product of the bourgeois century and its negation" as Moretti argues (Moretti 1983, 93).

From this perspective, Stoker's novel can be conceived as an early instance of twentieth-century vampire fiction just as much as it can be said to partake in the conventions of the nineteenth-century form. For as many commentators of vampire fiction have argued, the principle modification to the genre from nineteenth to the twentieth century is the expansion or amplification of the vampire threat from a solitary figure to a proliferous horde of the undead threatening to overrun civilization itself. The twentieth-century genre, unlike its antecedent, increasingly adopts a narrative dynamic wherein the vampire agent elicits such fear that its potential prey are compelled to abandon their personal or political differences and unite as a homogeneous community in opposition to this increasingly existential, as well as physical, threat. According to Stacy Abbott's analysis in *Celluloid Vampires: Life After Death in the Modern World* (2007), this shift reaches its apex at the point when what Paul Krugman calls the "Keynesian compact" (Krugman 2003, 96)—the historical deal between capital and labor that facilitated the unusual period of economic growth and stability from the immediate post-war years until the 1970s—began to break down as the advanced economies shifted from an industrial to a post-industrial model. According to Abbot, popular anxieties during this period, stemming from the social and political turmoil of the 1960s combined with the subsequent decline of American economic supremacy (OPEC crisis) and military infallibility (Vietnam), were reflected in the numerical proliferation of the undead in late twentieth-century Western cinema. For Abbot, then, this sea change within the vampire genre reflected a severe and deep seated crisis in normativity itself: "in the 1970s, a decade of intense change in American history—marked by Vietnam, Watergate, the Kent State Massacre, and the assassinations of Martin Luther King Jr., Malcolm X, and both John and Robert Kennedy—normality could no longer be restored: normality itself was deemed monstrous" (Abbott 2007, 80–1). Sue-Ellen Case stresses the same significance of this historical shift for the genre, though with more emphasis on the fear of nuclear and biological weaponry that permeated Cold War American culture. While the vampire-horde produced through biological experimentation appeared as early as Richard Matheson's novel *I am Legend* (1954), Case, like Abbott, argues that it was really in the 1970s that this narrative mechanism became the dominant generic trend:

> After the 50s, the lone vampire, or the family of vampires that threatened the human community, is replaced by a proliferation of the undead. Romero's trilogy illustrates the progression: in *Night of the Living Dead* (1968), a score of the undead threatens a family-unit-type group in a house; in the second film, *Dawn of the Dead* (1977), thousands of undead threaten a smaller, less-affiliated group in a shopping mall, one of the few material places remaining; and in *Day of the Dead* (1985), the undead have successfully taken over the continent, finally threatening what dwindles down to the basic heterosexual-couple-unit in a military–industrial complex. Successively, the undead have eliminated the family unit, claimed commodity reification for their own in the shopping mall, and defeated the military-industrial complex. (Case 2009, 82)

For these critics, the proliferation of the vampire into a mindless army of the undead reflected the breakdown of bourgeois norms amidst what Michel Crozier, Samuel Huntington, and Joji Watanuki (1975) infamously referred to as the "crisis of democracy" (Crozier, Huntington, and Watanuki, 1975). Like the multiplying hordes of "special interest groups" (civil rights activists, feminists, trade unionists, etc.) that threatened the hegemonic norms that had sustained twentieth-century industrial capitalism, the mid to late twentieth-century vampire genre displays a narrative structure whereby the monstrous itself seems to have gained the dominant position and increasingly threatens the "natural" human as such. Thus, far from being an agent of delightful subversion reveling in the gradually widening interstices of residual tradition, the post-industrial vampire can be read as an anxiety-saturated call to arms for a bourgeoisie whose very way of life seemed to be on the verge of collapse as oppressed populations of all kinds increasingly asserted themselves in political struggle.

While this diachronic account of the transformations within the vampire genre is intended as a form of cognitive mapping and a means to properly historicize the underlying conditions against which these generic shifts occurred, I want to stress that my criticism of the standard reading of Marx's vampire metaphors is situated as much in the synchronic dimension as in the diachronic. To re-iterate, it is not my intention to discover the 'true significance' of Marx's vampire metaphor nor definitively ascertain what Marx 'really meant' when using the metaphor. Rather, my aim has been to question the political efficacy of the vampire metaphor in the contemporary era when the connotations that orbit the theme of vampirism have shifted. As I have suggested, the central narrative convention of vampire (and by extension, zombie) fiction in the late twentieth century has been the multiplication or amplification of the vampire from a solitary figure to a mass horde of the undead threatening to consume the human as such. This permutation of the genre adopts a narrative structure wherein two agents—the human community and the undead horde—square off in a total or zero-sum conflict within an acute crisis format: the humans are compelled to destroy the undead in their entirety lest they themselves succumb to complete annihilation. Given the rigid parameters of this narrative form, any consideration of how the Marxian vampire metaphor imposes meaning onto the relation between the bourgeoisie and the proletariat today would surely want to question what type of political forms corresponds to this type of social relation and how this mode of political imagination relates to Marx's structural and historical understanding of the capitalist mode of production.

In his *Populist Reason* (2007), Ernesto Laclau suggests that it is precisely this type of scenario or narrative form (recalling the ideologies always take the form of a narrative) that leads to the development of a highly reactionary or populist form of politics. According to Laclau, the degree to which any political scenario results in what he calls an "institutionalist," or "populist," outcome depends on the intermix—or the degree of "totalization" —between a representational system's internal differentiation (drawn from Saussure's conception of languages as systems of "pure" difference, or difference without positive terms) and its imposed equivalency (which is simply that which provides the necessary degree of closure that enables representative or signifying systems, in the plural, to exist as such). A progressive "institutionalist" discourse, according to Laclau, "is one that attempts to make limits of the discursive formation coincide with the limits of the community," whereby "the universal principle of 'differentiality' would be the dominant equivalence within the homogenous communitarian space" (Laclau 2007, 81). In other words, a progressive or "institutionalist" politics does not allow its axis of equivalency to run roughshod over the play of differences within the political collective and, accordingly, radical and plural democracy is given discursive and ideological support.

At the other end of spectrum, a populist discourse is produced when the differences within the political community are entirely overcoded by an opposing force or element. As Laclau puts it,

> in the case of populism ... a frontier of exclusion divides the society into two camps. The "people," in that case, is something less than the totality of the members of the community: it is a partial component which nevertheless aspires to be conceived as the only legitimate totality. (Laclau 2007, 81)

As populist conditions reach extremity, the political collective not only crystallizes in its homogenous opposition to the perceived repressive power, but all manner of social and political grievances become irrationally condensed around the fictive antagonist (the oft-cited example being Nazi propaganda's ability to condense all of Germany's woes into the figure of cosmopolitan Jew). In these instances, the enemy will not only be perceived inaccurately as an outside intruder impinging on an otherwise functional system, but will also be entirely amplified in terms of its ideological force. As Laclau puts it, the intruder will "count less as the instrument of particular differential repressions and will express pure anti-community, pure evil and negation" (Laclau 1996, 42).

It is on these grounds that Marxist theory has always displayed considerable unease toward populist politics and why the standard reading of Marx's vampire metaphor warrants careful reconsideration. For if there could be said to be a defining element of populism, it would be the fallacious embrace of a form of "class essentialism": the conviction that some version of exogenous economic elite (aristocrats, cosmopolitan Jews, Wall Street financiers, etc.) is parasitically growing rich off the backs of an exploited working class. The ideological deficiency of populism, from a Marxist perspective, is not therefore based in its particular contents, which are in most cases based on very real grievances, but is rather grounded in the way in which these contents become articulated and expressed in class struggle. As Slavoj Žižek puts it, "for a populist politics, the cause of troubles is ultimately never the system as such but the intruder who corrupted it (financial manipulators, not necessarily capitalists, and so on)" (Žižek 2006a, 555). In other words, populism's narrative form, whatever particular content it embraces, always *performs* an externalizing reification of some "enemy" of the people. A basic tenet of Marx's analysis of capital, however, recognizes that economic crises are not evidence of exterior manipulation within an otherwise functional system, but are rather one of the fundamental mechanisms through which capitalism temporarily resolves, by deferring into the future, its structural contradictions. Crisis, then, as Žižek underscores through an analogy with psychoanalysis, is not an exception to the rule but is rather one of the basic characteristics of capitalist accumulation as such:

> For a Marxist (as for a Freudian), the pathological (deviating misbehaviour of some elements) is the symptom of the normal, an indicator of what is wrong with the very structure that is threatened in pathological outbursts. For Marx, economic crises are the key to understanding the "normal" functioning of capital; for Freud, pathological phenomena like hysterical outbursts provide the key to the constitution (and hidden antagonism that sustain the functioning) of a "normal" subject. (Žižek 2006a, 555–6)

The first critique of the standard reading of Marx's vampire metaphor offered here thus relates to the way in which this reading conforms to the ideological structure of populist politics: by creating an analog between the antagonism relating capital and labor and that conjoining the vampire and human in the literary or cinematic genre, the standard reading of Marx's vampire's fundamentally obfuscates the relationship between the capital and labor and risks endorsing what Žižek refers to as the "populist temptation." A second but related critique, however, points to the way in which this standard reading, by virtue of its populist structure, mimetically constructs the working class as pre-existing the intervention of capitalism on the world stage, in the same sense that the human characters in vampire fiction are understood to pre-date the appearance of the vampire threat. This implicit narrative presupposition distorts what is arguably the single greatest distinction between Marx's work and that of his predecessors in nineteenth-century political economy (Smith and Ricardo primarily).[5] In the final section of the essay, I return to the duality internal to Marx's vampire metaphor as discussed above and articulate this second critique of the Marxian metaphor by drawing attention to the vampire's transformative character in relation to the social or cultural abstraction inherent to commodity exchange.

Marx's vampires as cultural abstraction

In *All that is Solid Melts into Air* (1982), Marshall Berman asserts that two distinct discourses on modernity can be read into the works of Karl Marx, which he typifies as "modernization" and "modernism," or "solid" and "melting," respectively. For Berman, Marx's discourse on modernization, his "solid" discourse historically depicting socio-economic development in the West, is substantially documented and relatively uncontroversial. In this vein, Marx, like Weber and Durkheim after him, contributed greatly to our understanding of the genesis of industrial capitalism and compelled even its most apologetic proponents to carefully consider the implications of an economic formation built on class antagonism. Yet within this discourse on modernization, Marx's analytical usefulness is typically understood to end with the industrial age and his melodramatic assertions about the collapse of capitalism are dismissed as so much nineteenth-century romanticism. In contradistinction to the literature on modernization, however, Berman observes that Marx is hardly recognized at all within the literature on modernism,[6] despite his contemporaneity with such mainstays of literary modernism as Baudelaire, Flaubert, Wagner, Nietzsche, Kierkegaard, or Dostoyevsky. Marx's absence from this discourse is particularly strange, according to Berman, given the vivid and apocalyptic imagery one finds embedded within Marx's theoretical writings, particularly his incandescent passage from the *Manifesto of the Communist Party* (1848) describing modernity's irrevocable rupture with tradition: "All that is solid melts into air, all that is holy is profaned, and men at last are forced to face with sober senses the real conditions of their lives and their relations with their fellow man" (Marx 1978b, 476). For Berman, this passage from the *Manifesto* is but one instance of Marx's "melting discourse," a discourse which "pulls like an undertow against the more 'solid' Marxian visions we know so well" and not only captures the social and cultural experience of modernity as vividly as any modernist writer but additionally elucidates "the relationship between modernist culture and the bourgeois economy and society from which it [was] sprung" (Berman 1982, 89–90).

The thesis of this essay has similarly argued that there are two vampire metaphors in Marx, one "solid" and one "melting" as it were, and hence that there are at least two different interpretive avenues offered by this metaphor, two distinctive ways of conceptualizing capitalism through the imagery of the vampire. The standard reading of the vampire, which would constitute the "solid" version of the metaphor, is, as I have tried to demonstrate, accurate but problematic insofar as it is arrested at the point of analog in which the binary or antipodal antagonism between the vampire and the human is directly imposed on to the relation between the bourgeoisie and the proletariat as described by Marx. While this surface reading of the metaphor undoubtedly captures much of exploitation inherent in capitalist accumulation, its problematic character is two-fold. First, as I have already demonstrated, by mapping the antagonism between the vampire and the human directly on to that between the bourgeoisie and the proletariat, the vampire metaphor implicitly endorses a mode of reactionary–populist politics that scapegoats an interloper for system failures and thereby overlooks the faulty design of the system itself. In Marxian terms, this would be analogous to blaming individual capitalists, in moral terms, for the inducing systemic crises rather than recognizing that it is the system itself that produces these outcomes and that it is only by altering the fundamental axioms of the system that these structural failures can be addressed.

That said, a second inaccuracy implicitly encouraged by the standard or "solid" reading of Marx's vampire metaphor pertains to the historicity of capitalism itself, a premise upon which Marx insisted but his predecessors systematically overlooked. Nineteenth-century economists (and many of those in the twenty-first century, I would add), as Marx was fond of saying, have "a singular way of proceeding" when examining capitalist institutions of production and exchange:

> For them, there are only two kinds of institutions, artificial and natural. The institutions of feudalism are artificial institutions, those of the bourgeoisie are natural institutions. In this they resemble the theologians, who likewise establish two kinds of religion. Every religion which is not theirs is an invention of man, while theirs is an emanation of God ... There has thus been history, but there is no longer any. (Marx 1977, 175n)

The standard reading of Marx's vampire, I submit, implicitly taps into the same view of history adopted by bourgeois economists (and Christian theologians). For insofar as the "human" is conceived within the vampire genre's binary structure as on the side of the "natural," while the vampire is reciprocally coded as "unnatural," or in Marx's terminology "artificial," the aim of the human protagonists within the narrative conventions of twentieth-century vampire fiction is never ontologically transformative: rather, the human agents within the genre, particularly in the twentieth-century genre, are not only compelled to stave of total annihilation in the face of the vampire threat, but this effort is often melodramatically framed in terms of a duty to preserve the essence of humanity. While this type of narrative dynamic may make for entertaining and escapist cinema, it functions poorly as an analog for the relationship between the bourgeoisie and the proletariat in Marxist theory. For unlike the essential antagonism between the vampire and the proletariat, the proletariat cannot be said to oppose the bourgeoisie in the same fashion, insofar as the very category "proletariat" with which Marx deals is itself a sub-category of the larger notion of "capitalism" itself. And in those instances when the vampire stands in for the indeterminate article "capital," as it does in appearances of the metaphor in the *Grundrisse* and *Capital*, the metaphoric relation makes even less sense. For in what way can the working class oppose the economic force responsible for its very existence without submitting to potential and fundamental ontological transformation?

While this line of argumentation may seem to hinge on a rather technical distinction, the temporal and ontological inessentiality of the identity-category "proletarian" or "working class" in fact speaks to one of the core philosophical and methodological distinctions between Marxist and neoclassical approaches to economics. In Wolff and Resnick's *Economics: Marxian versus Neoclassical* (1987), the authors observe how neoclassical theory "employs a logic known in philosophy as 'deduction' [in which] new concepts or sentences are carefully deduced from prior ones ... From its entry points of human preferences, technology, and resource endowments, the concept of supply and demand for all commodities and resources is logically deduced or derived" (Wolff and Resnick 1987, 240). Based on this methodological approach, Wolff and Resnick are able to describe neoclassical economics as "essentialist" by virtue of the fact that the desiring individual, in combination with historically conditioned technologies and natural resources, is understood as the initial axiom from which all other economic phenomena are deduced and rooted: "supply and demand are reduced to whatever ultimately determines them: the entry-points of individual preferences, technology, and resource endowments. These three aspects of human nature form the basic concepts, the essences, to which all other concepts in neoclassical economics are logically reduced" (Wolff and Resnick 1987, 240). From the Marxian perspective, however, this methodology is based on the philosophically untenable premise that the desiring individual is not already conditioned, or overdetermined, by social and historical space but somehow enters the world *in toto* entirely prepared to engage in rational economic calculation. As Wolff and Resnick thus recognize, the Marxist approach to economics is contrastingly understood as "anti-essentialist" inasmuch as Marxism posits no solid foundations upon which logical deduction can axiomatically commence. Instead, Marxist theory understands that all the elements of an economic and social formation impinge on each other in complex and non-linear ways. "Marxian theory," they stress,

> employs as its connecting logic the anti-essentialist method called "overdetermination." In this approach, each concept of the theory is complexly linked, as both cause and effect, to all the other concepts of the theory. Thus, no concept of the theory can be reduced from or reduced to any other; no concept functions as essence. (Wolff and Resnick 1987, 241)

Unlike neoclassical economics, then, which would be absolutely paralyzed without the rational, utilitarian, and maximizing agent as the essential or axiomatic premise grounding the entire system, Marxist theory recognizes that subjectivity is fundamentally social and historical, and is therefore ontologically open in relation to the social conditions within which subjectivity as such is produced. By shifting the hermeneutic significance of Marx's vampire metaphor from its historico-political—or "solid"—instances to its more mature economic—or "melting"—uses, the metaphor not only subverts the populist potential of the metaphor by accentuating the fluid nature of capitalist society, but it also draws attention to one of the often overlooked elements of Marx's theory of capital: the deterritorializing effects exerted by capital on the cultural and social plane. For when confined strictly to the economic domain—which is already a specious abstraction in the Marxian view—capital, and the processes involved in commodification, is typically viewed as the form of modern mystification *par excellence*: it is the theology of bourgeois society and the autochthonous fetish from which all subsequent reifications are but mere extensions.[7] Recalling however that Marxism is a theory of social overdetermination rather than logical deduction, we cannot say therefore that commodification has an "essential" effectivity, since its effects in one domain may very well function differently elsewhere, and the interrelationships between these differential effects will necessarily overdetermine what we mean when we speak of commodification. And indeed, once analysis shifts levels in any attempt to grasp commodification more expansively as a social and cultural force, it is precisely this kind of dialectical reversal that occurs: what once appeared as the nucleus of capitalism's power for mystification becomes an equally powerful force for *demystification* in the socio-cultural realm. Of course, the nature of this dialectic was not lost on Marx who, with Engels, depicted the spread of capital across the social terrain as the clearing away of the fog of tradition and mysticism from which social relations for the first time become visible in their naked utilitarianism:

> Constant revolutionizing of production, uninterrupted disturbance of all social conditions, everlasting uncertainty and agitation distinguish the bourgeois epoch from all earlier ones. All fixed, fast-frozen relations, with their train of ancient and venerable prejudices and opinions, are swept away, all new-formed ones become antiquated before they can ossify. All that is solid melts into air, all that is holy is profaned, and man is at last compelled to face with sober senses, his real conditions of life, and his relations with his kind. (Marx 1978b, 476)

And it is according to this insight that cultural theory has often been compelled to face, with sober sense, the beneficial effects of commodification in the cultural domain at the same time that it decries the excesses and hypocrisies of the larger system. In one of the more cited instances of this recognition, Walter Benjamin (2008) observed that it was through commodification that art was at last freed from its parasitic relation to time, history, and ritual. Only through what Benjamin called the "liquidation of the value of tradition in the cultural heritage," arguably commodification's most endearing feature, could art begin to serve a properly political function (Benjamin 2008, 8).

Thus when Marx characterizes capital as a vampire, this metaphor should not simply be read as a straightforward denunciation of the immorality of capitalism—though this aspect of the vampire should, surely, not be wholly jettisoned—but rather as a further commentary on the emancipatory complexities rendered in the cultural domain by the spread of capital, as well as a bulwark against the populist narratives that strive anachronistically for the idyllic return to "a system of exchanges based on barter and/or ad hoc representations of value while dreaming of the return to an antediluvian world of use-values" that often accompany politic visions motivated by the concept of the "natural" (Hardt and Negri 2009, 295). While I have attempted to stay within the confines of the political economy in this reevaluation of the vampire trope, I would be remiss if I failed to point out that the efficacy of the vampire figure as just such a vehicle for anti-naturalist or anti-essentialist politics has long been registered in what is broadly referred to as post-humanist theory. And whereas I have earlier marshaled Sue-Ellen Case's queer depiction of the vampire as a subversive anti-normative figure in early modern literature as a foil for my own account, it seems just to return to a similarly queer account in order to square the vision of the economic vampire offered here with its more prominent post-humanist articulations. As part of her account of the sordid racial history of the United States, Donna Haraway (1997) finds good reason to tentatively side with the vampire. What is of particular interest for me, however, is the degree to which Haraway's comments on the vampire might just as well serve as a reflection on the vexed dialectics of capital's social and cultural effects:

> It is impossible to have a settled judgment about vampires. Defined by their categorical ambiguity and troubling mobility, vampires do not rest easy (or easily) in boxes labeled good or bad. Always transported and shifting, the vampire's native soil is more nutritious, and more *unheimlich*, than that. Deeply troubled by murderous ideologies since their modern popularization in European accounts of in the late eighteenth-century—especially racism, sexism, and homophobia—stories of the undead also exceed and invert each of those systems of discrimination to show the violence infesting supposedly wholesome life and nature and the

> revivifying promise of what is supposed to be decadent and against nature. (Haraway 1997, 215)

Critical accounts of the violence associated with racial and sexual identity grounded in notions of the natural have had more obvious recourse to adopt a nuanced view of the vampire than have Marxist analyses of capitalism. When National Socialists decried the parasitism of the Jews, when religious fundamentalists scream of sexual impropriety or when providentialists spew hatred toward immigrants in vampiric terms, the virtues of a reverse discourse of the vampire becomes clear enough. It is less obvious that the same should be said of struggles against the concentrated power of global capital. As I have aimed to demonstrate, however, the easy identification of capitalism with the vampire can be just as problematic as it is in these more notorious examples—and should be analyzed just as critically.

Notes

1 A "double bind," as conceived by Gregory Bateson et al. (1956), designates a communicational dilemma in which a subject is confronted with two opposing and mutually contradictory commands, without being able to clearly view the larger contours of the dilemma nor offered an avenue for opting out of the dilemma. Metaphor can be considered an instance of a double bind insofar as metaphor always hides some element of its referent as a function of its power of elucidation (it highlights and hides at the same time) but also because this property of metaphor is both rarely articulated and, as Lakoff and Johnson contend, metaphoricity cannot be purged from human cognition or language.

2 It should be noted that Marx never uses the vampire metaphor to describe "capitalism" for the simple reason that the term capitalism post-dates Marx.

3 French philosopher Louis Althusser (2009) famously argued that Marx's corpus is marked by an epistemological rupture that divorces his later, economically oriented work (e.g. *Grundrisse, Capital* vols 1–3) from his earlier, more humanistic texts (e.g. *The German Ideology, 1844 Manuscripts*).

4 The tendency to mark the transition from feudal to industrial–capitalist organization through forms of social and cultural anxiety or uncertainty is by no means confined to the vampire genre in late Victorian literature. For instance, it is striking the degree to which the classical detective fiction of Conan Doyle consistently finds its narrative impetus in aristocratic scandal, typically framed in terms of a necessity to rescue the good name or reputation of one noble family or another (indeed, Holmes' first recorded consignment meets this end). In a period when the industrial bourgeoisie had began to definitively supplant the landed nobility as the material hegemons of

English society (as elsewhere in Europe), all the aristocracy had left by way of social distinction was their residual cultural status (in Raymond Williams' sense of the term), and it is the tenuous nature of their symbolic capital that is the cause of much distress in Conan Doyle's narratives and the source of much employment for his enterprising detective.

5 See Althusser 2009, 101–31.

6 For exegesis on the distinction between modernity and modernism, see Harvey 1990, 10–38.

7 For the most developed theory from this perspective see Georg Lukács' "Reification and the Consciousness of the Proletariat" (Lukács 1971, 83–222).

5

Critical theory against the dispossession of needs: From perpetual crisis to social engagement

Tim Kaposy

One of the most repetitive, ubiquitous qualities of social life since the late 1960s is the frequency by which it is described as undergoing crisis. The word's meaning has been blunted with overuse, and its free association with any event gone awry—from the costs of energy and food to unemployment and financial malfeasance—has effectively diminished the concept's analytic acuity. Amid these reiterations is the curious way today's descriptions of social crisis are rarely accompanied by a convincing diagnosis. Though the anxieties and spectacles of catastrophe loom large, talk of crisis is perpetual and has different ramifications than in the past: despite evidence to the contrary, social conflict and disorder have come to be imagined as utterly ordinary and thus preventable.

Despite the surfeit of images of malnourishment, homelessness, environmental calamity, ethnic violence, and deadly viruses appearing before us in media headlines, the commentaries and discussions that follow recount a less alarming lesson: the continuity or end of these crises hinge on the willingness to adjust minor consumer habits, reallocate already abundant resources, and pursue plausible policy alternatives through local governments. We are encouraged to crest above the everyday fracas of media conjecture and "do your bit." Our shared crises are normal and, pundits suggest, solutions arise when these problems are treated with a dose of sensible discretion.

This logic was aired initially by intellectuals (primarily in the global North) who saw the collapse of the Berlin Wall as a reason to denounce and try to eliminate sociological traditions of thought that account for a large scale political economy. "I hope we have reached a time," remarked the pragmatist Richard Rorty in a 1995 article, "when we can finally get rid of the conviction ... that there must be large theoretical ways of finding out how to end injustice, as opposed to small experimental ways" (Rorty 1995, 4). It's known that global capitalism became orthodoxy after the cultural reorganization of post-socialist societies, which demonized State-based planning and curtailed the autonomy of populations from allocating resources before the market dictates the terms and conditions.[1] Less scrutinized, however, is a related illusion: how the universal laws of equivalency and value generated by global capitalism came to be thought of as small, widely beneficent, and, most consequential of all, sustainably self-correcting.

The curious notion that crisis requires sensible, menial responses amounts today to more than the declarations we hear from journalists and philosophers. Logic similar to Rorty's has seeped into the organizing protocols of the world's economic, environmental, medical, political, and social institutions. A cursory overview shows this mindset used in various guises across the map. National governments from Canada to South Africa tout "common sense" as the principle guiding intricate foreign policy and multi-lateral decision-making; NGOs such as Save the Children, Greenpeace, and Save Darfur simplify agendas on pamphlets and websites to parlay recognizable and definitively urgent predicaments of the day into determinate initiatives;[2] humanitarians and activists such as Melinda Gates, Mohammed Yunus, and David Suzuki espouse "simple solutions" to clear the ideological fog and restore the clamoring disjointed world to its equilibrium. Broad endorsement of the idea that minor choices will, for example, alleviate hunger or end poverty, raises innumerable questions concerning the *particular* way global crises are envisioned as mostly private problems under our noses waiting to be realized and dealt with accordingly.

What if crises persist today because, in part, the concepts that have the potential to illuminate their characteristics are consistently bypassed or are believed to be antiquated? Might it be the case that invidious global problems are the result of seemingly bygone structural issues such as class inequality, the geopolitical and gendered divisions of labor, and the anti-democratic centralization of political power *whose reckonings have never occurred in the first place*?

How then might our contention with these issues gain traction without simply reiterating crisis talk or curtailing potentially insightful forms of large-scale social thought and planning (i.e. those admonished by Rorty and others)? Let's turn to a more dynamic narrative of necessity—one that the self-anointed global humanitarians have avoided in favor of sounding the crisis alarm and preaching private responsibility.

How is crisis mediated?

Two questions must be posed to help us assess how the reiteration of crisis displaces us from the issues at hand. First, what forces shape the minutiae of sense perception and habituate the value of particular ideas and words over others (such as "crisis")? And second, conversely, how do cultural forms interrupt long-held habits and catalyze alternative values and vocabularies to make crises more understandable?

A national example is instructive here to help specify these questions. In his engagement with the history of the proletariat in Europe (that returns repeatedly to the above two questions), the theorist Jacques Rancière (2004a) names the relation of perception and social life "the distribution of the sensible." He describes it as

> a delimitation of spaces and times, of the visible and invisible, of speech and noise, which simultaneously determines the place and the stakes of politics as a form of experience. Politics revolves around what is seen and what can be said about it, around who has the ability to see and the talent to speak, around the properties of spaces and the possibilities of time. (Rancière 2004a, 13)

Rancière underscores the perceptual divisions that inflect interpretations of social experiences and, in some cases, further de-legitimate the claims made by already politically subordinated groups. As a result, large segments of populations, and often those seeking widespread change in how they're governed, are denied involvement in reckoning with the problems they face collectively every day.

In one of his earliest historical studies published in 1983, Rancière examines an archive of writings by the French proletariat in the 1830s. Workers' letters, journals, poems, and musical compositions attest to their protracted questioning of the fixity of their daily lives. "Emancipation," Rancière writes, "was not the affirmation of values specific to the world of labour. It was a rupture in the order of things that founded these 'values', a rupture in the traditional division [*partage*] assigning the privilege of thought to some and the task of production to others" (Rancière 2004b, 219). Many periods of history are witness to the revolts of populations whose aims do not achieve a concrete goal; rather, the preferred outcome of struggle is the elimination of the conditions of and divisions within struggle itself.

Revolts against repetitious struggle are often based in the very perceptual and linguistic norms by which social divisions are assumed to be irreversible. "Leaving the field open, for once," Rancière writes in his preface to *The Nights of Labor*, "we may come to see that the relationship between the order of things and the desires of those subjugated to it is a bit more complicated than scholarly treatises realize" (Rancière 1989, xii). Imperiled by symbolic de-legitimation and the fixity of their socio-economic subordination, artisan groups, wageless laborers, and women make their history visible (in part, by taking up new forms of representation or innovating and appropriating old ones) and thus reconfigure the relation of perception to possibilities within social struggle against the category of class created by intellectuals and institutional authorities.

Prior to Rancière, the relation of perception and social struggle was often named "mediation." Today contemporaries use the terminology of "media" or "mediascape" to conceive the technological structures that frame ideas, vocabularies, and images within the spaces of their ongoing interpretation and dispute. However, Rancière's account is usefully distinct because it expands both of these notions of mediation by pairing it with democratic social aims. That is, insurrectionist social critique and cognitive capacities are the basis for potential collective intervention against the fixity of daily struggle.

Aspirations for enduring equality must, at some untimely moment of urgency, contend with the necessarily indirect qualities of representational forms. Mediation is not something we should think of as an impediment to participation. Instead, as Fredric Jameson (1991) reminds us, interpreting mediation *enhances* one's ability to specify the implications of harried events. "My experience," Jameson argues, "is that you can't manage to think about things simply by deciding to, and that the mind's deeper currents often need to be surprised by indirection, sometimes, indeed, by treachery and ruse, as when you steer away from a goal in order to reach it more directly or look away from an object to register it more exactly" (Jameson 1991, 71).

In a similar sense, Rancière teaches us that any *social* reckoning with crisis ends not with a solution or failure (i.e. emancipation or a continued crisis). Insurrections engage the indirect, "participatory" characteristics of culture to see what particular forms and activities include or exclude participants for a more sustained struggle beyond the initial rebellion of a group. This may be why Rancière enlarges the problematic of "mediation" in his innumerable essays to delineate the spatial and temporal patterns of social inclusion and exclusion, and not just the immediate tactical use of a concept. Rancière directs his sustained attention to instances of unorthodox social solidarity that form against crises, and which, after the force of initial revolt and cooperation, causes its participants to "re-group" and grasp how they have come into being. "The apportionment of parts and positions," he writes, "is based on a distribution of spaces, times, and forms of activity that determine the very manner in which something in common lends itself to participation and in what way various individuals have a part in this distribution" (Rancière 2004a, 12). The value of Rancière's archival work in *The Nights of Labor* (1989) and his critique of theoretical practice in *The Philosopher and his Poor* (2004b) lies in their staging of the *normalization* internal to even the most egalitarian of social struggles. Rancière calls this process of normalization "consensus." Where normalization is often conceived as the 'absence' of social struggle, Rancière sees normalization as resulting from "apportioning" participation in space and time.

Furthermore, these two texts clarify that no direct correlation exists between the prevalence of political concepts in a culture (i.e. democracy, equality, freedom, liberty, etc.) and their social fruition. For example, today's reiteration of the word "equality"—which all, seemingly, agree is a *goal* of political struggle—for Rancière is an indication of an ill-fated belief that equality is something we ought to formalize, protect, or secure. On the contrary, he writes that "equality is a presupposition, an initial axiom—or it is nothing" (Rancière, 2004b, 223). The potential for equality thus exists *against* any formal consensus, any conferral in words, images, or artifacts that signal its "arrival" or determinate existence (i.e. think, for instance, of the belief that nations ensure "equality" because it is enshrined in their constitutional documents or laws).

Rancière's key question for us, then, is one similar to those faced by an earlier generation of social theorist: how might social participation "take place," even as a difficulty persists among artists, educators, activists, and citizens to admit that expression of one's political ideals may simply normalize and thus detract from social struggle? This question is made more vexing when one acknowledges the full scale of contemporary social life. What happens when a crisis is determined to be *unrestricted* to a national or local situation, such as revolutionary France, or Chiapas Mexico, but is intrinsically global? How do words and images gain the needed traction across linguistic and cultural divides so that the number of participants contending with the inequalities of material necessity increase? What type of consensus might arise in struggles against a global crisis?

The problematic of need *contra* crisis

> What has to be targeted by a politics of need ... is not only what we share in the way of basic needs, but in the causal relationship between the forms in which some are meeting those needs and the forms in which others are being deprived. (Kate Soper 1993, 129)

Take, for instance, the word "need." It is perhaps the most basic term used to characterize the transition from the identification of a crisis to the attempted implementation of a solution. How might one assess the historical valance of a word such as "need" today, when its use spans centuries, and, like a galloping horse, its power seemed best harnessed in earlier eras? What is a "need" today? Are not needs commonplace and simply chosen by the whim of each person in whatever situation he or she finds him or herself? Are we in agreement that what I need is rarely similar to what you need, and so forth? And finally, is it possible to delineate a stable problematic of need if many of us assume they consist of an aggregate of innumerable and disparate articulations of personal preferences?

Today the word "need" has a burnished density that is continually tread over and left out of circulation. Perhaps it is most useful to begin with the recognition that "need" is articulated in instructively contradictory ways. It circulates with both prosaic and highly connotative meanings. In the majority of its uses, "need" conveys a desire without circumspection, without forethought, and usually in reference to a defined object. It is a relative, banal descriptor used to signify an immediate purpose or aim. For example, I need a nail to connect a plank of wood to a tree. The concrete object is needed in order to create an intended effect and we point at it offhandedly. In other situations the term is resistant to definition and is the source of acrimonious disagreement.

Contested meaning occurs most often when need refers to the allocation of a resource for a group of people or to a non-human entity. For instance, the *New York Times* reports on the need to clean up the Gulf of Mexico after a British Petroleum drilling installation exploded in April of 2010. Over the next three months the well spilled approximately 180 million gallons into its waters. Debates concerning the exact extent of need guaranteed pages of editorializing. Who represents and is responsible for this massive body of water and surrounding ecosystem? Who accurately articulates the needs of the living beings within the Gulf, and who ultimately failed to meet their needs? Due to the impossibility of assigning a "proper" representative for all populations and non-human entities, the word "need" tends to be retracted from discussions in the media. And when the broader implications of the hemorrhaging oil were aired—i.e. the argument consistently made, "The gulf should remain a vibrant ecosystem for generations to come"—the environmental advocate was accused of tepid fantasy or exaggerated idealism.

Kate Soper's remark, flagged above as an epigram, teaches us, however, that if we wish to understand how need is an elementary quality of existence today, and not an antiquated project, then its formal characteristics beyond what you and I share in our separate articulations and disparate circumstances must replace the idea that need is synonymous with desire, choice, or compulsion. Need is much less an individual articulation of one specific *thing* than a fundamental *form* of coexistence whereby part of the group meets their needs and, perhaps as a result of this success, others are deprived. Only on this basis can we hope to adequately address and resolve seemingly interminable crises.[3]

Marx's problematic

Perhaps the tendency to represent needs strictly within the parameters of the human body is inevitable. A majority of the associations we have of eating, drinking, and protecting one's self are made in reference to one's body and the private struggle to survive. It is certainly easy to recognize how difficult it is to meet the most rudimentary of needs for each person. If meeting one's needs were simply a matter of how one's body acquires housing, food, goods, or energy—alone and in the absence of a broader human community—then many of us would fail to survive.

The most influential formalization of need that transcends the individual human body was made by Karl Marx. The uniqueness of Marx's "transindividual" outlook is noted by Étienne Balibar (2007). Marx differs from other theorists because, instead of asking "what are human needs?" he asks, "what conditions exist such that humans articulate, seek, acquire, deprive, and allocate needs"? Writing from the industrial epoch, Marx invites us to think in terms of changing social and material conditions that inform and make productive bodily needs. Balibar writes:

> The point is to reject both the positions (the *realist* and the *nominalist*) between which philosophers have generally been divided: the one arguing that the genus or essence precedes the existence of individuals; the other that individuals are the primary reality, from which universals are "abstracted." For, amazingly, neither of these two positions is capable

> of thinking precisely what is essential in human existence: the multiple and active relations which individuals establish with each other (whether language, labour, love, reproduction, domination, conflict, etc.), and the fact that it is these relations which define what they have in common, the "genus." (Balibar 2007, 31–2)

For Marx (1990, 1981), need is neither a pre-existent entity that strictly determines reality, nor is it strictly an acquisitive process through which an individual is ruled by compulsions. It is conceived as a material realm that shapes Marx's understanding of human freedom, especially his historical inquiries into labor organization and resource allocation. How one produces one's needs rather than having them dictated from elsewhere—an aspect of his notion of "freedom from necessity" —is a quintessential problematic of his dialectical thinking. Social problems are interpreted according to the particular situation (i.e. his analysis of the 1871 Paris Commune differs from his interpretation of the revolutions in 1848), and subsequently, Marx has no "philosophy of history" *per se* and instead his need problematic is scattered across his work to the extent that it has to be gathered together to make his problematic coherent.

In one of his early essays, Marx tells us that in relation to the earth and other beings the need of the human is to be

> a total being and as a total being his needs stand in a relation to the products of others—for the need for a thing is the most obvious, irrefutable proof that the thing is a part of my essence, that its being is for me and that its property is the property, the particular quality peculiar to my essence. (Marx 1991, 267).

Needs are imagined as an ongoing restriction that impedes humans from becoming "total beings." Differing from, say, Abraham Maslow (1987), Marx's underlying notion is that the possibility of becoming "total beings"—a consequence of first meeting their needs—is *not* simply predicated by personal conduct or whether or not one desires to survive or thrive. Instead this possibility arises through the productive reliance one has for the innumerable resources produced by others. The qualitative difference of Marx's view is that we *produce* needs and in so doing subject others to forms of production—especially unfavorable and debilitating forms of labor—that persist in order to meet the burgeoning number of needs that industrial life establishes.

The causal relation between meeting needs and their deprivation (noted by Soper in the epigram above) is located in this division of labor and its subsequent configuration of class formation. Need is a property of the relations that cut across personal preferences because resources are produced in a reliant and unequal manner. The form of need that Marx establishes is not nakedly primordial or subjective; it is located at the core of this difference between meeting a certain class's need and depriving needs from other parts of the population.

The point I want to stress here is that Marx shows that any need, however seemingly inextricable from the human body, is part of a system of production, circulation, and consumption that is rarely if ever immediate to oneself. Indeed, Marx's foregrounding of the commodity form in *Capital* Vol. I is the result of his perplexity in the face of intensely visceral, pseudo-religious experiences garnered by objects and the immense enterprise composed of years of work and enormous spaces facilitating this perceptual immediacy (Marx 1990). In specifying the relation of social life to the commodities produced and consumed, Marx stages need as an ongoing implication of one's material situation.

The realm of necessity

Marx differentiates between "natural needs," "necessary needs," "luxury needs," and "social needs."[4] Each category specifies a type of resource or product that is conferred with a different value depending on the way it is incorporated in a particular moment of capitalist social relations of use and exchange value. One of Marx's aims in creating these categories is to understand how these types are arranged in relation to one another. More specifically, he examines how this system of value is deemed legitimate and deployed across a social ensemble to reproduce the relations of production that are used to generate resources in the first place.

Marx argues that in order for a laborer to produce in an unimpeded, rote fashion, and in the way dictated to them, "natural needs, such as food, clothing, fuel and housing ... must be sufficient to maintain him in his normal state as a working individual" (Marx 1990, 133). Thus, an educated and healthy workforce underpins and is antagonistic with continuous production, and vice versa. One of the most instructive passages with respect to Marx's theory of need—displaying his impetus for having such a dialectical theory in the first place, rather than one that is exclusively economical—is found early in the first volume of *Capital*. Here need is a pre-condition of labor practices, while production is a pre-condition for the "realm" that (along with whatever externalities that may arise) provides capital the greatest probability to reproduce itself. He writes:

> [the worker's] natural needs, such as food, clothing, fuel and housing, vary according to the climatic and other physical peculiarities of his country. On the other hand, the number and extent of his so-called necessary means of subsistence, as also the manner in which they are satisfied, are themselves products of history, and depend therefore to a great extent on the level of civilization attained by a country; in particular they depend on the conditions in which, and consequently on the habits and expectations with which the class of free workers has been formed. (Marx 1990, 123–4)

Notice that need is formalized by Marx in a fundamental way: the ensemble of social relations determines and depends on material realms beyond what is perceivable for a subject. Marx uses the term "*zusammen*" (collective) to break from the "realist" and "nominalist" ontological dichotomy to argue, as Balibar does, that

> we have to think humanity as a *transindividual* reality and, ultimately, transindividuality as such. Not what is ideally "in" each individual (as a form or substance), or what would serve, from outside, to classify that individual, but what exists between individuals by dint of their multiple interactions (Balibar 2007, 32)

Therefore, needs are said to set the normal parameters of one's ability to act in accordance with others' preferences and demands. Capital is thus a category of specific *social relations* rather than a monetary unit of measure or currency, one that points toward a "realm … beyond the sphere of material production." Consider Marx again:

> The realm of freedom really begins only where labour determined by necessity and external expediency ends; it lies by its very nature beyond the sphere of material production proper ... This realm of natural necessity expands with his development, because his needs do too; but the productive forces to satisfy these expand at the same time ... The true realm of freedom, the development of human powers as an end in itself, begins beyond it, though it can only flourish with this realm as its basis. (Marx 1982, 958–9)

For Marx, human freedom is inextricable from the social and political struggle for meeting nutrition, housing, and so on. Whereas many political theorists consider freedom to be an issue related to one's political choices, personal expressions, and institutional affiliations, Marx argues that a "realm of freedom" opens up when needs are met evenly across the social ensemble.

Dispossession

The "realm of natural necessity" produced by late capital has a fundamentally different composition than in Marx's time. The epoch of imperialism from the late sixteenth to the early twentieth century was built upon a center-periphery geopolitical division whose burgeoning national antagonisms subsumed competing structures, such as the city-state and early modern trading companies. With time and increased innovation to further accommodate the dominion of capital, changes in corporate institutions (especially financial) have reshaped the means through which the regions of the world produce resources in order for populations elsewhere on the planet to survive. With further intensification, the struggles within local and national economies and their prospective reproduction have created a geopolitical arrangement that *international* rubrics only partially explained. "That new world-system moment," Jameson explains, was

> gradually laid in place since the end of World War II, [and] has been unveiled in discontinuous convulsions—the end of the 60s, the rise of the "third world" debt, the emergence first of Japan and then of soon-to-be-united new Europe as competing superstates, the collapse of the party state in the East, and finally the reassumption by the United States of a refurbished vocation as global policeman (Jameson 1992, 5)

"World systems theory" grew out of the inadequacies of earlier rubrics which had trouble mapping how these varied realms and conjunctures affected one another. As a result, problems of need can be produced virtually anywhere and predicaments of survival do not always coincide with national sovereignty or demographic patterns.

A prescient inflection of Jameson's analysis of the global scale of capitalism is presented by David Harvey (2003). Harvey's *The New Imperialism* is instructive for providing a useful interpretation of contemporary realms of necessity. In a chapter titled "Accumulation by Dispossession," Harvey examines how the shortage of food production within the global North occurred inexplicably in a time of the post World War II abundance. A crisis arose at this time because these sovereigns sought to reorganize the ways basic resources were exchanged, marshaling into existence a new way in which goods and services are produced, circulated, consumed, and discarded worldwide.

Harvey interprets this period as continuing the post-World War II structural adjustment programs set forth by Bretton Woods (1944), The General

Agreement on Tariffs and Trade (1947–93), and other transnational institutions that overhauled the political, legal, and economic rules for determining how people survive. Harvey earmarks this shift as the period in which many nation-states in the global South accrued debt and became beholden to a monetary and inter-political system that is not accountable to those whose lives are most affected. The global economy's influence in the States' handling of their domestic markets—where many basic resources are priced and allocated—is said to have reached unprecedented levels today.

The distinctiveness of Harvey's interpretation, however, lies in the belief that as these shifts redefine the ability of capitalism to incorporate and structure all aspects of daily life, its dynamic leaves a great deal "undefined" or "unknown" for future prediction. In a time when "boom and bust" cycles appear less likely to recur endlessly (i.e. where downturns will become a long-term norm), the economic cooptation of environmental, social, and cultural realms is conducted, according to Harvey, with a threatened, already maimed, and largely consenting populace as its witness and agent. Populations have immediate, incessant needs and yet lack readily available vocabularies and—*pace* Rancière—the means of participating to prevent the issue. This creates a pragmatic gap and into this gap floods a constant raft of images, sounds, and narratives that buoy a tentative understanding of our social crises. Harvey emphasizes an examination of the *geographical* dimension since World War II based on the premise that if we are to challenge and reconstitute these processes, the *social* dimension of dispossession will be explicit in an optimal participatory sense. Put differently, the forms of dispossession noted here cannot be allowed to recur in abstract form—*realms* of necessity must be interrogated and made concrete to others with models which demonstrate how processes of food, energy, housing, and others interrelate. Harvey notes:

> Struggles over dispossession occur on a variety of scales. Many are local, others regional and still others global . . . The targets and objectives of these struggles are diffuse, very much a function of the inchoate, fragmentary and contingent forms taken by dispossession. Destruction of habitat here, privatization of services there, expulsions of the land elsewhere, biopiracy in yet another realm—each creates its own dynamic. (Harvey 2003, 174)

Arguably, the virtue of *The New Imperialism* is the eschewal of popular synthesizing concepts, such as "neoliberalism" or "crisis," that tend to subsume a thorough economic critique of the disjointed scales of global capitalism. The "new imperialism" is based on labor manufacturing statistics, finance trends, growing evidence of the influence of debt and stagflation, and the falling rate of profit throughout the corporate world of Japan, Germany, England, and the United States (despite off-shoring and out-sourcing growth strategies). No one explanatory model or concept within Harvey's reach is sufficient to conceive of where global capitalism, after the economic control of these countries has migrated elsewhere, is leading us economically.

Sounding out the spectacle

The mediation of crisis takes place within many of the world's international economic, educational, humanitarian, and environmental institutions such as the International Monetary Fund, The World Bank, The European Union, and UNESCO. But the gradual elimination or narrowing of alternative representations and spaces also occurs uneventfully in the apparently innocent and plural cultural activities we might assume to have no relation to global coexistence.

Sustaining a normalcy of meeting needs has a national provenance that has fragmented and splintered out beyond these predictable geographies and timelines. In recent French history, "*le spectacle*" became the term associated with the onslaught of commodities bringing about a regression of perceptual capacities and the dissolution of standards of living. The year 1967 saw not only Guy Debord's demonstrative manifesto and film montage responses to pervasive social alienation (see Debord 1994); Jacques Tati's "Play Time," which was screened in the same year, dramatizes a technologically baffling and humdrum Paris circulating with tourists and comical high jinks butting up against the prearranged furniture of enjoyment (see Tati 2001). Listen closely to the final sequences of Tati's film and one will hear the dull moans of surmising and perplexity of Monsieur Hulot amid "the inhuman unloveliness of the glass walls and décor" (Jameson 1992, 194). Where Debord's didacticism reaches unexpectedly comedic levels in his montage film, Tati's use of physical folly is an indication of the limits of personal initiative and maneuvering within the spectacle. Kristin Ross notes, "*vieux Paris* has disappeared and the whole movie transpires in the vague, airport-condo terrain of prefab industrial space" (Ross 1995, 173). Tati's film serves up no lesson in particular *except* that the world of the spectacle is a world with no instruction to be had and without anything in particular to learn. Is not Hulot enacting for us the space of linguistic dispossession via commodification?

Inheritor of a world spectacle and observant of both Debord's didactic iconoclasm and Tati's ludic dramaturgy, Jean Baudrillard describes "the ideological genesis of needs" in the dominion of myths arising in advertising and other seductions of popular culture. Baudrillard's point is that these myths compel subjects to believe, as did Abraham Maslow,[5] that needs consist of an order of primordial forces waging war within their body. "Needs," Baudrillard argues, "are a function induced (in the individual) by the internal logic of the system itself, by its process of reproduction and survival. In other words, there are only needs because the system needs them" (Baudrillard 1981, 82). Commodity fetishism in late-capital culture allows for Baudrillard to envision ways that categories of interpretation or analytical thought are evacuated at the moment of encounter with the objects one consumes. In terms of the need for housing, for example, one intuits the house's exchange value and symbolic connotations, both of which alter one's capacity to grasp its infrastructure:

> Is a house an object? Some would contest this. The decisive point is to establish whether the symbolism of the house (sustained by the shortage of housing) is irreducible, or if even this can succumb to the differential and reified connotations of fashion logic: for if this is so, then the home becomes an object of consumption ... The definition of an object of consumption is entirely independent of the object themselves and exclusively a function of the logic of significations. (Baudrillard 1981, 67)

When the built environment becomes thoroughly commodified (as in Tati's Paris) and shelter is abstracted into exchange value, its function becomes inextricable from the representations that animate and mystify it.[6] In defiance of aggrandizing claim or admonishment, Tati and Baudrillard seem to ask: How best might we test out the predicaments of need in utterly detailed fashion, attendant to the geographies of anecdote, color, voice-over and pleasure to more exactly register how and why global capital has come to work in this muted manner?

* * *

No one category is sufficient for understanding how populations become dispossessed of the capacity to eat, cohabit, and so on. However, it is clear cities are the primary scale adjudicating need. Over the course of the twentieth century, they have demonstrated an increasing tendency to dictate how other spaces and processes evolve. Urban sovereignty is readily explicit in many theories of globalization, but this focus omits accounts of rural, maritime, atmospheric, and oceanic spaces—since scant work has been produced examining their relation. How, for instance, does the need for housing complicate projects for ensuring the population eats nutritiously or breathes well? Furthermore, how does the reliance of cities on other spaces reorganize the intermediary realms of sea-faring trade and energy prospecting?

Dispossession is a concept often used to describe the sustained military and cultural extension of colonial and imperialist incursion of one nation into another territory for the purposes of societal and material reorganization. The contemporary dynamic of dispossession written here differ slightly from its more prevalent colonial or imperialist ones. This twist is not an implied dissolution of the residual structures of violence and domination that generated modern modes of social and material production, but an attempt to understand the way the dispossession of need has bled out beyond national parameters through the capillaries of all social bodies, periphery and centre, in order to exclude populations according to how they feel, see, say, think, and exist in the world ("Play Time" is a demonstrative example). If we have many ways to specify issues surrounding and redirecting the energies of crisis-talk, the problematic I have explored is but one.

While dispossession's philosophical underpinning in the liberal tradition from John Locke and Friedrich Hayek to Hernando de Soto has enabled the transformation of all things into private property, I am giving attention to an expropriation of a second order in which the continuity and depth of dispossession is an imperative of culture itself (and not just an effect of being written into the protocol of law and socio-economic institutions).[7] The continuity of dispossession in this way has the alarming tendency to erase its own history from both immediate visual perception and historical memory. One of the imperatives for foregrounding *need rather than crisis* is to counteract this erasure in an effort to provide resources for participants against current economic orthodoxy and for a future no longer mired in the experiments of humdrum dispossession.

Notes

1 For a thorough study of post-socialist property relations, see Verdery (2003).

2 On the egregious misinterpretation of the civil war in Darfur on the behalf of the "Save Darfur!" movement, see Mamdani (2009). On "commonsense" governance in Canada and South Africa see respectively Healy (2010) and Gevisser (2007).

3 For example, in 2010, the Agricultural Development Economics, Food and Agriculture Organization of the United Nations reported that 925 million people did not have enough to eat and malnutrition was ranked as the world's greatest health risk (Food and Agriculture Organization of the United Nations 2010).

4 Agnes Heller (1976) differentiates Marx's theory of need in terms of necessary needs, social needs, and radical needs. This differentiation seems more hermetic to me because it elides the issue of how value is determined on a daily basis. See the first chapter of her book, *The Theory of Need in Marx*.

5 Published in 1954, *Motivation and Personality* (1987) delineates a hierarchy of needs in four stages. The acquisition of one stage of bodily need is the precondition for acquiring the next. They are: physiological need, safety of the body, social belonging, and esteem. The first stage of need—physiological need, driven by the attainment of food and water—allows for the possibility of securing a feeling of safety for the person, and so on. Maslow differentiates the stages of need by arguing:

> there are real psychological and operational differences between those needs called "higher" and those needs called "lower." This is done in order to establish that the organism itself dictates hierarchies of values, which the scientific observer reports rather than creates ... The basic needs arrange themselves in a fairly definitive hierarchy on the basis of the principle of relative potency. Thus safety need is stronger than the love need, because it dominates the organism in various demonstrable ways when both needs are frustrated. (Maslow 1987, 97–8)

6 Baudrillard's (1981) critique is less incisive when he makes reference to "the system" as the source of myths pertaining to consumption. The value of Marx's work pertains to utterly precise naming and locating where needs are produced, mediated and threatened to be deprived.

7 The texts I note here are synonymous with attempts to justify private property as the basis for freedom: John Locke's *Second Treatise on Government* (2002 [1690]), Friedrich von Hayek's *The Road to Serfdom* (2006 [1944]), and Hernando de Soto and Francis Cheneval's *Realizing Property Rights* (2006).

6

Finance and the social time of aging: Toward a synthesis

Justin Sully

The world's population is growing older at a rate and on a scale that is historically unprecedented. Between 1950 and 2000, the percentage of the world's population over the age of 65 grew from 8.3 per cent to 10.1 per cent. During the first 50 years of this century, from 2000 to 2050, demographic projections suggest we will see this number swell to just over 21 per cent of the world's population (United Nations 2002, xviii). The United Nations' 2002 report on World Population Aging puts the facts of the matter succinctly: "Increases in the proportions of older persons (60 years or older) are being accompanied by declines in the proportions of the young (under age 15). By 2050, the number of older persons in the world will exceed the number of young for the first time in history" (United Nations 2002, xxvii). These conclusions have long been accepted fact in the population studies community. In these circles, the process of population aging is widely recognized as ranking with events like the Black Death, indigenous American "depopulation," and European industrialization as an epochal demographic event in the history of human life on the planet. The past decade in particular has witnessed a growing stream of prognostication about the apocalyptic future of aging societies, beginning with the World Bank's 1994 report "Averting the Old Age Crisis" and ballooning into countless high-profile policy documents and works of popular non-fiction.[1] Given the unprecedented nature and the scale of this demographic process, its effects will be marked at all levels of social life. The most common alarmist response to this new form of "population crisis" focuses predictably at the level of national interests—for example, the capability of aging states to maintain military hegemony, economic growth, and social security. In the midst of the debt crises and austerity programs ushered in by the financial crisis of 2008, the concrete economic and political impact of population aging is evident today. In the face of immense challenges and the growing discourse of crisis, a sense of the broader, systemic, and even cognitive transformations associated with population aging tends to get pushed out of view.

We know that the broad demographic transformations that have led to aging population—namely, increased life expectancy and lower total fertility rate—have been apparent in many European countries for, at least, the last hundred years. By the mid 1960s, however, almost all advanced industrial societies had reached a point where life expectancy had increased and fertility levels had dropped to a level that would lead inevitably toward an older society. Over the last decades of the twentieth century, numerous developing nations and regions (e.g. China, South East Asia, Latin America) made rapid transition to low birth rates and toward the aging populations that are, at the beginning of the 2000s, already posing significant challenges for national and regional economies across Europe, Japan and, to a lesser extent, North America.[2] Given the now global scale and significance of this process, and the extent to which it entails such an overdetermination of economic, sociological, cultural, and even biological causes and effects, it is notable that contemporary social theory has largely ignored it.

To some extent, this is no surprise. Population has long been a suspect category for social theory. Karl Marx's famously derogatory critique of Malthus, and the associated attack on the concept of population as being itself an especially pernicious example of the "bad abstraction" of social relations, is perhaps the most formative moment in a break between social theory and the analysis of concrete demographic trends.[3] At the same time, the field of modern population science has on the whole been comparatively slow to integrate the theoretical turns that have shaped the social sciences—including the most conspicuous examples of demography's late (or non-) adoption of postcolonial theory, the so-called constructivist critique of institutional knowledge, and recent feminist and gender theory. But even this pervasive theoretical promotion of population as the primary site of a new mode of bio-power has taken very little interest in the *content* of contemporary demographic discourse itself. Indeed, there is reason to wonder whether the power to "make live and let die" that Foucault et al. have elevated to the dominant modality of social control requires adjustment in the light of the contemporary situation, where fewer and fewer are made to live (i.e. born) and more and more are allowed to live longer than they ever have.[4]

In short, there is room to make a case for taking a closer look at official discourses of population crisis and aging today. Population aging presents a range of challenges, both conceptual and analytic, for contemporary social theory. In this chapter I will focus on two of these challenges. First, I will explore the challenge posed by the temporal form of aging as a mass, demographic process and its uncertain relationship to the still axiomatic assumption of continuous (population) growth. What kind of temporality is projected in the future of an aging society? How is the modern fantasy of infinite (economic) growth being reshaped to contend with a mass biological and demographic behavior that fits, at the very least, uncomfortably with this imaginary? Second, I will explore the analytic challenge raised by the relation of this new demographic condition and the concurrent economic financialization of the capitalist world system. In light of the on-going systemic economic crisis and widespread dissemination of population anxiety and alarm, these two approaches offer a way toward staking out some of the ill-defined points of contact between existing approaches to social theory and the radical new face of the "problem of population."

The crisis discourse of aging

Discourses about population behavior have long functioned as a powerful, if often deeply suspect, mode of representing a social totality. To speak about population aging, in particular, is to make a complex claim about social time and its political ontology, one that rests in part on the projective impulse of statistical demography itself and, in part, upon the temporal trajectory plotted by the idea of age and aging. Though social and political theorists today are likely to nominate globalization, financialization, or the environmental unsustainability of current patterns of growth as the most significant social processes defining the horizon of the political, even a passing glance at the current and projected demographics demonstrates the importance of including population aging on this list. The points of connection between the former, more familiar global processes and the condition of world population aging are mentioned more and more often as practical challenges in both popular and expert political and economic analyses. Yet there remains a relative absence of synthetic accounts of their relation and codetermination. In social and cultural theory, where such synthetic account are often produced today, the problem of aging has indeed begun to merge with a cluster of existent and emergent fields of inquiry, including gender, disability, immigration, health, and science studies, as well as other topics subsumed under the porous category of the "biopolitical." With the exception of the political-economic approaches in critical geronotology, contemporary theories of aging remain largely focused at the level of the subject and leave the global or systemic view of *population* aging as an introductory footnote to studies of aging as a subjective or sociological condition.

One of the more remarkable features of the popular interpretation of world events today is the manner in which the available narratives that give coherence to public debate—for instance, globalization, financial crisis, or ecological catastrophe—pinpoint the novelty of our contemporary moment in processes that are at the same time, paradoxically, widely accepted as having always already been there. For instance, insofar as globalization or climate change are imagined as eventful, it is not in terms of their sudden discovery or arrival, but rather in terms of their continuity with the past and their gradual development through which they make urgent, epochal claims upon the present. In other words, what appears eventful about these macro-logical narratives is ascribed more to their concretion of an inherent limit of an existing system than their break or incompatibility with this order. What is peculiar here is not so much the endogenous formation of these "new" global conditions (something that is in a sense inevitable), but their structural or logical continuity with the existing order. The attempt to conceptually manage this contradiction is readily apparent. Consider, for instance, the historiographical acrobatics of the theorists of globalization, applying increasingly fine-grained distinctions to identify the contemporary newness of social, economic, and cultural processes that most theorists will also (often simultaneously) agree stretch back centuries. Whatever the nature of the critical or normative procedure that follows from these discourses, everyone can agree that the existing order, which we can simply call capitalism, contains an impulse to territorial expansion (among others) and that this growth has tended to produce destructive and traumatic transformative effects for the societies and ecosystems it happens to enclose. Indeed, however we conceptualize the origins, causal relations, or consequences of these processes (expansion, growth, integration), they remain the most recognizable signs of progress we possess.

What may distinguish the problem of population aging from discourses like globalization and ecological deterioration, then, is the extent to which it might be seen to represent a definite conceptual interruption, rather than an expansion or exacerbation of what are essentially expected features of modernity and of capitalist growth more generally. Set against ecological crisis, globalization, and other recognizable modes of imagining social totality today, population aging represents a global narrative of a social whole that is distinguished by its dramatic incommensurability with any modern rationality of social time or progress. While diminishing fertility rates and lengthening life cycles extend logically from an available concept of development and social progress, the total effect of these combined processes, namely demographic aging, fits less easily. Population aging signifies at the same time a process of decline (of fertility rates, for example) and the expected process of continuous growth (the world's population will continue to grow in absolute terms, at the earliest, well into the second half of this century).

To clarify this point, consider the distinction between demographic aging and absolute population decline. Viewed in terms of its temporal structure or logic, the prospect of an absolute decline in population, while reversing the propulsive logic of modernity and the classical momentum of capital accumulation, is in a larger sense still structurally contained within the parameters of the productive–destructive mechanics of capitalist progress. Decline functions as the possible negation of the coincidence of population-growth and expanded capital accumulation. This is apparent at the level of economic thought, where continuous population growth remains, for the most part, axiomatic (though this is certainly beginning to change). It is, however, even more profoundly true at the level of the symbolic, where (particularly following European industrialization) decline and entropy help to form the dialectic kernel of creative destruction that remains the (ever less-sustainable) condition for the reproduction of our economic system.

By comparison, the crisis discourse of population aging gives shape to a figure of social time that cuts ambiguously across the structuring polarities of growth/decline, expansion/contraction, more/less. The idea of population aging describes both *and* neither population growth and/nor population decline: today's aging societies continue to increase in absolute size, but it is a *kind* of growth that we have not previously seen, as characterized, paradoxically, by numerous signs and figures of decline. For instance, one can point to declines in total fertility, and to the (at least perceived) capacity of aging population for productivity, innovation, and economic growth. To contemplate the implications of a social futurity characterized by progressive agedness exposes the epistemic fragility of a wide range of assumptions guaranteed by the untroubled identity of fertility and futurity, crystallized in the cliché "the children are the future," or in what Lee Edelman (2005), in a quite different register, has provocatively called "reproductive futurism" (Edelman 2005, 16–17). Arguably, though, population aging is a process that exceeds its etiology and cannot be reduced to diminishing fertility rates or lengthening life spans, however causally related they are.

The temporal construction of aging as a demographic process demands attention at the level of its effects. The social time contained in the concept of aging as a collective, demographic process exerts a potentially powerful reorientation of the way subjects and the societies to which they belong imagine themselves and their future. Population aging is a deeply political discourse, one invested in projecting a radically other figuration of futurity. While identifying the anticipatory traces of this cognitive shift is possible through a more cultural approach to the problem, examinations of the economic sphere provide evidence that this shift already has tremendous social purchase. Adopting a mode of social theorization more concretely informed by political economy grows naturally from the macroscopic view of demographic aging. Though it is often precisely the suturing of population behavior to economic calculation that pushes social analysis toward reactionary alarmism, to begin with the social or cultural logic of population aging reframes the analysis of the economic in a way that brushes against the grain of expected anxiety about scarcity, security, and sovereignty; anxiety that tends to underwrite the crisis discourse of population.

Financing old age

Part of what makes assessing these demographic changes so complicated is the way they are embedded within wholesale transformations of the regime of capital accumulation that have occurred over the past forty years, namely, since the world systemic crises of the late 1960s and 1970s. The relationship between population aging and changes at the level of the social reproduction of capital are far from autonomous developments. Indeed, it is increasingly difficult to understand one without taking the other into account. To help focus and deepen our understanding of the convergence of demographic aging and capital accumulation, let's quickly review the entanglement of pensions in post-industrial, financialized economies (see Haiven, chapter 3).

Begin with the longer historical evolution of contemporary finance. The recomposition of the capitalist world system that came out of the economic turbulence of the 1970s was accompanied by immense popular anxiety surrounding overpopulation, fitting a new scale and rhetoric to old fears about the sustainability of growth and the carrying capacity of the Earth. In retrospect, part of what makes the demographic imagination of this period so interesting is how few of its dreams of demographic catastrophe were realized. As an ideological project, population alarm during this period cannot be separated from the effort to structure production and to resuscitate the levels of profitability enjoyed by capital in the decades after World War II. The field of popular culture sought to express and, in different ways, contain the economic crises of the 1970s. In particular, science fiction and "popular non-fiction" texts underlined the manipulation of alarmist discourses of overpopulation, which project an image of undifferentiated, global population growth to explain the fact of radically uneven distribution of demographic behavior globally.

If there is something in the rhetoric of population crisis during the 1970s that is symptomatic of the re-organization of the time and space of production that also takes place during this moment, it is the way in which the *location* of the so-called population bomb, despite all data, became so hard to identify. Whether we attribute this social or cognitive shift to the after-effects of decolonization, the emergent influence of ecological perspectives, the ideological–strategic interests of the cold war, or the ideological–strategic interests of capital in crisis, it is apparent that sometime in the late 1960s and 1970s, the rate of increase among populations in India or Nigeria suddenly appeared as if it were universal—and so appeared threatening to members of Western, advanced capitalist nations. How else to explain the broad appeal and popular success of the demographic post-apocalyptic film *Soylent Green* (Fleischer 1973), or American best sellers *The Population Bomb* (Ehrlich 1968) and *Famine 1975!* (Paddock 1967)? There is nothing new about the alarm over population growth being sounded most loudly where it is least in evidence. Indeed, it is the consistency of this incongruity that historically has served so effectively to expose the class-interest of Malthusian and eugenicist movements. Yet there is something decidedly different about the scale of this operation following the crises of the 1970s.

To return to these documents of alarm about overpopulation today puts into further relief the fact that, rather than ushering in an expansion of labor-intensive production, the expected explosion of the "population bomb" was accompanied instead by almost continuous high unemployment and a steady movement of capital away from traditional industrial production and toward managerial, financial, and communication industries (cf. Brenner 2009; Duménil and Lévy 2004; Harvey 1991; Lipsietz 1987). In light of these changes, the available means for grasping the relationship of population and economic production are put into question. The migration of capital further and further from investment in traditional production to more spatially distributed circuits of production (as well as the increasingly virtual modes of speculation) helps to fragment and undermine the familiar calculation of population growth and industrial production. Analytic concepts like Marx's "industrial reserve army" that sought to identify population growth as a factor in (or effect of) the exploitation of wage labor no longer capture the far looser relationship of industrial labor and the productivity of capital that applies after the globalization of production and the growing financialization of capital. This is not only a matter of the globalization of production and the heightened mobility of capital. As the hegemonic form of capital accumulation appears increasingly abstract and delinked from material production, the behavior of populations of labor—their numeric growth or decline, in particular—appears gradually more external to economic processes.

The precipitous growth and structural transformation of pension savings and pension funds that begins during this period of crisis provides a fascinating nexus of the contradictions in this historical development. Peter Ferdinand Drucker's 1976 book *The Pension Fund Revolution* was among the first to identify the disjuncture between the new role of pension funds and the then-existent parameters for understanding capital accumulation. In *The Pension Fund Revolution*, Drucker argued that:

> if "socialism" is defined as "ownership of the means of production by the workers" [...], then the United States is the first truly "Socialist" country. Through their pension funds, employees of American business today own at least 25 percent of its equity capital, which is more than enough for control ... [and] by 1985 (probably sooner), they will own at least 50—if not 60—percent of equity capital. Ten years later, or well before the turn of the century, their holdings should exceed around two-thirds of the equity capital (that is, the common shares) plus a major portion—perhaps 40 percent—of the debt capital (bonds, debentures, and notes) of the American economy. Inflation can only speed up this process. (Drucker 1996, 1)

Drucker's early projection of the growth of pension investment and its broader political, economic, and cultural implications is illuminating, both for what he got right and for what he got wrong, but also for what he was unable to conceive. Despite the broad accuracy of Drucker's book in identifying the long trend toward absolute growth of pension funds and, in very a general way, recognizing the importance that pension funds would come to possess, the social and political consequences that he imagined have not materialized. By the end of the twentieth century, assets in some individual pension funds had grown large enough to compete and even exceed the value of the largest multinational corporations.[5] A recent and widely cited survey of global pension markets placed the value of pension fund assets (a narrow, yet illustrative measure) in the 13 largest national markets at $26.5 trillion in 2010 (Thinking Ahead Group 2011). Though it is difficult to put such an immense figure into perspective, at the beginning of 2012, the total value of sovereign wealth funds was estimated at $4.8 trillion and the immense pool of foreign debt owned by China stood at approximately $2.6 trillion (see Sovereign Wealth Fund Institute 2012). Perhaps more significant than the sheer size of pension funds is the fact that even as these funds reach record highs nearing 30 trillion in assets globally, the very great majority of these pension funds remain underfunded (Kollewe and Inman 2011).

Brett Neilson (2009) has recently argued that, amidst the ongoing failures of financial markets, a critical analysis of the emergence of the financialized regime of capital accumulation must do more to acknowledge the degree to which "pension funds were at the leading edge of this process" (Neilson 2009, 352). Echoing this, Robin Blackburn (2007, 2004) and other critical historians of pensions have insisted that the scale or quantitative growth of pension funds has proven less significant than the changes to the way that pensions are funded, structured, and managed. With the privatization of pension funds and their integration into new circuits of financial speculation—securities, derivatives, hedge funds—pensions have become complexified to a degree that has rendered policy holders passively dependant on the expertise and good intentions of fund managers. More disturbingly, perhaps, the movement of a significant portion of global pensions toward privatized or semi-privatized investment funds has functioned to invest the personal earnings of working people in the maintenance of banking and finance industry, shoring up the traditional interests of a capitalist class (see Kingwell, chapter 7). Coinciding with the emergence of a new dominance of finance capitalism, the potential for the democratization and redistribution of ownership that Drucker saw in the growth of pensions has thus been realized, instead, as a distribution or socialization of *risk*, in which an individual or a family's savings for their later years becomes effectively leveraged against, and/or subsumed within, the volatility of the market.[6]

In his study, *The Cold War in Welfare*, Richard Minns (2001) takes a close look at the rapid expansion of defined-contribution pension funds—as opposed to the historically more common defined-benefit, state, or employee pension. Minns traces the parallel growth of these privately managed, defined-contribution schemes and the re-emergence of finance capitalism in the last decades of the twentieth century. Minns notes a connection that many will be intimately familiar with after the immense hemorrhaging of the value of pension funds in the market crashes of 2008:

> international financial flows do not emanate solely from the financial transfers arising from trade or corporate surpluses. Financial flows also spring from how we pay for the maintenance of a large and growing proportion of the population as defined by a certain stage in life. Indeed, the role of pension funds suggests a new paradigm of economic analysis whereby "social" provision through flows of finance for income security has augmented international financial flows. "Social security capital" is now as important as other sources of capital, if not more so as more and more people are encouraged in one way or another to save privately for their retirement. It is a key element in fuelling the expansion of financial markets. (Minns 2001, 33)

Repositioning pensions, not as a symptom or side-effect but as a crucial condition of possibility for the late twentieth-century's deregulation and globalization of the flow of capital, Minns' analysis (subsequently extended in Robin Blackburn's two book-length studies on pension reform[7]) has profound implications not only for the way in which pensions are situated in relation to finance capitalism's reproduction, but also for the way we theorize the social significance of population aging.

While the social and cultural life of pensions themselves, like population aging, have yet to receive the treatment by social theorists that their economic significance deserves, one of the places that this discussion is beginning to take place is in the critical attention (energized by the on-going financial crisis of 2008) now being given to the relationship between finance capital and society (see Haiven, chapter 3). The beginnings of a social theory of financialization that has emerged in the past decade warrant re-consideration in light of the growth and reform of pension funds and the aging populations that have been, in a sense, integrated into the growth of finance. Though we are all, in the wake of a financial meltdown, perhaps too well aware of the complex forms that financial speculation has come to assume, it is worth returning to the basics. Finance capital, in essence, describes money capital (sometimes "bank capital"), as opposed to "real capital" or capital goods (i.e. capital already invested in production or on its way, as a commodity, toward being realized again as money). Finance is, strictly speaking, a necessary element of any capitalist economic system. Following Rudolph Hilferding's *Finance Capital* (2006 [1910]), the term finance capital has been used more specifically to describe the moment that, as industry becomes more and more dependent on bank credit and financial investment, finance capital itself becomes gradually delinked from industrial production, creating increasingly complex instruments for generating profit on a stock of capital at an ever greater remove or abstraction from industry and real property.

Attempts to periodize the development of capitalism as an economic system over the course of the twentieth century have come to view the changing role and composition of finance capitalism as key to understanding the cycles and development of capitalism. Giovanni Arrighi's *The Long Twentieth Century* (1994) provides one of the most compelling and influential periodizing accounts of capitalism and the twentieth century in particular in terms of the cyclical pattern of finance capital's structural dominance and retreat as a mode of capital accumulation. This periodizing account proves particularly useful for explaining the shift between two very different regimes of production and capital accumulation between the 1960s and 1980s. From this point of view, a wide range of political–economic transformations that take place over this period are made legible within a broader historical framework:

the increasing dominance of monetarist fiscal policy and the associated push toward the reduction and privatization of social welfare institutions at the state level, the new technologies of transnationally distributed and flexible production, the institution of a supranational consensus founded in a floating currency exchange, and the gradual abolition of international barriers to capital investment. By the end of the twentieth century, the world system that had grown out of the crashes and contractions of the 1970s could be recognized as a globalized return of finance capitalism.

The historical lateness of finance capitalism

Efforts to produce a historical narrative that organizes these transformations into a coherent social and economic period has drawn productively on the cyclical account of the rise and fall of finance in order to locate recognizable trends. Beginning with Marxist interventions into what were largely aesthetic theories of postmodernism in the 1980s and 1990s, the still-emerging content of social and cultural theories of finance capital provide a means not merely of dating, but also of interpreting the characteristic features of this conjuncture.

Theoretical explorations of the relationship between finance capital and culture over the past twenty or so years have tended to stress three structuring linkages: (1) the full enclosure or subsumption of social and cultural activity within economic systems that occurs with the deindustrialization of advanced capitalist nations, and the expansion of culture as a site for investment and speculation; (2) a new cognitive and aesthetic degree of abstraction that is most apparent at the level of cultural production, suggesting a changed relationship to representation and "the real" that mirrors the growing abstraction of value that accompanies the precipitous growth of new instruments of financial speculation (securities, derivatives, shorts, futures, swaps); (3) a new preoccupation with epistemological or cognitive distributions of space–time that register across numerous spheres of cultural production, responding in different ways to the new global movement of capital, on the one hand, and changed temporality engendered by the growing dominance of new technologies and instruments of financial speculation on the other. Of these major themes or points of articulation, it is the third linkage of space–time that I want to emphasize. The notion of a spatial and temporal condition specific to the dominance of finance capital provides a route to finally return to the conceptual problems of population aging with which I began, and also to the way in which the contemporary situation of pensions and retirement saving might provide a means of concretizing and focusing these problems.

Fredric Jameson's (2003) account of the temporal dimension of what he variously names late capitalism, postmodernism, or globalization represents one of the more influential theoretical touchstones for theorizing the social effects of the contemporary economic domination of finance capital. Among the most important concepts that recur in Jameson's analysis is that of a temporal "reduction to the present" that he describes at length in an essay of 2003, "The End of Temporality." Jameson outlines this concept in a passage worth quoting at length:

> The dynamics of the stock market need to be disentangled from the older cyclical rhythms of capitalism generally: boom and bust, accumulation of inventory, liquidation, and so forth, a process with which everyone is familiar and that imprints a kind of generational rhythm on individual life. From [these older cyclical rhythms], then, is to be distinguished the newer process of the consumption of investment as such, the anxious daily consultation of the listings, deliberations with or without your broker, selling of, taking a gamble on something as yet untested ... The narrowing and the urgency of the time frame need to be underscored here and the way in which a novel and more universal microtemporality accompanies and as it were condenses the rhythms of quarterly "profit taking" (and is itself intensified in periods of crisis and uncertainty). The futures of the stock market—whether in the literal and traditional sense of investments in crops and other seasonal goods not yet in existence or in the more figurative sense of derivatives and speculations on the company reports and the exchange listings—these "futures" come to be deeply entwined with the way we live our own individual and collective futures generally ... Rather than a period of style, therefore, it seems more desirable to stage the "end of temporality" as a situation faced by postmodernity in general and to which its artists and subjects are obliged to respond in a variety of ways. This situation has been characterized as a dramatic and alarming shrinkage of existential time and the reduction to a present that hardly qualifies as such any longer, given the virtual effacement of that past and future that can alone define a present in the first place. (Jameson 2003, 703–8)

In these characteristically expansive observations, Jameson's suggestion that we read finance capital's social effects in terms of a "virtual effacement" of past and future is compelling and aligns with growing apprehension of what Randy Martin calls (2002) "the financialization of everyday life." The linkage between the dominance of a new form of finance capital and a "narrowing" or "shrinking" of the temporal rhythms of modernity also offers an interesting route by which to return to the speculations on the social time of population aging with which I began.

In light of the extraordinary role of pension and "grey capital" in the formation and reproduction of what is named here simply as finance, there is room to wonder whether this new mode of accumulation and its concomitant temporal "reduction to the present" should be, as Jameson recommends, so quickly "disentangled" from "older cyclical rhythms of capitalism"—even as a strictly heuristic operation. Indeed, among the more remarkable implications of thinking through finance capitalism in light of the aging of populations is the extent to which it begins to illuminate a new kind of "generational rhythm" imprinted on individual lives. What would it mean to think the experience of time adequate to today's finance capitalism, not only in terms of a quickening of the comparatively sleepy, intensive rhythm of industrial capitalism, but in terms of a radically altered "generational rhythm" of capitalism being wrought by population aging? More challenging still, how might these two temporal logics be grasped synthetically, as concordant dimensions of an entirely different kind of time? Alongside the light speed of digitized financial markets and the capture of social futures enabled by new instruments of financial speculation, population aging hints at a radically new tempo being introduced to social relations by changes in life cycle. Without putting into question the accuracy of Jameson's diagnosis of a "reduction to the present," the temporal rhythm of an aging population with its implied time of neither growth nor decline adds new sense of the *lateness* of late capitalism.

Demographic time, financial time

With the 1994 publication of the World Bank's document "Averting the Old Age Crisis: Policies to Protect the Old and Promote Growth," the projective narrative of aging societies was made sensible to a wider public, outlining political–economic implications that give shape to a radically new scenario for the capitalist imagination of disaster. Subsequent high-profile pieces in *Foreign Policy* and *The Economist* and numerous special reports over the past decade have focused alarm, thrusting the rhetoric of a "grey dawn" and a global "baby bust" into wider circulation.[8] Most of these pieces begin with a version of the same journalistic hook:

> Not so long ago, we were warned that rising global population would inevitably bring world famine ... Instead, the global growth rate [of population]

> dropped from 2 percent in the mid-1960s to roughly half that today, with many countries no longer producing enough babies to avoid falling populations. Having too many people on the planet is no longer demographers' chief worry; now, having too few is. (Longman 2004, 54)

Setting aside how such statements obscure the degree to which the (growing) number of people on the planet still poses decisive ecological and economic challenges and will continue to for some time, what is noteworthy about these repeated comparisons of the contemporary aging "crisis" with the 1970s alarm about overpopulation is the way in which this naming of the absolute reversal in the trajectory of the "population crisis" becomes, in effect, a way of establishing an equivalence between the two under the sign of "crisis." Indeed, the (quite simply false) implication that with the emergence of a 'new' crisis (aging), the old one (overpopulation) has been overcome, tends to builds upon this questionable equivalence a teleology, reaffirming the durability of the ideological alchemy of capital accumulation, wherein "[e]very limit becomes a barrier to be overcome" (Marx 1993, 418). As critical explorations of the recent development of pension funds make clear, there is no lack of evidence that population aging has in fact already been transformed into an immensely profitable frontier for capital, at the same time that the immense pools of cheap, disposable labor that remain of the 1970s "population bomb" continue to ensure profit margins for investment in globalized industrial production. Yet while capital adjusts as quickly as ever to the latest crisis, the paradoxes produced in the attempt to turn population decline into a surmountable figure of "crisis" and growth rise just as consistently to the surface.

"The future is older than the past," reads the witty title above a graph in a recent issue of *Foreign Policy* depicting the dramatic increase projected over the coming 40 years of the portion of the world's population over the age of 65 (see Longman 2011). A postmodern proposition if ever there was one, paradoxical dicta such as this one typify the current demographic crisis discourse and its projection of a mass figure of a future decline—or, still more ambivalently, an aged future—that fits uncomfortably within the essentially modern temporal trajectory of continuous growth that it attempts to resuscitate. We must wait and see whether or not Marx's observation that "an increasing population appears as the basis of accumulation as a continuous process" (Marx 1972, 477) proves accurate at the level of political economy. But whether examined at the level of the economic or the cultural, symptoms of this looming contradiction are already apparent, as an imaginary of continuous growth forces us to contend with the certainty that the coming century will bring older societies. Popular resistance to austerity measures being forced into effect today in the European union represents only the most recent sign of these contradictions. The emerging contradictions and the new affiliations of class and age (and, something I have not touched on, race) that are resisting the socially immiserating interests of the financial industry, expose the urgency of these analytic challenges for social theory. Key among these challenges, as I have begun to suggest here, is the work of understanding the temporal dimension of these systemic changes and the uncertain figure of social time that emerges between the temporality of finance and the temporality of demographic aging.

The anachrony that exists between these two social processes begins to suggest the deep implications opened up by a re-examination of demographic features of the current conjuncture. Indeed, there is room to wonder whether the particular rhythm or time scale of demographic behavior is commensurate with that of social and economic theory, where there remains a pervasive misunderstanding of the manner in which, for instance, changing birth rates translate (at the length or duration of generations) into changed workforces. Within the crisis narratives elaborated from demographic projections, there is, on the one hand, the projective alarmist time of a sort of scientistic future in which populations are imagined to follow the same instantaneous timescale of an expansion or depression of the market. Following Jameson's thesis of a temporal "reduction to the present," I propose that we unconsciously tend to treat demographic data of a region or nation-state much like the quarterly report or projected earnings of a corporation, as though the increase or decline of vital statistics of a population (birth rate, life expectancy) are figures on a ledger that can be budgeted and balanced on a schedule of financial quarters or years. Against this financial logic of population, these changes, even under the most forced and artificial conditions (e.g. a national one-child policy), remain determined by the generational time of the biological reproduction of a species, in which, for example, a fertility "boom" will echo into the future in twenty-five- to thirty-year interval even as the total fertility of the same population might decline. Thus, while the specific case of population aging and decline shapes the imagination of a social future that appears radically opposed to the continuous growth axiomatic of modernity and the social reproduction of capital, there is also a deeper way in which the archaic, generational, perhaps even species-time of collective, increasingly global population behavior resists incorporation into the linear temporality of growth or decline.

In arguing that we pay closer attention to the broader social and even deep cognitive effects ushered in by population aging and its discursive reproduction, it is crucial to underline the extent to which such a methodological revaluation ought to remain suspicious of any historiographical practice of isolating and, in a sense, ontologizing the demographic behavior itself as a way of encompassing or determining the totality of a moment. It is, indeed, precisely through a critical apprehension of the positivist premise of demographic projections that it becomes possible to theorize what population aging is productive of. By examining population aging through its ongoing incorporation into circuits of capital accumulation and its parallel narrativization as a source of crisis, we avoid contributing to a positioning of aging as a problem requiring management, and thus throw light on the deeper rationalities and contradictions at work. My concern has been to suggest how certain fundamentally discrepant levels of social time appear when attending to population aging in light of its relationship to its socio-economic context. Beyond this particular problem of the time of finance and the time of aging is a broader case for the importance for social theory to critically address demographic aging and its discursive production as crisis.

Notes

1 For a representative sample, see: Peterson, *Grey Dawn* (1999); Longman, *The Empty Cradle* and *Born To Pay* (2004); *The Economist*, "A World of Methuselahs" (2009c) and "Ageing in the Rich World" (2009a); BBC's "Ageing Issue: 'Ticking Time Bomb'" (2008). For criticism of these views, see Gee and Gutman, *The Overselling of Population Aging* (2000); and Mullan, *The Imaginary Time Bomb* (2000).

2 For contemporary accounts of current theory of demographic transition, see: Aries, "Two Successive Motivations" (1980); Caldwell, "Toward a Restatement" (1976); Galor and Weil, "Population, Technology, and Growth" (2000); Lesthaeghe, "The Second Demographic Transition" (2007).

3 On the problematic legacy of Marx's denunciation of Malthus, see Wally Seccombe's "Marxism and Demography" (1983).

4 For a lucid exploration of the implications of population aging for the contemporary theorization of biopolitics, see Brett Neilson's "Globalization and the Biopolitics of Aging" (2003).

5 "By 2000 the largest US money managers, ranked by asset value, were Fidelity Investments with $1,074 billion under management, Barclays Global Investors ($784 billion), State Street Global Advisers ($681 billion). [...] Around the time of these valuations General Electric, the world's most valuable company, had a market worth of $460 billion and Microsoft a market capitalization of $353 billion" (Blackburn 2004, 121).

6 A much longer account of this process would be required to give a sense of the unevenness that underpins this general trend when considered globally. For a succinct summary see Nielson, "Ageing and Globalization" (2009, 350–2).

7 *Age Shock: How Finance Is Failing Us* (2007) and *Banking On Death, Or Investing in Life: The History and Future of Pensions* (2004).

8 For a small sample of such articles and reports, see *The Economist's* "Ageing in the Rich World" (2009a), "A Slow-Burning Fuse" (2009b), and "A World of Methuselahs" (2009c).

7

The work idea: Wage slavery, bullshit, and the good infinite

Mark Kingwell

Before Occupy Wall Street and its various offshoots took centre stage in the fall of 2011, it was remarked, if not exactly often then at least poignantly, that there had not been, in the wake of 2008's economic meltdown, any sustained political critique of the system or individuals responsible for the collapse. No general strikes. No riots or mass demonstrations. No protest songs, angry novels, or outbreaks of resistant consciousness. In contrast to the Great Depression of the 1930s, the "recession" or "correction" or "setback" (choose your *status quo* euphemism) of 2008 had barely impinged on the popular media.[1]

Even the special class of idleness-under-duress fantasy film has disappeared without a trace: there is no contemporary equivalent of the heroes of those great 1930s and 1940s freedom-from-work Hollywood comedies: Cary Grant and Katharine Hepburn in *Holiday* (George Cukor 1938), or Joel McCrea in *Sullivan's Travels* (Preston Sturges 1942). "I want to find out why I'm working," says the Grant character, a self-made man, in the former film. "It can't be just to pay the bills and pile up more money." His wealthy fiancée—and her blustering banker father, seeing a junior partner in his son-in-law—think it can be just that. Which is why Grant goes off with the carefree older sister, Hepburn, on what might just be a permanent holiday from work. In *Sullivan's Travels*, Hollywood honcho McCrea goes in search of the real America of afflicted life—only to conclude that mindless entertainment is a necessity in hard times. Childlike joy and freedom from drudgery is more, not less, defensible when unemployment rates rise. But there is no Preston Sturges for our own day.

The reasons are puzzling. The collapse proved every anti-capitalist critic right, though without anything much changing as a result. The system was bloated and spectral, yes, borrowing on its borrowing, insuring its insurance, and skimming profit on every transaction. The FIRE sector—finance, insurance, real estate—had created the worst market bubble since the South Sea Company's 1720 collapse and nobody should have been surprised when that latest party balloon of capital burst. And yet everybody was. It was as if a collective delusion had taken hold of the world's seven billion souls, the opposite of group paranoia: an unshakable false belief in the reality of the system. As a result of that, in the wake of the crisis, awareness of the system's untenability changed nothing. The government bailout schemes—known as stimulus packages, a phrase that belongs easily in the pages of porn—effectively socialized some failing industries, saddling their collapse on taxpayers, even as it handed over billions of dollars to the people responsible for the bloat in the first place. Unemployment swept through vulnerable sectors in waves of layoffs and cutbacks, and "downturn" became an inarguable excuse for all manner of cost-saving action. Not only did nothing change in the system, the system emerged stronger than ever, now just more tangled in the enforced tax burdens and desperate job-seeking of individuals (see Kaposy, chapter 5). Meanwhile, the role of gainful occupation in establishing or maintaining all of (1) biological survival, (2) social position, and, especially in American society, (3) personal identity was undiminished.

Capitalism is probably beyond large-scale change, but we should not waste this opportunity to interrogate its most fundamental idea: work. A curious sub-genre of writing washed up on the shore of this crisis, celebrating manual labor and tracing globalized foodstuffs and consumer products back to their origins in toil.[2] The problem with these efforts, despite their charms, is that they do not resist the idea of work in the first instance. The pleasures of craft or intricacies of production have their value; but they are no substitute for resistance. And no matter what the inevitabilists say, resistance to work is not futile. It may not overthrow capitalism, but it does highlight essential things about our predicament—philosophy's job ever.

My contention in this chapter is that the values of work are still dominant in far too much of life; indeed, that these values have exercised their own kind of linguistic genius in creating a host of phrases, terms, and labels that bolster, rather than challenge, the dominance of work. Ideology is carried forward effectively by many vehicles, including narrative and language. And we see that this vocabulary of work is itself a kind of Trojan horse within language, naturalizing and so making invisible some of the very dubious, if not evil, assumptions of the work idea. This is all the more true when economic times are bad, since work then becomes itself a scarce commodity. That makes people anxious, and the anxiety is taken up by work: *Don't fire me! I don't want to be out of work!* Work looms larger than ever, the assumed natural condition whose "loss" makes the non-working individual by definition a loser.

* * *

Consider the nature of work. In a 1932 essay called "In Praise of Idleness," Bertrand Russell is in fact more incisive about work than he is about idleness, which he seems to view as the mere absence of work (in my terms, defended elsewhere, that is slacking rather than idling).[3] Russell defines work this way: "Work is of two kinds: first, altering the position of matter at or near the earth's surface relatively to other such matter; second, telling other people to do so. The first kind is unpleasant and ill paid; the second is pleasant and highly paid" (Russell 2004 [1932], 3). Russell goes on to note that "The second kind is capable of indefinite extension: there are not only those who give orders, but those who give advice as to what orders should be given" (Russell 2004 [1932], 3). This second-order advice is what is meant by *bureaucracy*; and if two opposite kinds of advice are given at the same time, then it is known as *politics*. The skill needed for this last kind of work "is not knowledge of the subjects as to which advice is given, but knowledge of the art of persuasive speaking and writing, i.e. of advertising" (Russell 2004 [1932], 3).

Very little needs to be added to this analysis except to note something crucial which Russell appears to miss: the *greatest work of work* is to disguise its essential nature. The grim ironists of the Third Reich were exceptionally forthright when they fixed the evil, mocking maxim "*Arbeit Macht Frei*"—work shall make you free—over the gates at Dachau and Auschwitz. One can only conclude that this was their idea of a sick joke, and that their ideological commitments were not with work at all, but with despair and extermination.

The real ideologists of work are never so transparent, nor so wry. But they are clever, because their genius is, in effect, to fix a different maxim over the whole of the world: work is fun! Or, to push the point to its logical conclusion, *it's not work if it doesn't feel like work*. And so celebrated workaholics excuse themselves from what is in fact an addiction, and in the same stroke implicate everyone else for not working hard enough. "Work is the grand cure of all the maladies and miseries that ever beset mankind," said that barrel of fun Thomas Carlyle (Carlyle 1969, 455). "Nothing is really work unless you would rather be doing something else," added J. M. Barrie (1930), perhaps destabilizing his position on Peter Pan. And even the apparently insouciant Noël Coward argued that "Work is much more fun than fun" (Coward 1963). Really? Perhaps he meant to say "what most people consider fun." But still. Claims like these just lay literary groundwork for the *Fast Company* work/play maneuver of the 1990s or the current, more honest compete-or-die productivity language.

Work deploys a network of techniques and effects that make it seem inevitable and, where possible, pleasurable. Central among these effects is the diffusion of responsibility for the baseline need for work: everyone accepts, because everyone knows, that everyone must have a job. Bosses as much as subordinates are slaves to the larger servo-mechanisms of work, which are spectral and non-localizable. In effect, work is the largest self-regulation system the universe has so far manufactured, subjecting each of us to a generalized panopticon shadow under which we dare not do anything but work, or at least seem to be working, lest we fall prey to an obscure disapproval all the more powerful for being so. The work idea functions in the same manner as a visible surveillance camera, which need not even be hooked up to anything. No, let's go further: there need not even be a camera. Like the prisoners in the perfected version of Bentham's uber-utilitarian jail, workers need no overseer *because they watch themselves*.[4] There is no need for actual guards; when we submit to work, we are guard and guarded at once.[5]

Offshoots of this system are somewhat more visible to scrutiny, and so tend to fetch the largest proportion of critical objection. A social theorist will challenge the premises of inevitability in market forces, or wonder whether economic "laws" are anything more than self-serving generalizations. These forays are important, but they leave the larger inevitabilities of work mostly untouched. In fact, such critical debates tend to reinforce the larger ideological victory of work, because they accept the baseline assumptions of it even in their criticisms. Thus does work neutralize, or indeed annex, critical energy from within the system. The slacker is the tragic hero here, a small-scale version of a Greek protagonist. In his mild resistance—long stays in the mailroom, theft of office supplies, forgery of time cards, ostentatious toting of empty files—the slacker cannot help but sustain the system. This is resistance, but of the wrong sort; it really is futile, because the system, whatever its official stance, loves slackers. They embody the work idea in their very objection.[6]

* * *

None of that will be news to anyone who has ever been within the demand-structure of a workplace. What is less clear is why we put up with it, why we don't resist more robustly. As Max Weber (1958) noted in his analysis of leadership under capitalism, any ideology must, if it is to succeed, give people reasons to act. It must offer a narrative of identity to those caught within its ambit, otherwise they will not continue to perform, and renew, its reality. As with most truly successful ideologies, the work idea latches on to a very basic feature of human existence: our character as social animals jostling for position. But social critics are precipitate if they argue that all human action was motivated by tiny distinctions between winner and loser. In fact, the recipe for action is that recognition of those differences *plus* some tale of why the differences matter and, ideally, are rooted in the respective personal qualities or "character" of winner and loser.

No tale can be too fanciful to sustain this outcome. Serbs and Croats may engage in bloody warfare over relatively trivial genetic or geographical difference, provided both sides accept the story of what the difference means. In the case of work, the evident genius lies in reifying what is actually fluid, namely social position and "elite" status within hierarchies. The most basic material conditions of work—office size and position, number of windows, attractiveness of assistant, cut of suit—are simultaneously the rewards *and* the ongoing indicators of status within this competition. Meanwhile, the competition sustains itself backward via credentialism: that is, the accumulation of degrees and certificates from "prestigious" schools and universities which, though often substantively unrelated to the work at hand, indicate appropriate elite grooming. These credentialist back-formations confirm the necessary feeling that a status outcome is *earned*, not merely conferred. Position without an attendant narrative of merit would not satisfy the ideological demand for action to seem meaningful.

The result is *entrenched* rather than *circulating* elites. The existence of elites is, in itself, neither easily avoidable nor obviously bad. The so-called Iron Law of Oligarchy states that "every field of human endeavor, every kind of organization, will always be led by a relatively small elite" (see Michels 1915; Rothbard 1995, 4). This oligarchic tendency answers demands for efficiency and direction, but more basically it is agreeable to humans on a socio-evolutionary level. We like elite presence in our undertakings, and tend to fall into line behind it. But the narrative of merit in elite status tends to thwart circulation of elite membership, and encourage the false idea that such status is married to "intrinsic" qualities of the individual. In reality, the status is a kind of collective delusion, not unlike the one that sustains money, another key narrative of the system.

At this stage, it is possible to formulate 'laws'—actually law-like generalizations—about the structure of a work idea company, which is any company in thrall to the work idea, including (but not limited to) bureaucracies. Parkinson's

(1955), Pournelle's (2005), and Moore's (2000) Laws of Bureaucracy may be viewed as derivatives of the Iron Law, understood as ways in which we can articulate how the system sustains itself and its entrenched elite. While expressly about bureaucracies, these generalizations speak to the inescapable bureaucratic element in all workplaces, even those that try to eschew that element. In short, they explicate the work idea even as that idea works to keep its precise contours implicit.

Parkinson's Law is minimalist in concept but wide in application. It states: "There need be little or no relationship between the work to be done and the size of the staff to which it may be assigned" (Parkinson 1955). This despite the lip-service often paid to the norm of efficiency. Parkinson also identified two axiomatic underlying forces responsible for the growth in company staff: (1) "An official wants to multiply subordinates, not rivals"; and (2) "Officials make work for each other." The second may be more familiar as the Time-Suck Axiom, which states that all meetings must generate further meetings. And so at a certain threshold we may observe that meetings are, for all intents and purposes, entirely self-generating, like consciousness. They do not need the humans who "hold" them at all, except to be present during the meeting and not doing anything else.

Examining the company structure at one level higher, that is, in the motivation of the individuals, the science fiction writer Jerry Pournelle proposed a theory he referred to as Pournelle's Iron Law of Bureaucracy. It states that "In any bureaucracy, the people devoted to the benefit of the bureaucracy itself always get in control and those dedicated to the goals the bureaucracy is supposed to accomplish have less and less influence, and sometimes are eliminated entirely" (Pournelle 2005). In other words, just as meetings become self-generating, so too does the company structure as a whole. *The company* becomes a norm of its own, conceptually distinct from whatever the company makes, does, or provides.

Once this occurs—most obvious in the notion of "company loyalty," with the required "team-building" weekends, ballcaps, golf shirts, and logos—there will be positive incentives for position-seekers to neglect or even ignore other values ostensibly supported by the company. More seriously, if Pournelle's Law is correct, then these position-seekers will become the dominant position-holders, such that any norms outside "the company" will soon fade and disappear. The company is now a self-sustaining evolutionary entity, with no necessary goals beyond its own continued existence, to which end the desires of individual workers can be smoothly assimilated.

Moore's Laws take the analysis even further. If a bureaucracy is a servo-mechanism, its ability to process an error signal, and so generate corrective commands and drive the system away from error, is a function of the depth of the hierarchy. But instead of streamlining hierarchy and so making error-correction easier, bureaucracies do the opposite: they deepen the hierarchy, adding new error sensors but lessening the system's ability to respond to them. Large bureaucracies are inherently noisy systems whose very efforts to achieve goals make them noisier. Thus, Moore concludes, (1) large bureaucracies cannot possibly achieve their goals; as a result, (2) they will thrash about, causing damage (Moore 2000).

He suggests five further laws. The power wielded by bureaucracies will tend to attach above-mean numbers of sociopaths to their ranks. Hence (3) large bureaucracies are *evil*. Because the mechanism of the system increases noise as it attempts to eliminate it, system members in contact with the rest of reality will be constrained by rigid, though self-defeating rules. Thus (4) large bureaucracies are *heartless*. They are also (5) *perverse*, subordinating stated long-term goals to the short-term ambitions of the humans within the system; (6) *immortal*, because their non-achievement of goals makes them constantly replace worn-out human functionaries with new ones; and finally (7) *boundless*, since there is no theoretical limit to the increased noise, size, and complexity of an unsuccessful system.

* * *

So much for elites looking backward, justifying their place in the work idea, and finding ever novel ways of expanding without succeeding. Pournelle's and Moore's laws highlight how, looking forward, the picture is considerably more unnerving. The routine collection of credentials, promotions, and employee-of-the-month honors in exchange for company loyalty masks a deeper existential conundrum—which is precisely what it is meant to do.

Consider: It is an axiom of status anxiety that the competition for position has no end—save, temporarily, when a scapegoat is found. The scapegoat reaffirms everyone's status, however uneven, because he is beneath all. Hence many work narratives are miniature blame-quests. We come together as a company to fix guilt on one of our number, who is then publicly shamed and expelled. *Jones filed a report filled with errors! Smith placed an absurdly large order and the company is taking a bath!* This makes us all feel better, and enhances our sense of mission, even if it produces nothing other than its own spectacle.

Blame-quests work admirably on their small scale. At larger scales, the narrative task is harder. What is the company for? What does it do? Here, as when a person confronts mortality, we teeter on the abyss. The company doesn't actually do much of anything. It is not for anything important. The restless forward movement of companies—here at Compu-Global-Hyper-Mega-Net, we are always *moving on*—is work's version of the Hegelian Bad Infinite, the meaningless nothing of empty everything.[7] There is no point to what is being done, but it must be done anyway. The boredom of the average worker, especially in a large corporation, is the walking illustration of this meaninglessness. But boredom can lower productivity, so a large part of work's energy is expended in finding ways to palliate the boredom that is the necessary outcome of work in order to raise productivity: a sort of credit-default swap of the soul. Workaholism is the narcotic version of this, executed within the individual himself. The workaholic colonizes his own despair at the perceived emptiness of life—its non-productivity—by filling it in with work.[8]

It can be no surprise that the most searching critic of work, Karl Marx, perceived this Hegelian abyss at the heart of all paid employment. But Marx's theory of alienated labor, according to which our efforts and eventually our selves become commodities bought and sold for profit to others, is just one note in a sustained chorus of opposition and resistance to work.[9] "Never work," the Situationist Guy Debord commanded, articulating the baseline of opposition.[10] Another Situationist slogan, the famous graffito of May 1968, reminded us that the order and hardness of the urban infrastructure masked a playful, open-ended sense of possibility that was even more fundamental: *Sous les pavés, la plage!* Under the paving stones, the beach!

Between Marx and Debord lies the great, neglected Georges Sorel, a counter-enlightenment and even counter-cultural voice whose influence can be seen to run into the likes of Debord, Franz Fanon, and Che Guevara; but also Timothy Leary, Jack Kerouac, and Ken Kesey. Like many other radical critics, Sorel perceived the emptiness of the liberal promise of freedom once it becomes bound up with regimentation and bourgeoisification of everyday life. Sorel was a serial enthusiast, moving restlessly from cause to cause: a socialist, a Dreyfusard, an ascetic, an anti-Dreyfusard. In the first part of the twentieth century he settled on the labor movement as his home and proposed a general strike that would, in the words of Isaiah Berlin (who had tremendous respect for this against-the-grain thinker):

> call for the total overthrow of the entire abominable world of calculation, profit and loss, the treatment of human beings and their powers as commodities, as material for bureaucratic manipulation, the world of illusory consensus and social harmony, or economic and sociological experts no matter what master they serve, who treat men as subjects of statistical calculations, malleable "human material," forgetting that behind such statistics there are living human beings. (Berlin 1980, 320)

In other words, late capitalism and all that it entails.

One might wonder, first, why such resistance is recurrently necessary but also, second, why it seems ever to fail. The answer lies in the evolutionary fact of *language upgrade*. In common with all ideologies, the work idea understands that that victory is best which is achieved soonest, ideally before the processes of conscious thought are allowed to function. And so it is here that language emerges as the clear field of battle. Language acquisition is crucial to our evolutionary success because it aids highly complex coordination of action. But that same success hinges also on the misdirection, deception, control, and happy illusion carried out by language, because these too make for coordinated action. Thus the upgrade is at the same time a downgrade: language allows us to distinguish between appearance and reality, but it also allows some of us to persuade others that appearances are realities. If there were no distinction, this would not matter; indeed, it would not be possible. Deception can only work if there is such a thing as truth, as Socrates demonstrated in the first book of Plato's *Republic*.[11]

Jargon, slogans, euphemisms and terms of art are all weapons in the upgrade/downgrade tradition. We should class them together under the technical term *bullshit*, as analyzed by philosopher Harry Frankfurt (2005). The routine refusal to speak with regard to the truth is called bullshit because evasion of normativity produces a kind of ordure, a dissemination of garbage, the scattering of shit. This is why, as Frankfurt reminds us, bullshit is far more threatening, and politically evil, than lying. The bullshitter "does not reject the authority of the truth, as the liar does, and oppose himself to it. He pays no attention to it at all. By virtue of this, bullshit is the greater enemy of the truth than lies are" (Frankfurt 2005, 61).[12]

Work language is full of bullshit. But by thinking about these terms rather than using them, or mocking them, we can hope to bring the enemy into fuller light, to expose the erasure that work's version of Newspeak forever seeks. Special vigilance is needed because the second-order victory of work bullshit is that, in addition to having no regard for the truth, it passes itself off as innocuous or even beneficial. Especially in clever hands, the controlling elements of work are repackaged as liberatory, counter-cultural, subversive: you're a skatepunk rebel because you work seventy hours a week beta-testing videogames. This, we might say, is meta-bullshit. And so far from what philosophers might assert, or wish, this meta-bullshit and not truth is the norm governing most coordinated human activity under conditions of capital markets. Thus does bullshit meet, and become, filthy lucre; and of course, vice versa.

As the work idea spins itself out in language, we observe a series of linked paradoxes in the world of work: imprisonment via inclusion; denigration via celebration; obfuscation via explanation; conformity via distinction; failure via success; obedience via freedom; authority via breezy coolness. The manager is positioned as an "intellectual," a "visionary," even a "genius." "Creatives" are warehoused and petted. Demographics are labeled, products are categorized. Catch phrases, acronyms, proverbs, clichés, and sports metaphors are marshaled and deployed. Diffusion of sense through needless complexity, diffusion of responsibility through passive constructions, and elaborate celebration of minor achievements mark the language of work.

And so: Outsourcing. Repositioning. Downsizing. Rebranding. Work the mission statement. Push the envelope. Think outside the box. Stay in the loop. See the forest *and* the trees. Note sagely that where there is smoke there is also fire. Casual Fridays! Smartwork! Hotdesking! The whole nine yards! Touchdown! You-topia!

These shopworn work idea locutions have already been exposed, and mocked, such that we may think we know our enemy all too well. But the upgrade/downgrade is infinitely inventive. Even this glossary cannot be considered the final word on wage-slave verbiage. The work of language-care is never over.

* * *

You might think, at this point, that a language problem naturally calls for a language solution. The very same inventiveness that marks the ideology of work can be met with a wry, subversive counterintelligence. Witness such portmanteau pun words as "slacktivism" or "crackberry" which mock, respectively, people who think that forwarding emails is a form of political action and those who are in thrall to text messages the way some people are addicted to crack cocaine. Or observe the high linguistic style of office-bound protagonists from Nicholson Baker's *The Mezzanine* (1988) and Douglas Coupland's *Generation X* (1991) to Joshua Ferris's *Then We Came to the End* (2007) and Ed Park's *Personal Days* (2008).

These books are hilarious, and laughter is always a release. But their humor is a sign of doom, not liberation. The "veal-fattening pen" label applied to those carpet-sided cubicles of the open-form office (Coupland) does nothing to change the facts of the office. Nor does calling office-mateyness an "air family" (Coupland again) make the false camaraderie any less spectral. Coupland was especially inventive and dry in his generation of neologisms, but reading a bare list of them shows the hollow heart of dread beneath the humor.[13] Indeed, the laughs render the facts more palatable by mixing diversion into the scene of domination—a willing capitulation, consumed under the false sign of resistance. This applies to most of what we call slacking, a verb at least as old as 1530, when Jehan Palsgrave asked of a task-shirking friend "Whye slacke you your busynesse thus?" (Palsgrave 2003, 720)

That is the main reason it is essential to distinguish idling from slacking. Slacking is consistent with the work idea; it does not subvert it, merely gives in by means of evasion. As John Kenneth Galbraith pointed out a half-century ago in *The Affluent Society* (1958), such evasion is actually the pinnacle of corporate life:

> Indeed it is possible that the ancient art of evading work has been carried in our time to its highest level of sophistication, not to say elegance. One should not suppose that it is an accomplishment of any particular class, occupation, or profession. Apart from the universities where its practice has the standing of a scholarly rite, the art of genteel and elaborately concealed idleness may well reach its highest development in the upper executive reaches of the modern corporation. (Galbraith 1958, 95)

Galbraith's "idleness" is not to be confused with genuine idling, of course; the "concealed" that modifies his use of the word shows why. A slacking executive is no better, and also no worse, than the lowliest clerk hiding in the mailroom to avoid a meeting. But neither is idling, which calls for openness and joy.

And so here we confront again the Bad Infinite at the heart of work. What is it for? To produce desired goods and services. But these goods and services are, increasingly, the ones needed to maintain the system itself. The product of the work system is work, and specters such as "profit" and "growth" are covers for the disheartening fact that, in Galbraith's words, "[a]s a society becomes increasingly affluent, wants are increasingly created by the process by which they are satisfied" (Galbraith 1958, 129). Which is only to echo Marcuse's and Arendt's well-known aperçus that the basic creation of capitalism is *superfluity*—with the additional insight that capitalism must then create the demand to take up such superfluity.[14] Galbraith nails the contradiction at the heart of things: "But the case cannot stand if it is the process of satisfying wants that creates the wants. For then the individual who urges the importance of production to satisfy the wants is precisely in the position of the onlooker who applauds the efforts of the squirrel to keep abreast of the wheel that is propelled by his own efforts" (Galbraith 1958, 125).[15]

Still, all is not lost. There is a treasure buried in the excess that the world of work is constantly generating: that is, a growing awareness of a *gift economy* that always operates beneath, or beyond, the exchange economy. Any market economy is a failed attempt to distribute goods and services exactly where they are needed or desired, as and when they are needed and desired. That's all markets are, despite the pathological excrescences that lately attach to them: derivatives funds, advertising, shopping-as-leisure. If we had a perfect market, idling would be the norm, not the exception, because distribution would be frictionless. As Marcuse (1964) saw decades ago, most work is the result of inefficiency, not genuine need.[16] This is all the more true in a FIRE-storm economy. Paradoxically, idling is entirely consistent with capitalism's own internal logic, which implies, even if it never realizes, the end of capitalism. This insight turns the Bad Infinite of work into a Good Infinite, where we may begin to see things not as resources, ourselves not as consumers, and the world as a site not of work but of play.

The great Marxist and Situationist critics of work hoped that critical theory—accurate analysis of the system's pathologies—would change the system. The latest crisis in capitalism has shown that it will not. But a system is made of individuals, just as a market is composed of individual choices and transactions. Don't change the system, change your life. Debord's "Never work" did not go far enough. Truly understand the nature of work and its language, and you may never even think of work again.

Notes

1 There are some important exceptions. I will note just three here: Jonathan Dee's novel *The Privileges* (2010), a sly satire of the blithe arrogance of one couple who swim through the economic collapse; Chris Lehmann's collection *Rich People Stuff* (2010), which lampoons the favoured tropes and preoccupations of one-percenters; and Roger D. Hodge's angry screed about the Obama administration's complicity with minimizing the responsibility of Wall Street for the collapse, *The Mendacity of Hope* (2010). One complicated example is the hit 2010 film *The Social Network* (directed by David Fincher), which tells the story of Facebook 'inventor' Mark Zuckerberg in the unspoken context of the early 2000s bubble. But the film can't decide whether it is a revenge-of-the-nerds celebration or a moralistic slam of internet-age sharp dealing.

2 See, for example, Matthew Crawford, *Shop Class as Soulcraft* (2009) and Alain de Botton, *The Pleasures and Sorrows of Work* (2009). Andrew Ross summarizes the political puzzle posed by these books: "It is an unfortunate comment on the generous intellects of these two authors that they do not see fit to acknowledge, in their respective surveys of working life, the nobility of those who resist" (Ross 2009, 16).

3 I argued for a distinction between idling and slacking in "Idling Toward Heaven: The Last Defence You Will Ever Need," (Kingwell 2008), later adapted as the Introduction to *The Idler's Glossary* (Kingwell and Glen 2008).

4 The working principle behind Bentham's "panopticon"—that subjects under surveillance will become their own agents of discipline—garnered much attention in the later writings of Michel Foucault, who saw the same principle at work at large across the institutions of modern capitalist society. In *Discipline and Punish* he writes:

> [Bentham's panopticon] set out to show how one may "unlock" the disciplines and get them to function in a diffused, multiple, polyvalent way throughout the whole social body ... It programmes, at the level of an elementary and easily transferable mechanism, the basic functioning of a society penetrated through and through with disciplinary mechanisms. (Foucault 1977, 208–9)

5 One could cite, in support here, the analysis of Gilles Deleuze (1992). Deleuze notes three modes of social structure: sovereign states (pre-modern); discipline societies (modern); and control societies (postmodern). Whereas a discipline society moulds citizens into subjects through various carceral institutions—schools, armies, prisons, clinics—a control society can be radically decentred and apparently liberated. The difference in the world of work is between a factory and a business. A factory disciplines its subjects by treating them as a body of workers; this also affords the opportunity of organizing and resisting in the form of unionized labour. A business, by contrast, treats employees like hapless contestants on a bizarre, ever-changing game show—something like Japan's "Most Extreme Elimination Challenge," perhaps—where they are mysteriously competing with fellow workers for spectral rewards allocated according to mysterious rules. The affable boss who invites you over for dinner is a paradigm case: Is it business or pleasure? Who else is invited? Does it mean a likely promotion, or nothing at all? Thus does business invade and control the psyche of the worker, precisely because obvious mechanisms of discipline are *absent*.

6 Corinne Maier's otherwise excellent *Bonjour Laziness*, especially on the language of work, is unstable on this point. She acknowledges the work system is impervious to challenge, and yet finally urges: "rather than a 'new man', be a blob, a leftover, stubbornly resisting the pressure to conform, impervious to manipulation. Become the grain of sand that seizes up the whole machine, the sore thumb" (Maier 2005, 117). This confused message would seem to indicate insufficient grasp of the slacker/idler distinction.

7 In his *Science of Logic* (1812–16), Hegel characterizes the "bad infinite" as that which is "never ending" (such as an extensively infinite series of numbers—or, more appropriately, the never ending toils of Sisyphus in Camus' novel). This is contrasted against conceptions of infinity as being "end-less" (such as a closed circle) which, for Hegel, represents a *totality* insofar as it incorporates both the infinite and the finite.

8 More extreme measures can be imagined. In J. G. Ballard's novel *Super-Cannes* (2000), bored executives at a sleek French corporate park are advised by a company psychiatrist that the solution to their lowered output is not psychotherapy but psychopathology: once they begin nocturnal sorties of violence on immigrant workers and prostitutes, productivity rates soar.

9 In his *Economic and Philosophical Manuscripts of 1844* (1959), Marx characterizes four types of alienation of labour under capitalism: alienation of the worker from (1) the product of labour, (2) from the act of labouring (3) from him/herself as a worker, and (4) from his/her fellow workers.

10 "Ne travaillez jamais" was inscribed on Rue de Seine's wall in Paris by Debord in 1953 and was later, much to Debord's disappointment, reproduced en-masse as a "humorous" postcard (Debord 1963).

11 This is one implication of the celebrated exchange between Socrates and Thrasymachus in *Republic*, book I, 340b–344c (see Plato 1997).

12 See Harry Frankfurt, *On Bullshit* (2005), a huge international bestseller which was in fact a repurposed version of a journal article Frankfurt had published many years earlier, included in his collection *The Importance of What We Care About: Philosophical Essays* (1988).

13 See, for example, Jonny Fink (1996).

14 Arendt famously distinguishes *work*, *labour*, and *action*—the three aspects of the *vita activa*—in her magnum opus, *The Human Condition* (2008 [1958]). In this schema, labour operates to maintain the necessities of life (food, shelter, clothing) and is unceasing; work fashions specific things or ends, and so is finite; and action is public display of the self in visible doings. Work as we are discussing it in the present essay is obscurely spread across these categories. As a result, Arendt could indict the emptiness of a society free from labour—the wasteland of consumer desire—but could not see how smoothly the work idea would fold itself back into that wasteland in the form of workaholism.

15 Compare a more recent version of the argument, in the nihilistic words of the Invisible Committee, a group of radical French activists who published their anti-manifesto, *The Coming Insurrection*, in 2009:

> Here lies the present paradox: work has totally triumphed over all other ways of existing, at the same time as workers have become superfluous. Gains in productivity, outsourcing, mechanization, automated and digital production have so progressed that they have almost reduced to zero the quantity of living labour necessary in the manufacture of any product. We are living the paradox of a society of workers without work, where entertainment, consumption and leisure only underscore the lack from which they are supposed to distract us. (Invisible Committee 2009, 46)

It is perhaps no surprise that the authors, viewing this superfluous majority as set off against the self-colonizing desires for "advancement" in the compliant minority, suggest that the current situation "introduces the risk that, in its idleness, [the majority] will set about sabotaging the machine" (Invisible Committee 2009, 48).

16 In his *One-Dimensional Man* (1964), Marcuse distinguishes between "true needs" (i.e. those necessary for survival; food, clothing, shelter) and "repressive needs" (superfluous commodities; luxury items, status symbols, etc.), arguing that a worker's ability to purchase "repressive" items gives him or her a false sense of equality to oppressors and, more seriously, turns individuals away from recognizing the true inequalities of society.

8

The uniqueness of late capitalism: Biopower and biopolitics

Kezia Picard

> [B]iopower was without question an indispensable element in the development of capitalism. (Foucault 1978, 140–41)

> Biopower is a form of power that regulates social life from its interior, following it, interpreting it, absorbing it, and rearticulating it. (Hardt and Negri 2000, 23–4)

Late capitalism is often identified as different from its previous variants for its attention to expressive individuality and diversity (Hardt and Negri 2000; Nealon 2008; Niedzvieck 2004). In this chapter I examine Foucault's notion of biopower, the theorists who employ it, and how it has changed with the emergence of late capitalism. Associated with this change are a number of structural shifts within late capitalism that include, but are not limited to, the importance of immaterial labor, the global flows of monies and commodities, the widespread use of communications technologies that link disparate locales and mobile populations (whether through international travel or as migrant laborers), the financialization of capitalism, and, again, an insistence on constituting ourselves as unique and diversely situated individuals. This signals the intensification of biopower that, as Foucault's (1978) work has long illustrated, functions against the backdrop of previous incarnations of capitalism, disciplinary power, globalized power relations, and colonialism. In what follows I examine how the use of biopower has intensified mostly in response to the destabilization of previous variants of capitalism and how it absorbs ever more characteristics of human life into capitalist economic processes. At the same time I would insist that opportunities to resist capitalism remain, opportunities that are inadvertently generated by capitalism itself. To this end I outline the differences between biopower and what Maurizio Lazzarato (2002) calls a "biopolitics from below."

I begin with an examination of the history of biopower and its current incarnation that exhorts us to produce ourselves as unique and diverse individuals, and then turn to discuss shifts in capitalism (e.g. financialization) that are associated with the intensification of biopower. Next I outline the differences between biopower and biopolitics, and close with a brief consideration of the recent "Occupy Movement." My basic aim: to assess the possibilities of resistance to and within capitalism.

The emergence of biopower and individuality

Hal Niedzviecki (2004) has written extensively about the recent shift in capitalism toward the active production of individuality. He argues that the requirement to express our uniqueness has become so intense that individuality is, ironically, now the new conformity, a kind of inescapable commandment (see p. xvi). He points to the rise of the internet (and now social media), do-it-yourself culture, reality television, the use of rebellion in advertising as well as a whole host of celebrity chefs, bartenders, hairstylists, bloggers, and other self-styled experts who have achieved fame through their own "special" talents as part of a general cultural trend to recognize everyone's uniqueness. This expectation of nonconformity and uniqueness highlights the intensification of previous instantiations of biopower that worked to produce individuals in specific homogenizing ways. Foucault (1978) argues, for instance, that since the eighteenth century, capitalism has employed biopower to direct "the performances of the body . . . with attention to the processes of life" (Foucault 1978, 139). The emergence of biopower is tied to capitalism and its requirement for a productive, efficient, healthy, and sane population by and through its continuous and routine management of the human body. This corresponds to capitalism's deep-going concern to generate a vast, efficient, controllable, and productive workforce that is indispensible to its overall success (see Kingwell, chapter 7).

The history of capitalism's reliance on biopower is bound up with a corresponding history of capitalism's seemingly never-ending expansion that results from its need to increase profits, control natural, and human resources, and promote continuous growth. Expansion is necessary to capitalism because it is only by extending its limits (i.e. the places that it operates, the nature that it uses, and the people that it exploits) that it can absorb additional resources and grow profits year after year. As Michael Hardt and Antonio Negri (2000) point out, capitalism's quest for expansionism is evident in its relationship to a colonial project that sought vast material and financial wealth through the "superexploitation" of colonial territories and the indigenous peoples who inhabit them (Hardt and Negri 2000, 122). Capitalism must, in other words, push against its limits in order to grow and this has historically been achieved through territorial expansion that requires an engagement with the people who live in those territories. To manage this colonial situation, biopower was put into play to hierarchically order colonized populations and organize indigenous peoples in opposition to a supposedly superior colonializing power (see Morgensen 2011). Biopower was fundamental to capitalism here because it functioned to produce specific *kinds of individuals* that facilitated the management and hierarchization of large and diverse populations (what Foucault refers to as to as the process of individualization i.e. the creation of one's gender, class, race, ethnicity, sexuality as well as workers, bosses, doctors, patients, students, teachers, etc.). Unsurprisingly, as capitalism today continues to extend its limits, its use of biopower has similarly expanded and intensified.

Unlike the earliest forms of biopower that "fixed individuals within institutions but did not succeed in consuming them completely in the rhythm of productive practices and productive socialization," the contemporary version of biopower effectively transforms all facets of human life and experience into resources for capitalist exchange (Hardt and Negri 2000, 24). Biopower under contemporary capitalism seeks to manage individuals in increasingly subtle and commonplace ways by engaging each person as a *unique* individual. Whereas previous forms of capitalism employed biopower to produce fixed, homogeneous identities, biopower under a "postmodern" form of capitalism helps produce "hybrid identities, flexible hierarchies, and plural exchanges" (Hardt and Negri 2000, xii–xiii). The focus here is on one's unique and special individuality, an expansion that Foucault calls "the Californian cult of the self," that now permeates our lives (1983a, 245). Biopower today infiltrates the most mundane, and the most profound, aspects of human life. This is illustrated, for example, in an interest in memoirs as a literary form which gives preference to the personal; the fact that "home is the new work and play space of our time" (Nealon 2008, 86); the popularity of grunge in the 1990s which "was absolutely dedicated to some notion of subjective authenticity and the revelation of personal experience" (Nealon 2008, 87); and "the triumph of student-centred process pedagogies" that, among other things, make "education personally 'relevant' to the students" (Nealon 2008, 88). More recently, social media such as Facebook and Twitter amplify such individuality by allowing and encouraging users to widely broadcast their unique preferences and accomplishments.

The shift to the production of a multiplicity, and fluidity, of unique identity does not, however, mean that biopower no longer orders, manages, and hierarchically arranges individuals. Instead the spread of biopower coincides with the *increased flexibility and adaptability* of capitalist regimes of management and hierarchization. And yet, even though biopower may instigate the production of individuality and difference (or uniqueness), it is not necessarily a liberatory practice. For, as Chicchi (2010) points out, biopower seeks to incorporate all facets of human life (such as relationships, emotions, interaction, creativity, cooperation, languages, and communication) into capitalist economics to better control and regulate them. Biopower is thus no longer simply about the creation of a healthy, controllable, sane body; it seeks to manage what could be viewed as mundane aspects of human life, such as relationships, communication, creativity, and problem solving (see Lazzarato 2002; Lucarelli 2010; Marazzi 2008; Virno 2004). More specifically, biopower is integral to the shifting requirements of capitalism that have moved toward what Maurizio Lazzarato (1996) terms "immaterial labour" and the emergence of financialized capitalism. For these reasons, biopower no longer seeks to produce homogeneous conformity but seeks to produce uniqueness, diversity, and difference.

Immaterial labour and financialized capitalism

The intensification of biopower resonates with late capitalism's need for "a social control compatible with democratic societies where order is based on the formalized participation of great masses" (Lucarelli 2010, 120). As capitalism shifts away from Fordist production regimes and toward immaterial labor, the use of biopower increases because it is adept at managing the diverse and heterogeneous populations of late capitalism without recourse to overtly oppressive power relations. As opposed to the industrial or modernist capitalism that preceded it, "postmodern" or late capitalism is characterized by a kind of labor that is dependent upon cooperation (e.g. teamwork), communication (e.g. dialogue), and creativity (e.g. innovation). This is the basis for Lazzarato's work on immaterial labor that, he rightly claims, requires the magnification of biopower because it not only helps produce material goods, but also seeks to exploit less-tangible human qualities associated with the intellectual work of innovation, dialogue, and teamwork. While an awareness of the relationship between creativity and capitalism is not new, as is clear in Theodor Adorno and Max Horkheimer's (2002) famous work on the culture industry, it is now integral to *all* labor and industries. Considerations of creativity and communication, for example, pervade the workplace and the workforce, as the use of collaborative software, the corporate retreat weekend, the insistence that employees participate in teamwork exercises, and strategies of "creative management" come to the fore. Indeed, this is Richard Florida's (2004) argument when he describes the rise of a "creative class" which has "evolved economic and social systems that tap human creativity and make use of it as never before" (Florida 2004, xiii [see Dufresne and Sacchetti, chapter 9]). It is not only an explicitly creative "class" that makes use of immaterial labor, for even sectors such as manufacturing and manual labor rely on communications technologies to fulfill orders, to problem solve, or even simply to organize schedules in creative and efficient ways.

Immaterial labor is thus ever more present as we labor in our workplaces; but it is also ever more present as we labor in our homes and everywhere else wireless data networks are available. As mentioned, social networks such as Twitter and Facebook are consistent with contemporary biopower as users continually broadcast—and in the process produce and reproduce—their own personal tastes, relationships, and experiences. Yet the constant stream of user updates, the continuous addition of "friends," the never-ending "liking" of things around the internet, and the steady insertion and sharing of links does more than produce a unique identity, as corporations cull invaluable information about "user-generated content ... [that] is the very dynamic driving new revenue streams" (Coté and Pybus 2007, 100). The virtual goods and services that users produce through their *unpaid* labor (of linking, liking, sharing, and uploading) make use of human dialogue, cooperation, and creativity to generate profit; they make, namely, use of immaterial labor. Moreover, because this immaterial labor can take place outside working hours and anywhere a network is available, it renders the distinction between work and leisure obsolete. Late capitalism aims to "*put to work the entire lives* of workers" by expanding both production and consumption into every aspect of an individual's life (Marazzi 2008, 50).

Concomitant with the shift to immaterial labor is the growth of financialized capitalism. The salient place of finance is linked to the end of the Bretton Woods System in the early 1970s, the subsequent liberalization of financial markets, and the introduction, widespread acceptance, and enormous short-term profitablity of complex financial instruments. Like immaterial labor, financialized capitalism makes use of biopower insofar as it is associated with "the diversion of savings from household economies to stocks and securities" (Marazzi 2008, 21). Personal and communal earnings are increasingly put into the service of complex financial instruments leading to the new "massification of stock market investment" that allow anyone to participate in, say, widely available methods of online trading (Marazzi 2008, 16). This "massification" illustrates an intensification of biopower as private and public economies collapse into each other in the incessant expansion of capitalist profit and gain. But this collapse also speaks to the similarities between immaterial labor and financialized capitalism in their reliance on human communication, cooperation, and creativity.

The necessity of communication, in particular, is understood as a crucial component of both financialized capitalism and immaterial labor. Paolo Virno (2001) identifies language itself as a primary component of post-Fordist capitalist production because "the dialogic word is installed at the very heart of capitalist production" and at the very heart of the machinations of labour (Virno 2001). In this way, all labor within late capitalism takes place in what Virno calls the "talkative factory," as all labor makes use of human language and, by extension, of communication. As a result, financial exchange is only possible through the continual chatter of contemporary life that is spread through communications technologies, media, and social networks. Such chatter is necessary as financiers weigh, consider, and discuss the risks and benefits of potential investments by surveilling global communications. But as Marazzi (2008) points out, financialized capitalism is not merely dependent upon communications technologies because it is coextensive with language. It is its own *convention*, it is "*language itself as means of production and circulation of goods*" (Marazzi 2008, 48; author emphasis). Just as all post-Fordist labor takes place in a talkative environment, financialization also takes place in a talkative environment as investors cooperatively and creatively make investment decisions in the context of an increasingly complex, global economic system. Within late capitalism language thus becomes productive in capitalist terms in that it not only facilitates but also constitutes the interaction, communication, and cooperation that capitalism requires to survive.

The quest for never-ending profit and relentless expansionism is foundational to capitalism in general, without which it would quickly falter. As the locales of non-capitalist spaces shrink and opportunities for expansionism decrease, capitalism expands more and more into the interior of human life. Financialization and immaterial labor are illustrative of contemporary capitalism's quest to turn every aspect of human life, i.e. communication, cooperation, and creativity, into a vehicle for expansion and growth. As capitalism shifts from Fordist labor and manufacturing to immaterial labor and financialization, the application of biopower helps manage every aspect of everyday life. For unlike previous variants of capitalism that relied on mechanization, industrialization, and manufacturing and a fixed sense of place and identity, contemporary capitalism relies on digitization, globalization and communication and a fluid sense of place and identity. As a result, biopower helps produce the heterogeneity, cooperation, and creativity that those shifts require. It is worth repeating: industrial capitalism required a homogeneous workforce to insert into mechanized factories; contemporary practices of financialization and immaterial labor are associated with heterogeneity and workers who creatively problem solve, practice teamwork, and are comfortable with a talkative environment.

The intensification of biopower aids in capitalism's expansionary quest as it regulates and centralizes the human characteristics required by late capitalism. This process of expansion and adaptation is perhaps best described by Gilles Deleuze and Felix Guattari (1984) as a process of deterritorialization through which capitalism works at opening up exterior limits and then ensconcing those limits within its own boundaries. As capitalism expands and shifts, it must continually redefine itself in relation to new limits and challenges. According to Deleuze and Guattari, the concomitant process to deterritorialization is *reterritorialization* through which capitalism must absorb, and respond to, the limits that it opens up. The intensification of biopower is likewise akin to a deterritorializing practice that seeks to open up the interior limits of human life and reterritorialize the limits it opens up by deploying methods of hierarchically ordering and arranging diverse individuals.

Resistance: Thinking through biopower and biopolitics

The intensification of biopower complicates resistances to capitalism because the goals of those who endeavor to increase human opportunity and decrease racism, colonialism, patriarchy, heterosexism, classism, and other forms of prejudice can be consistent with the production of multiplicity and uniqueness that is central to postmodern capitalism. So, for example, contemporary advertising makes use of cultural symbols of rebellion, while protest is presented as a media event where a kind of commoditized dissent does not threaten capitalist exchange.[1] And yet biopower is not oppressive in a straightforward, top-down manner for it is not a power that says "you must not" (Foucault 2007, 154). It is an invisible power that, because it exhorts us to constitute ourselves as unique individuals, is productive. Recall that as the use of biopower has deepened within postmodern capitalism it has shifted from the production of particular kinds of individuals that are easily inserted into homogenizing institutions to the production of unique and diverse individuals. Furthermore, today's biopower—as it produces uniqueness and diversity—seeks to open up the interior characteristics of human life as a new limit into which capitalism can expand. Capitalism must absorb and neutralize anything that destabilizes and threatens its survival. Nonetheless, when capitalism opens up a new limit and is thusly deterritorialized, there is a moment of destabilization before that limit is reterritorialized (to the benefit of capitalism). The profusion of diversity and uniqueness on which postmodern or late capitalism and current modes of biopower relies inevitably produces such destabilizing effects precisely because they cannot instantaneously reabsorb the limits that they open up. In short, there is a time-lag between deterritorialization and reterritorialization, a space of unpredictability, a time of uncertainty. This in-between space means that resistance can be reconceived as something other than the usual recognizable symbols of overt rebellion or protest. It follows that resistance reconceiving in this way runs counter to the dominant understanding that resistance is an intervention from *outside* capitalism (Lotringer 2004, 17).

Recognizing that capitalism generates its own resistances or instabilities means that it is possible to exploit that instability. Resistances exist because capitalism is continually under threat, perpetually shifting, and challenged by the very characteristics that sustain it. Moreover, as Foucault (1978) argues, power and resistance are coextensive, and because power is everywhere, resistance is similarly everywhere (Foucault 1978, 95). It is for this reason that Foucault did not view the omnipresence of power relations (including biopower) as necessarily oppressive. Instead he pointed out that because power is omnipresent "everything is dangerous, which is not exactly the same as bad. If everything is dangerous, then we always have something to do" (Foucault 1983a, 231–2). This means that power relations are *never static or stable* for they are always shifting in response to various threats and instabilities. Although capitalism is continually expanding, it cannot explicitly foreclose the possibility of resistance because its own stability and the stability of the power relations on which it depends cannot be guaranteed. However, the corollary is that resistance cannot be guaranteed for it is similarly shifting and unstable.

And so, when late capitalism seeks to open up all aspects of human life to realize additional profit it cannot always immediately absorb what it opens up. Here the distinction that Lazzarato (2002) makes between bio*power* and bio*politics* helps illustrate that there will always be shifting remainders that cannot be fully assimilated by capitalism. Biopower is distinct from biopolitics, according to Lazzarato, because biopower is a form of power that individualizes, manages, and hierarchically arranges populations whereas biopolitics focuses on human characteristics and relationships that emerge from below. While biopower seeks to use human life as a tool for capitalist economics, biopolitics recognizes that human life is embedded within shifting and unstable power relations that originates from humans, rather than institutions, governments, or corporations. This means that even as the application of biopower is intensified and human life is increasingly embedded within capitalist economic processes, capitalism becomes reliant upon a biopolitics that it cannot explicitly control for its continued survival for *it is not human life itself*. That is, biopower cannot entirely lay claim to the creativity, individuality, communication, cooperation, and diversity that supports contemporary postmodern capitalism. Distinguishing between biopower and biopolitics in this way helps highlight a form of resistance that emerges in those moments when capitalism changes its character.

Resistance *is* possible, therefore, within postmodern capitalism and biopower if we consider that "[t]he true act of revolt against the system is a kind of disappearing act" (Niedzviecki 2004, 225). Rather than creating the kind of unique and diverse identities that contemporary capitalism demands and that biopower encourages, it is possible for us to refuse to broadcast our identities, talents, and opinions by embracing, say, facelessness. Facelessness can be viewed as an attempt to engage in biopolitics by "refus[ing] what we are" (Foucault 1983b, 216). Anonymity, then, is a tool that contributes to biopolitics. To cultivate anonymity is not, to be clear, the equivalent of "dropping out" of the system as it entails a radical engagement with the kinds of characteristics that contemporary capitalism requires. This tactic is advocated by The Invisible Committee, an anonymous group of activists and theorists based in France who self-consciously act and write without identifying themselves either collectively or individually. "To be socially nothing is not a humiliating condition," they write, or "the source of some tragic lack of recognition ... but is on the contrary the condition for maximum freedom of action" (The Invisible Committee 2009, 113). The Invisible Committee suggests that resisting the uniqueness and the recognition of such uniqueness required by recent capitalism is a difficult task as it demands that we resist without the usual public validation that is an ingrained part of contemporary protest. Being anonymous affords the ability to remain undetected. Moreover, refusing the charms of validation helps anonymous agents generate connections between communities and grass-roots groups, as the saliency for unique individualism and its public recognition or validation fades to the background. Such connections are a necessary precondition for developing resistance as a biopolitics from below.

Late capitalism strives to close off a biopolitics from below in its quest to control, regulate, and exploit human communication, cooperation, and creativity. That a biopolitics from below exists is certain, even if it is difficult to describe. Nonetheless, I would like to suggest that a biopolitics from below should seek to engage those facets of human life that explicitly rouse in us the acknowledgement that we are not individuals in isolation. This is important not only because it counters the contemporary insistence on individualized uniqueness, but also because it acknowledges that human life is both personal *and* communal. For what is communal and shared about human life cannot be abstracted from our personal identities. Donna Haraway (1991) argues that because our identities are always partial and partially produced we are "able to join with another, to see together without claiming to be another" (Haraway 1991, 193). This partialness contributes to biopolitical resistances because it necessitates making connections beyond ourselves and opens up the possibility that we can join with others to resist, even for a moment, the capitalist order of things.

The Occupy/(Un)Occupy Movement

And so, does the Occupy Movement of 2011–12 signify an emergent threat to capitalism? Can the Occupy Movement be interpreted as a biopolitics from below? It is no doubt too soon to assess its effects, but with its rallying cry of "We Are The 99%," the Occupy Movement explicitly acknowledges the structural changes associated with globalization, financialization, and the decline of Fordism that have made life within late capitalism increasingly precarious. Housing bubbles burst, workers choose not to retire after having lost their pensions, jobs are outsourced, debt is endemic, and inequities are reinforced. In opposition to inequity, the Occupy Movement insists on a collective and "leaderless resistance movement with people of many colours, genders and political persuasions" (#OWS 2011). This insistence on a leaderless and non-hierarchical movement is suggestive of a biopolitics from below, since it actively engages in the production of new forms of human life, relationships, and interactions. Primarily influenced by the revolutionary tactics put to use in the Arab Spring uprisings of 2011, the Occupy Movement consists of numerous interrelated movements that—though they seek to "occupy" local spaces—connect and cooperate with a wider, more globalized movement. The Occupy Movement, recognizing the effects of biopower's subsumption of human life, also establishes sites that seek to Occupy University, Food, Student Debt, Research, Libraries etc., to allow the aspects of human life that have become absorbed by those institutions to exist in ways not always tied to capitalist calculations.

Despite the promise of the Occupy Movement, the instability of all power relations means there is no guarantee that it will succeed. Occupy Wall Street was forcibly ended, a fate shared by other protests. True, evicted sites relocate or return to re-Occupy, but any widespread impact on capitalism has so far been unrealized. Capitalism will again seek to absorb and even commodify what exists at its limits. Perhaps the more pressing threat to the Occupy Movement comes from the criticism that it does not actually represent the 99 per cent—and so re-inscribes the kinds of exclusions, ordering, and hierarchies that are essential to capitalism (see Bagsak 2011; Walia 2011; Yee 2011). When participants of the Occupy Movement examine its embeddedness within biopower—such as the decision to change the name of the Albuquerque movement to (Un)Occupy in the recognition that, as a colonized territory, it is already forcibly occupied; or the acknowledgement that leaders from the American Civil Rights Movement have something to teach Occupy organizers—it demonstrates a clearer possibility of developing a biopolitics from below (see National Council of Elders 2011; (un)Occupy Albuquerque 2011). In these instances, the refusal of *what we are* should take the form of joining together in the way that Haraway (1991) advocates. Or again, the Occupy Movement could be viewed as an opening to a biopolitics that recognizes the partialness of each identity; the necessity of cooperating and communicating with each other; and, perhaps, the need to resist the common injunction to broadcast our uniqueness instead of our communal connections. Perhaps the Occupy/(Un)Occupy movement, or something like it in the future, can help us imagine new ways for human life to exist for itself. If for a moment—or more.

Note

1 Shortly after the 2011 student protests in London a commentary in *The Guardian* pointed out that high-street retailer Topshop began selling t-shirts with the slogan "the students are revolting" (O'Hagan 2011).

9

Place, creativity, and Richard Florida: On the aesthetics of economic development

Todd Dufresne and Clara Sacchetti

Why people live in some places and not in others has been the subject of much debate over the last two decades (Krätke 2010; Peck 2011), which is perhaps surprising. By the 1980s it was widely believed that modern technologies would level the labor market; that access to the means of production (e.g. land, equipment, and knowledge) had heralded a new and better kind of democracy; and that computer technology in particular had undermined the need to gather, live, and work in expensive cities. Certainly there have been amazing transformations in how we think about the notion of place, i.e. country, home, community, neighborhood, and its connection to making a living. Physical places, we are still told, matter little in a contemporary world increasingly marked by the fluidity of virtual spaces, electronic media, e-learning, e-conferencing, social media sites, webcasts, and so on. Yet place still seems to matter to our working lives or, better put, a good place to live and work still seems to trump the advantages of a virtual or cyber space. And this is nowhere more true than in those unlovely wastelands of our post-industrial landscape, which beg for more frank discussions of the aesthetics of economic development.

The dominant pop theorist of the importance of the economy and place is Richard Florida (2004), guru of city planning and economic development most famous for his work on "the rise of the creative class." We argue that the most interesting and ultimately suggestive aspect of his work is found between the lines of his discussion of creativity, place, and the spectral aspects of capitalism. Our claim is that Florida is curiously ambivalent about social theories of late capitalism that help us understand an economy that increasingly moves beyond the machinations of material production. On the one hand he accepts the parts of social theory that rationalize his view of creativity, while on the other he rejects the parts of social theory that compromise his own authority as a public intellectual, policy-maker, and city planning consultant. This ambivalence boils down to a reluctance to deal adequately with the problem of representation in a postmodern era; of how we conceptualize the practices and meanings of the "new economy," interchangeably referred to as the knowledge economy, late capitalism, and contemporary capitalism (Castells 2010; Comaroff and Comaroff 2000).

In this chapter we unpack Florida's work on the creative class, measure it against competing theories, and consider the importance of place for economic development. We suggest that no one has noticed how Florida negotiates, or fails to negotiate, what Jean Baudrillard (1983) calls "third order simulation" as it concerns late capitalism: "the generation by models of a real without origin or reality" (Baudrillard 1983, 2; see 105–6). Finally, we will avoid a cheap, knee-jerk rejection of Florida's contribution as just the latest neoliberal strategy for economic development (see Kapferer 2010; Peck 2011), and attempt to salvage the potentially positive effects that flow from the spectral features of the "new economy." Our overall aim in these regards is to open up a critical dialogue between contemporary theories about the social and economic realms of everyday life and the recent ascendancy of the "creative class" discourse.

Place-based theories of economic development: An overview

It was only a few decades ago that Western academics, urban planners, policy-makers, and corporate leaders believed that long-term economic prosperity was dependent upon the availability and extraction of non-renewable natural resources that lay in close proximity to natural transportation routes, like water, or built transportation routes, like canals, railways, and highways (see Harvey 1992). Similarly, they believed that establishing a strong manufacturing base best propelled progress, modernization, and the generation of surplus revenues. And they had every reason to accept these beliefs, since modern Europe and North America were developed on the basis of, and flourished according to the logic of, this "old economy" thinking (Lash and Urry 1987; Lipietz 1987). It is a well-known story: people followed the firms who followed the resources; and then people followed the factories that followed the firms that followed the resources.

It is just as well known that contemporary urban life does not always tally so well with these old economy models. The decline of resource-driven industrial cities, the advance of global assembly lines, and the extensive use of technology have devastated the social and economic health of a strong working class and economic equality within society (Levinson 2011). At the same time, some cities have not just weathered the demise of the "old economy," but have thrived and prospered. Among observers, these cities—from smaller centers such as Austin, Portland, and Seattle to larger centers such as London, Milan, and New York City—suggest novel models for economic development in the face of post-industrial decline and decay.

Why some places in the global North continue to prosper while others decline is at the heart of a lively debate about the economy today, an economy proclaimed to be more reliant on brain power and ideas than on physical labor and tangible goods (Peck 2011). Two basic and competing theories of economic growth have emerged in this regard. The first theory, associated with Michael Porter (2000), holds that similar firms tend to "cluster" in a given city or region for easy access to markets, resources, and talent. Clustering is an effect of old-fashioned competition between firms that encourages the development of new technologies through the continuous transfer of intra-firm knowledge by a highly mobile and porous labor pool. The "clustering firms" theory assumes, like older models of economic development, that the firms, like planetary bodies, inevitably pull knowledge workers into particular locales. This pull is what accounts for the economic prosperity of particular cities and regions and repeats the taken-for-granted notion that industry comes before (and so makes possible) place.

The second theory iterates the clustering idea, but with a crucial difference. It holds that economic prosperity is determined primarily by the clustering of *talent* in a given city or region. For it is talent that best explains the locational decision of firms and businesses, a logic that reverses the causal relation espoused by Porter. Three variations on this theme stand out:

- the human capital theory;
- the social capital theory; and
- the creative class theory.

Edward Glaeser's (2000) "human capital" theory suggests that highly educated people drive economic development through the application of their education, skill, and talent. Glaeser, a knowledge-based economy theorist, fails, however, to explain why knowledge workers are attracted to particular places and not to others. Robert Putnam's (2000) "social capital" theory holds that regional economic growth is tied to the formation of social networks that encourage people and firms to maintain strong connections with each other. Unlike Glaeser, Putnam attempts to explain why some places attract knowledge workers while others fail utterly. Like Glaeser, however, Putnam ignores the attitudes of the workers he describes, who reject rigid communities and networks in favor of flexible, dynamic, semi-autonomous, and culturally diverse relations. This leads us, finally, to Richard Florida's thesis about the "rise of the creative class." According to Florida, education and social networks do not adequately explain the linkages between economic prosperity and regional development. Theorists who focus solely on these linkages, Florida argues, have hitched their wagons to "the so-called New Economy and the Internet age," a mistake that has them fetishizing "technology and virtual worlds, the notion that this stuff could make anyone rich quick and solve all our problems" (Florida 2004, xviii–xix). What is required, Florida contends, is a longer-term view of prosperity and an analysis of the locational decisions of creative workers—those people who use creativity to earn a living by generating new ideas (for products or as solutions to problems). Florida's sweeping conclusion: Human creativity drives economic revolution and accounts for the major socio-economic and political transformations in history. Florida even contends that creativity made possible the agricultural revolution, which involved a move away from nomadism toward human settlement; the subsequent rise of systematic and large-scale trading; the intensification of job specialization and the social division of labor; and, more recently, the rise of industrial capitalism.

On the one hand, the grandiosity of this narrative in some ways echoes Karl Marx's own, which identifies not creativity but the application of human labor to the natural world as the driving force of progress in history, all of which he equates with the ur-domain ("base" or "substructure") of economics itself (see Marx and Engels 2002). And, as in Marx, it is possible to interpret Florida's discussion of creativity as a contemporary take on human nature, what Marx calls *Gattungswesen*—"species being" or "essence" (see Marx 1933). After all, Florida conceives of creativity as a continuously renewable resource that is innate to all human beings and which serves as the ground of society, culture, politics, and economics.

On the other hand, the labor of Florida's so-called "creatives" is far less earnest, programmatic, and positivistic than it is in Marx. For while creatives refuse the status quo by playing with and/or breaking the rules of, say, hegemonic corporate culture, they engage less in strategy and resistance than in tactics and subversion (de Certeau 1984); less in negation (i.e. the "work of the negative" as first theorized by Hegel in 1807; see Hegel 1977) than in playful celebration of alternative hipsterdom. This is a "revolution," therefore, not from below, as in Marxism, but from the middle and above; a revolution, as in Marx, that occurs within capitalism, but unlike Marx, not for some future communist utopia but for the betterment of neoliberalism or capitalism itself (see Gibson and Klocker 2005; Peck 2005). Creatives thus exist only to the extent that creativity is nurtured and prioritized by a creative economy—a circularity, however vicious or virtuous, that Florida applauds, since it best explains the positive relationship between place and economic development today.

Florida's thesis is that creativity pulls in the creative class that, in turn, pulls in the firms. Or again, Florida believes that creative people cluster around creative people who cluster together in places that have a creative buzz. If, then, for the other "talent cluster" theorists like Glaeser and Putnam we are describing gravitational forces of attraction, with Florida creativity functions more like a black hole: it sucks all economic activity inside it.

Florida's creative places

Florida insists that creative workers are the most important group in society because, although they comprise only 30 per cent of the work force in North America, they produce 50 per cent of its wealth. Florida claims that the factors that ground the locational decisions of twenty-first-century creative workers—what he refers to as the "Super Creative Core," the engineers, computer scientists, writers, actors, musicians, architects, and makers of culture and public opinion, and the "Creative Professionals," the lawyers, bankers, managers, and physicians who provide services for those in the Super Creative Core—are the keys to future economic wealth. For, as mentioned, the clustering of the creative classes supposedly determines the long-term economic prosperity of a particular locale, country, city, neighborhood, or region in today's economy.

Place, Florida discovered, figures strongly with the members of the creative class. Not surprisingly, this emphasis suggestively puts Florida in good company with other contemporary scholars of place who argue that it is an important consideration in our globalizing world (Gupta and Ferguson 1997; Soja 1989). In the social sciences place is no longer regarded simply as a setting where economic and geo-political power is exercised amongst the elite; nor is it regarded simply as a background of and for culture and identity, the place where people mindlessly reproduce "their culture" and root their sense of self. Instead, place is viewed as a much more dynamic and critical factor in the construction of identity, culture, ethnicity, gender, race, nationalism, etc. A sense of the place of home can, for example, be critical in producing a safe haven from gender and racial oppression (see Ben-Yoseph and Rosen 2009). Groups of people who come together on the basis of their shared ethnicities in a locale that is not their natal homeland are attuned to place and the way it affects their ability to secure employment, educational, health, and leisure resources in the pursuit of their everyday lives (see Glenn, Bouvet, and Floriani 2011). Generations of people who electronically communicate with partners, competitors, Facebook friends, etc., from across the world no longer simply see themselves as part of a single nation state, region, or city but as part of a virtual global landscape, engaged in cross-cultural learning and the fusion of multiple perspectives, insights, and ways of being that no longer rely strictly on one's own home, homeland, locally specific community, and physical locale (Plunkett 2011). Place is not simply an empty vessel that is, as Soja (1989) notes, a container for everyday life; it informs, shapes, and helps fashion the machinations of life.

Against this broad, contemporary scholarly literature, it is not surprising that Florida draws attention to how place is interrelated to the economic aspect of life more generally and to economic development more specifically. Yet he contends that place is in fact not crucial in and of itself but for the buzz it creates, the greater level of creativity it engenders and, by extension, its prospects for economic development. Florida's creatives routinely cluster in "broad creative ecosystems" (Florida 2004, xxiii) that are diverse, vibrant, and awash in interesting architecture, history, recreation, street-life, and "just-in-time" leisure activities. "Buzzing cities," as Jamie Peck (2011) summarizes Florida's thesis, "can anticipate cumulative growth, but staid, hierarchical, and suburbocentric cities, where the buzz is off, can only slide into the rustbelt of the knowledge economy" (Peck 2011, 42). In other words, creatives reside in cities and regions that are cosmopolitan, open for work and play 24/7; places far removed from the usually aesthetically challenged locales of post-industrial society, and that are invariably judged to be shabby, neglected, non-cosmopolitan, and decidedly unlovely.

Working off census data and interviews, Florida forges his argument on the basis of a series of indices that highlight strong correlations (not causal links) between the diversity of a given place, high-tech success, and the residential decisions of the creative class. Diversity is measured by three now well-known indices:

- "Bohemian Index," a measure of a region's proportional national share of employment in artistic occupations, including writers, film producers, dancers, composers, musicians, actors, and visual artists;

- the "Mosaic Index," a measure of a region's foreign-born residents; and
- the "Gay Index," a measure of a region's share of gay male couples relative to the nation's share.

Of these admittedly limited and limiting indices (what of, for example, non-immigrant ethnics and other genders with same-sex identifications?), Florida discovered that the single best predictor of economic prosperity in the U.S. is the presence of a large gay community, a simple measure of tolerance and urbanity. And so, for example, of the 50 metropolitan areas surveyed in 2001, Florida found strong correlations between diversity and high-tech success so that "hot" economy places like San Francisco (1st), Boston (2nd), Seattle (3rd), and Austin (14th) were 1st, 8th, 6th, and 3rd on the Gay Index; 8th, 9th, 1st, and 10th on the Bohemian Index; and 4th, 9th, 15th, and 19th on the Mosaic Index. The upshot: find the artsies, gays, and immigrants, and you will find either creative economy wealth or the *foundations* for creative economy wealth.

Given these findings Florida is less sanguine about theories of late capitalism that suggest that the old economy connections between place, work, and leisure have destabilized and have become irrelevant in our current hyper-electronic age. Theorists of place contend that new telecommunications and transportation technologies—e.g. internet, fax, telephone, mass air travel, and high-speed trains—have radically altered our usual relationships with time and space (Appadurai 1992; Hannerz 1989; Harvey 1992). They suggest that we no longer have to be at work in order to do work because in our post-Fordist world we work, live, and play in cyberspace. Florida is openly skeptical of these "utopian prophesies" and "happy talk" (Florida 2004, 24). He does not find these supposedly asocial cyborgs, the creative class, stuck at work in their parents' basements. Instead he finds a new class of people deeply interested in what he refers to as "quality of place," which he emphatically distinguishes from "quality of life" (see Florida 2004, 231–4).

Yet not just any "quality of place" will do. Florida is much more circumspect in this regard, arguing that cosmopolitan places (see below) in particular are harbingers of economic prosperity. Florida writes about how members of the creative class "turn down jobs, or decide not to look for them, in places that did not afford the variety of scenes they desired—music, art, technology, outdoor sports" (Florida 2004, 224). Apparently creatives are not simply or primarily attracted to the old economy perks of salary, benefits, job status, and job advancement; perks that belong to vertical labor markets. Creatives rather prefer the weak attachments and job flexibility of "thick" horizontal markets, characteristics that fit well (some think too well) with management philosophies under late capitalism. They are attracted to places that bolster their creativity and give them the chance to exercise their creativity in multiple ways with multiple firms.

Moreover, overworked creatives increasingly act like tourists in their own cities, hard-pressed as they are to find time to act like tourists in other cities. Consequently they demand a place that is full of vibe, energy, buzz, and unique entertainments. Such vibe is tied to the "third places" of contemporary life; places, like coffee shops and bars, that are neither home nor work but nonetheless sustain loosely knit communities. As Florida claims, these communal spaces stave off the instabilities of home life engendered by our serially monogamous blended families (see also Pinsof 2002; Rampage 2002). But they also help mitigate some of the risks ingrained in the very horizontal job market creatives prefer and the promiscuous job-hopping they endure. In the face of these instabilities, third places give rise to a host of positive attributes that Florida charts: "reliable human contact"; the "pleasure of good company and lively conversation"; "the interplay of culture and ideas"; "excitement and energy"; and "a mix of influences" that includes music and food (Florida 2004, 226). In short, Florida's creatives prefer to live, work, and play in a cosmopolitan place "where anyone can find a peer group to be comfortable with, and also find other groups to be stimulated by; a place ... where outsiders can quickly become insiders" (Florida 2004, 227).

A cosmopolitan place is one that has a "unique mix of urban grit, renovated buildings, commingling of new and old, fashion ladies and bag ladies" (Florida 2004, 228). It is not about living in and amongst real historic buildings in established neighborhoods, or engaging in novel activities and alternative music scenes amidst the suddenly awesome bums and bag ladies. At least, it is not just that. It is rather more focused on the often unexpected or unpredictable experiences of the novel. Perhaps not surprisingly, then, the cosmopolitanism of place is defined against the unlovely, uninteresting, mono-cultural, generic, white bread experiences of big-box stores, chain restaurants, and nightclubs. If, finally, "quality of place" means anything, it means *not that*—the crux of an aesthetic revulsion in the face of the mass produced. Ultimately it is this quality of place that, for Florida, best explains why some cities and regions have prospered while others have declined. Quality of place is thus contingent upon what he refers to as an "interrelated set of experiences":

> Many of them, like the street-level scene, are dynamic and participatory. You can do more than be a spectator; you can be part of the scene. And the city allows you to modulate the experience: to choose the mix, to turn the intensity level up or down as desired, and to have a hand in creating

> the experience rather than merely consuming it. The street buzz is right nearby if you want it, but you can also retreat to your home or other quiet place, or go into an urban park, or even set out for the country. This is one reason canned experiences are not so popular. A chain theme restaurant, a multimedia circus sports stadium or prepackaged entertainment and tourism district is like a packaged tour. You do not get to help create your experience or modulate the intensity: it is thrust upon you. (Florida 2004, 232)

Hence the rise of "creative cities," places like Seattle, that Florida can and does hold up as concrete exemplars of successful economic development.

Place misplaced: Or, where to find an economy of pure representation

Actually, though, Florida's rejection of virtual or cyber-space in favor of "quality of place" goes only so far. For clearly a quality, even a quality of place, is not the same thing as a built space. It is no thing at all. In fact, Florida goes to great lengths to distance his notion of place from any particular built environment. Partly, no doubt, this is because the creative class is supposed to care little about old economy "amenities" like opera houses, convention centers, musical theatres, and sports arenas. They care about local flavor or scene, a vibe that is irreducible to any particular built space, most especially branded, packaged, and predetermined space. Once again, creatives care less about jobs than job opportunities; less about infrastructure than ideas and debate; less about packaged experiences than novel encounters. So out with Disney and in with Indie.

But while a given flavor or scene, like the feel of a city or the buzz it occasions, may or may not be virtual, it most certainly is imaginary and spectral. Of course, this realization is ironic, since although Florida explicitly invokes place as the best way of distinguishing his analysis from, first, the other "talent cluster" theorists like Glaeser, and second, social theorists of late capitalism (rarely named), he actually says very little about it. That's because "place," however ubiquitous and essential in his work, is really a misnomer. Florida's constant recourse to elusive energy, buzz, vibe, feel, quality, flavor, and so on is an attempt to represent the characteristics of places that attract creatives. That is to say, Florida desperately tries to *quantify the qualitative*—literalize the elusive qualities of creativity, name the aesthetic qualities of creative scenes. Yet he is also quick to point out that these qualities are irreducible to any given or predetermined set of characteristics. "There is no one-size-fits-all strategy," he writes in his new Preface of 2004, adding: "the development of such environments cannot be planned from above" (Florida 2004, xxiii). This makes sense, since what is cool one minute is not cool the next, the content of buzz being subject to the whims, not primarily of the market place, but of the culture brokers, the hipsters and artists who make it all possible in the first instance.

If creativity really is the foundation of and for capitalist wealth, then of course the artist is the ideal kind of "entrepreneur"—at once the latent past, manifest present, and tantalizing future of all market-based wealth. And so it follows that, as Daniel Pink quips in *The Harvard Business Review*, "the MFA is the new MBA" (Pink 2004) in so far as it is the artist who plays around with and subverts the existing rules of the knowledge game. It is the artist who creates the scene, generates the buzz, and fires the creative imaginations of others. And so forget the convention centers, Florida insists, and support the next Hendrix or Warhol. Free the artists to do what they have always done: create and manipulate the actual built spaces around them in unpredictable, creative, and finally profitable ways, thus refashioning the underused and derelict sites cast aside by the old economy. Art and artistry thereby become the dominant force around which twenty-first-century economics revolves.

This revelation about the artist-hero is bound to sound fanciful to many or perhaps most observers. Artists do not extract and then refine gold and oil, traditional old economy standard-bearers of wealth in the West. They produce and manipulate knowledge and images, among them truth and beauty. Consequently their overt recognition in Florida's work on economic development is certainly a remarkable, even stunning, turn of events. One can debate the finer points. But Florida is, albeit unwittingly, right about this much: today we find ourselves in the third order simulacra Jean Baudrillard (1983) described presciently decades ago. That is, what Florida struggles to represent—quantify and literalize—is *an economy of pure representation*, where exchange among its members is much ado, literally, about no thing, nothing. My vibe for her feel. Your flavor for his buzz. Our idea for your money—in each case a currency of floating desires and mutual illusions (see Haiven, chapter 3). Such is the variously called post-Fordist, new economy, knowledge economy, contemporary capitalist, postmodern, or late capitalist world in which we live, work, and play today (Castells 2010; Comaroff and Comaroff 2000; Harvey 1992; Jameson 1983).

If so, it can't be surprising that there is no irreducible "place" in the creative economy from which Florida or anyone else could offer up a model, an exemplar, according to which all others could be judged and then replicated ad infinitum. There is no one brand, no ground, only pure simulation:

vibe, buzz, feel, quality, energy, flavor, and so on. That is not to say that there are no actual places in which the creative class clusters. Florida is right to name them: London, Toronto, Boulder, etc. But these places are more about ideas and experiences than about qualities, amenities, and buildings. As Baudrillard might conceive it, these are cities that are not so much launched into orbit around an economy of creativity, but are sucked right into it—no longer real, but "hyperreal." Cities, in short, that have radically outstripped the (nonetheless still abstract) security once provided by natural resources, ultimately by the gold reserve, and have replaced them with the insecurity of an unhinged consumer culture driven by creativity and its twin, desire. In the most simplified terms, these are the successful places that have transitioned their economies from the notion of a material, natural resource, or manufacturing economy to one that stresses an elusive culture-based economy; places that have transitioned from mechanical (factory) reproduction to idiosyncratic consumption; places where, in a word, the only resource worth investing in is human creativity.

And so the artist, once thrown from the Republic of reason, now runs the show, and runs the show *as show*, as pure spectacle. This is in fact Florida's great achievement—and the most fundamental reason why he has generated so much controversy and, indeed, hatred among his detractors. More than any economist or urban planner working today he has done his best to capitalize (in both senses of the word) on just this transition to spectral capitalism, where "creativity" is the impossible name for that which Western thought, beginning with Plato, has done its best to exclude. Creativity is in this sense the poet within, or perhaps the sophist, unleashed by a late capitalism that is decades beyond another era's artistic fantasy, namely, the rational *homo economicus* of modernism. It's over and the pundits of economic development don't quite know what to say or think—or how to profit from it.

At the same time, Florida's own creative and entrepreneurial interests (allowing, for the moment, if contingently, that particular pairing to stand) have led him elsewhere than to a full-blown recognition of the simulated, spectral, abstract, delirious culture of contemporary capitalism. He is a marketing guru and widely sought out and highly paid public speaker who has the ear of influential people everywhere, including city planners and politicians from nearly all levels of government. It is probably no surprise, then, that Florida goes only so far in recognizing the specular nature of his own speculations. It's facetious but no doubt true to say that postmodernism doesn't pay as well as handy prescriptions for leaders looking for help with revitalizing their neglected downtown cores. Clearly everyone's artistry has its limits.

But actually our criticism is very limited, and not at all dismissive of Florida's overall achievement. We certainly take our stand on different grounds than Florida's many other critics, whose complaints include (without exhausting) the following: questionable use of statistics and controversial Indexes (Christophers 2007; Rausch and Negrey 2006; Tepper 2002); happy appropriation of indie-groups, like gays and artists (Barnes et al. 2006; Binnie and Skeggs 2004; Kapferer 2010; Markusen 2006); lack of serious regard for the issues of social marginalization and inequality, including the hot-button subjects of gender, race, and sexual orientation (Atkinson and Easthope 2009; McCann 2007; Slater 2006; Thomas and Darnton 2006); neoliberal bias (Gibson and Klocker 2005; McGuigan 2005; Peck 2011, 2005); conservative bias and its pitfalls (Boschken 2003; Goonewardena and Kipper 2005); cookie-cutter prescriptions for urban reform (Comunian, Faggian and Li 2010; Hansen and Niedomysl 2009; Krätke 2010; Mcgranahan and Wojan 2007; Oakely 2004; Scott 2006); intellectual naivety (Elliot 2003; Gibson and Klocker 2004); and even Florida's envy-inducing reputation and speaking fees as public lecturer (Markusen 2006; Peck 2005).

Unlike these critics and many more besides, and without diminishing their often valuable contributions to our understanding of urban growth and creativity, we are rather more interested in the slippages that function in Florida's work between the material and ideational; built and imagined; place and experience; quantity and quality; literal and figurative. For our claim is that these slippages are the inevitable consequence of *any analysis of aesthetics and economic development*, and a reflection of the specular or hyperreal version of capitalism that exists today (Baudrillard 1983; Bell 1979; Jameson 1983). The truth about Florida is therefore prosaic, mundane: he inevitably, repeatedly, and rather unwittingly deconstructs his own concepts and claims. Florida does, and does not, advocate actual built places. Florida does, and does not, invoke a category of the novel that is irreducible. Florida does, and does not, name creativity itself. Florida does, and does not, prescribe solutions for the purposes of a marketing machine (his and his clients'). Florida does, and does not, cross the limits of a materialist economics into (for the sake of shorthand) a postmodernist philosophy.

This is not a criticism, or simply a criticism. We are rather claiming that what is best in Florida is his realization (to invoke Gertrude Stein's apt phrase) that there is "no there there" in traditional economics; that something called "creativity" has indeed become the gold standard in much of the West today; but that creativity is in fact irreducible to a given occupation or place; that being independent or alternative means, literally and figuratively, going your own way and not that of others; but that this independence is also a cliché and, therefore, inauthentic and no guarantee of economic success; that economics may indeed be driven by something other than human reason; but that a metaphysics of creativity (and here is the rub) is less the salvation of economics-as-science than it is its destruction as such. Clearly creativity is no more apt to put economics on a solid foundation than was an overinflated, if delusionary, model of rationality. But creativity's failure in this regard is also its triumph, since an economics of creativity, precisely because it is irreducible, draws us back, not to labor and therefore productivity, but to the fantastical coupling of desire and consumption. And as such it draws us back to a consideration of social theory and its treatment of place.

What is to be done?

There is, of course, a real danger that behind our kind of rumination lurks nihilism and defeatism. After all, if buzz is irreducible and cannot be programmed, then action to improve our cities according to that logic may seem pointless. But the fact that Florida's work implies uncertainty as it concerns ineffable qualities like "cool," as well as supposedly effable inquiries like economics, doesn't mean that forgotten industrial cities are doomed to oblivion. It could just as easily mean the opposite. For if no one knows which way the winds of fashion will blow—including economists, whose success is restricted to a prescient form of retrospection—then invention and reinvention is owned by no one. Consequently, what is potentially significant about an *aesthetics of economic development*, inspired by Florida but fuelled by an awareness of the slippages between physical and fantastical places, is that it seeks its validation elsewhere than with economists and city planners. Above all it seeks itself where it is, in the conditions it finds itself in, and in the people for whom creativity is a ready and useful home.

All of which brings us back to those decidedly unlovely parts of the post-industrial wasteland that remain serious problems for late capitalism. The revolution Florida charts, and the lives that creatives live, may seem a distant reality for the people inhabiting, for example, the American rust belt. Far from having transitioned to a hyperreal economy of creativity and human desire, these regions stumble forward, grounded as they have long been on the earth itself, doing their best to extract an honest dollar from a rock or tree—mineral, fiber, and 2x4. Maybe these regions will get lucky. Maybe the bohemians, with their unique ability to manipulate the norms of aesthetics, will transform their post-industrial wastelands into a new definition of authenticity: Detroit as the *art brut* of the creative economy. Incredibly, that is not entirely far-fetched: many artists are already attempting this and we watch their progress with great interest and enthusiasm.

But, once again, an appreciation of the situation does not need to imply that people should just wait, hope for the best, and continue to do nothing. The part of Florida's project that grates the most on earnest old-style Lefties is the invocation that everyone needs to become "entrepreneurial," to wit, newly duped cogs in the machinery of late capitalism. Although we share some of these concerns, our position is quite different. In our opinion there is simply no choice but for society to unleash the potential of its citizens and to create "creatives." The supposed slavery of such well-educated, well-fed, and spiritually fulfilled hipster mass-individuals is therefore, for us, a cringe-inducing projection of stunning condescension, at least four decades past its 'best before' date in the heyday of Herbert Marcuse's *One-Dimensional Man* (1964). A less grandiose goal than Marxist revolution for the dispossessed proletariat is the actual empowerment of individuals and regions that are indeed being left behind by a newer, consumption-oriented, spectral capitalism. And what we need is what we get with Florida: the aforementioned "revolution from the middle and above." This requires, fortunately or not, the active participation of all classes in a journey toward whatever form of creativity suits them. And of course it also requires and deserves political support of every possible kind.

So although Florida sometimes slips on his own conceptual terrain, we have to admire him for an attempt that is, alas, the best we got. The trick, taught by Jacques Derrida (1991), is to subject concepts to a certain interpretive rigor; Derrida calls it a "duty" and "responsibility," for example, the duty to *think* and to consider our relational responsibility to the *Other* (Derrida 1991, 108). But this trick is incomplete if one avoids the crucial second step: affirming one's complicity (for instance, one's complicity in capitalism) even as one insists on "free" choice and taking a brave step beyond what one could ever predetermine in advance of acting (see Derrida 1981, 40–3). In short, one takes a chance.

For his part Florida takes a chance, many of them in fact, and in some ways falls short. That, however, is the glory of a creative act done publicly. Certainly the (after all inevitable) failure of every act of creation in no way nullifies the attempt. Just the opposite, since one act, no matter how botched, is the condition of another act, to wit, a response.

So, then, what is to be done in the depressed locales skipped over by the "new economy"? Why not raid what has worked, and avoid what has failed, and take a chance on this elusive concept of creativity? Like many other communities, these places could proactively encourage the economic development of aesthetics. Take three conceptually tame, but in everyday practice actually wild, recommendations for challenged regions: (1) they could invest some real money in the arts, broadly conceived, and in artists; (2) they could encourage the development of Florida's three Ts: technology, talent, and tolerance, and; (3) they could invest heavily in their local universities and colleges, the one built site (or place) that Florida concedes will generate new wealth in smaller cities and regions. Why is that? Because although a university is an actual built place, its main function, if not its identity, is the creative production, and distillation, of ideas. Not accidentally, it's also a haven for a diverse and risk-taking segment of the population that includes bohemians, foreigners, and gays. Smart, informed, and visionary leadership at the university, fully supported by the community, is needed to improve the local scene of smaller cities across North America and Europe.

Obviously this is just a start. Above all, economically challenged nations, regions, cities, and communities need to stop thinking that a resource or manufacturing based-economy is a sure-fire solution to chronic decline and decay in the twenty-first century. It isn't. Leaders need to fully realize that an economy cannot live on rocks, wood, and factories alone. The good news is that it never could—and never has. There has always been a creative class living, working, and playing in the old economy regions. It's well past time that this group emerged as the central concern of strategies for economic development. For the alternative is, indeed, already very well scripted: this precious resource, like the natural resources that once fuelled the economy, will dwindle just as assuredly as have the minerals, the fiber, and the 2x4s. It's called brain drain.

Put perhaps too quickly, we are claiming that the solution lies in embracing an alternate representation of the economy. To this end urban planners and economists could do far worse than looking to social and cultural theorists who know a thing or three about representation in an age of late capitalism; who think with responsibility about productive and destructive slippages between the real and the idea, the material and immaterial, the concrete and fantastical. Arguably 'navel gazing' of this sort is a very good starting point to begin rethinking what late or contemporary capitalism looks like and what its positive and negative effects are for everyday life.

10

Franco "Bifo" Berardi and the future of capitalism: "*We have to run along the line of catastrophe*"

Andrew Pendakis

Franco Berardi is an important theorist of contemporary economic culture and a personal vector of political energy known to significant pockets of Left activists, organizers, students, and squatters all over the world. His work deals primarily with the political economies of "post-industrial" or "cognitive" capitalism, a focus that derives in part from the rich political struggles and intellectual legacy of Italian autonomist Marxism. He was kind enough in February of 2012 to answer questions posed to him across an ocean by a stranger.

* * *

Pendakis: There was a time, not so long ago, when unemployment could be imagined as the phenomenon most likely to directly volatilize existing social relations. The classic images of idleness and social wastage—bodies grouped in immense, jittery crowds or queues—rendered powerfully intelligible arguments (almost unphraseable today) about the inherently inefficient nature of a system which regularly leaves entire masses of its abstract human labor power and potentiality "unused." Mass unemployment clearly and crisply illustrated the idea that "capitalism wasn't working" (even as full employment and an end to the business cycle seemed to have been achieved in the Soviet Union). Much has changed, however, since unemployment was closely monitored by Keynesian politicians on both the left and right as the indicator most likely to win or lose an election. As early as 1979, Stuart Hall would famously note that being unemployed was no longer a reliable predictor of political affiliation. Class compositions have altered, leaving the sight lines of redundancy less clear than they once were. The collective transparency and "bare-life" of the soup line has been replaced in part with unemployed people in their mid-thirties thrown out across social space in the basements of their parents' homes. At the same time, much of the homogeneity that one might imagine as necessary to codify a consciousness of shared situation has been complicated by privatized, customized forms of cultural pleasure. What do you make of this conjuncture? Can unemployment function as a spur to politics in the West in the same way it has in places like Argentina, where new cultural and organizational forms sprang up to counteract the vacuum created by the loss of income and wages, but also the temporal rhythms of secure employment?

Bifo: *Unemployment is an effect of the capitalist perversion of the technological increase of productivity. The submission of the general intellect and of its technological output to the interests of profit and to the obsessive pursuit of accumulation is continuously transforming progress and discovery into impoverishment, and freedom into misery. The worker's interest in the reduction of work time and the intellectual ability to reduce the necessary time for production did converge in the 60s and 70s, making possible the revolution of information technology and the transformation of labor into info-labor. However, the opportunity of a general emancipation from exploitation and from salary was lost and reversed by neoliberal ideology and the counter-revolution of the 80s. The effect of this counter-revolution is massive unemployment and, now, after thirty years of neoliberal dictatorship, the generalized collapse of modern civilization and of the very infrastructures of social life.*

Unemployment is producing the condition for a social explosion opening the way to the revolutions of Egypt and Syria, and to the riots of London and Rome. The trend of increased unemployment cannot be reversed because society does not need work anymore. We have worked too much the last 500 years, and too much has been added to too much during the last 30. But capitalism is using the deadly blackmail of salary, and pushing people to work more, therefore pushing an increasing number of people into unemployment.

Only when society understands that we need to reduce the time of work, only when we are rid of the capitalist paradigm itself, will intellectual and technological progress cease to be a curse and become what it always already was: a source of freedom and wealth and well-being.

Pendakis: At first quietly, but then very obstreperously, the last decade has moved us squarely into a conjunctural and ideological space very far from that registered at the height of Clinton's "frictionless" 90s. That something is ending or beginning right before our eyes is an experience particularly remarkable for the generation (of which I am a part) who grew into consciousness at the very apex of the boom and its logics. Viewed from the perspective of a whole gamut of dwindling essential liquids and substances (oil, soil, water, cheap food, etc.), the classical era of infinite growth (and perpetual externalities) would appear to be over. Even analyzed away from its indispensable ecological considerations, many now doubt the capacity of today's "post-industrial" capitalism to generate the growth, stability, and employment necessary for its continued social legitimacy. Across a spectrum ranging from invocations of mass immiseration and social disruption to worries about blatant new forms of political authoritarianism, our moment is now very easily encoded within certain Left circles as terminal ("end times"). Though there is a great deal to recommend this position, I wonder if you might speculate a little about the possible futures of capitalism—that is, about the possibilities within the present conjuncture for retrenchment and evolution of the present neoliberal consensus (or some variation on it). What new "capitalism with a human face" can you see either thriving or limping across the next century? Are there, for example, technological conditions (in genetics or nanotechnology, for example) or new regimes of growth which you can imagine relaxing the existing tensions within the global system? Are there forms of politics that you can see evolving out of the present consensus that would function to regulate or manage our moment's changes? How convinced are you, for example, by those who imagine the possibility of a steady state capitalism, one modeled say on some extended variation on Japan?

***Bifo**: I do not see any "human face" of capitalism. In the past—for instance during the Clinton era, the age of the net economy and the dot.com boom—an expansion was possible and an alliance was established between venture capital and the emerging cognitive work force. But that alliance is over forever: financial capitalism has destroyed for good the social conditions that made possible a free expression of the creative class in the 90s. No new technological cycle will be able to rescue capitalism. Biotechnology and nanotechnology will possibly develop under the control of the military and will become tools for the tyrannical control of society in a time of generalized civil war.*

Financial predation is literally devastating the future. Look at what is happening in Greece: in order to pay an imaginary debt the Greeks are depleted of their physical, intellectual, and infra-structural resources. GNP is falling everywhere and debt is increasing. There can be no way back, when the intellectual resources of a country are predated and dissipated. In the 80s and in the 90s, research and the educational system were incremented, now they are de-financed and privatized to death.

Yes, it's true, Japan has been able to survive in a condition of no-growth for more than a decade. I don't think that Europe will be able to do the same, as the internal situation of the European countries is absolutely different from the ethnic, cultural, and social point of view. War and violence will explode everywhere in Europe in the coming years. As the price of energy becomes unsustainable, relations with the Middle East and with Russia are destined to fuel war. Nazism is the destiny of Europe.

Pendakis: How do things stand between postmodern irony as a dominant interpretive mode or "structure of feeling" and the possibility, now increasingly forecast by Marxists and liberals alike, of a long deflationary period ahead? Is there a distinction to be draw between irony and cynicism? Was the age of the surface in part dependent for its integrity on the relative stability of capitalist growth or can we imagine an interregnum in which the old media and cultural forms continue to prop up and sustain postmodern subjectivities? In Greece, for example, sociologists are noting remarkable demographic trends specific to an era of austerity: as wages and opportunity in the city dry up, many young and unemployed are moving back to family homes and farms in the country, where kinship networks and possibilities of subsistence are readier to hand. Perhaps, in other words, the half-century hold of the city on the country stands to be troubled or reversed in the next century. What are some of the possible cultural outcomes of this or other such shifts?

Bifo: *I refuse the post-modern conceptualization of irony that you mention. Post-modernism is more or less equally irony and cynicism, with both understood as cultural and linguistic modes of disenchantment. This is a refusal also made by Sloterdijk, for instance, in his* Critique of Cynical Reason. *Of course irony can be an expression of cynicism, but irony and cynicism should not be confused in any case.*

Cynicism is deceived moralism, a judgment of behavior that depends on a fixed system of (moral) values. Dialectical materialism, the philosophy of the past century, implied a form of moralism. Anything (progress, socialism, etc.) that moves in the direction of history is good; whatever opposes the movement of history is bad. Post-68 cynicism results from a painful awakening. It says: "since the truth has not been fulfilled, we'll align ourselves with the untruth." And this is where irony and cynicism differ. Ironic discourse never presupposes the existence of a truth that will be fulfilled or realized. Irony implies the infinite process of interpretation, whereas cynicism results from a (lost) faith. The cynic has lost his or her faith; the ironist never had a faith to begin with. In Jankelevitch's words: "[I]rony is never disenchanted for the good reason that irony has refused to be enchanted"(Jankelevitch 1964, 15–16).

Neither irony nor cynicism believes in the true foundation of law. While the cynical person bends to the law while mocking its false and pretentious values, the ironic person escapes the law altogether, creating a linguistic space where law has no effectiveness. The cynic wants to be on the side of power, even though he doesn't believe in its righteousness. The ironist simply refuses the game, recreating the world on the basis of language that is incongruent with reality. Whereas mass cynicism (Zynismus) is aggression, both suffered and inflicted, irony is based upon sympathy. While cynical behavior pivots upon a false relation with interlocutors, irony involves a shared suspension of reality. The use of irony implies a shared sense of assumptions and implications between oneself and one's listeners. Irony cannot be conflated with lying. As Jankelevitch writes: "Lying is a state of war, and irony is a state of peace. The liar is not in agreement with the cheated. The gullible consciousness is late in relation with the lying consciousness, which is trying to maintain its advantage. Irony, instead, is crediting the interlocutor of sagacity and treats him/her as a true partner of true dialogue. Irony incites intellection, and is calling a fraternal echo of understanding" (Jankelevitch 1964, 63–4).

Unfortunately, the cult of competition is inciting cynicism in those who are marginalized from the game. The language of the movement has to be ironic because irony is the construction of solidarity and of empathy outside the citadel of capitalist power. I think that the collapse of the capitalist civilization and the following breakdown of consumerism will open the way to a wave of ironic post-consumerism and frugality.

Pendakis: Khrushchev's promise to "bury" the West in socialist productivity and efficiency, as well as the viability of the kinds of "mixed-economies" envisioned in places like Britain and Sweden in the 50s, were undermined both by their own material failings (as well, paradoxically, by their own successes), but also by the discursive power of neoliberal imaginings of the market as an unthinkably nuanced and responsive form of distributional intelligence. Planning—still obviously functional on the level of the multinational enterprise or even nationally in the domain of monetary regulation—came to be imagined as inherently totalitarian, the violent subordination of actually existing diversity by the grayness and hubris of the Idea. In fact, we can in part trace back to this political genealogy the contemporary popular and theoretical fetish of an action without thought (see Gladwell 2005), the notion that "thinking things through" only disrupts the keener intelligence of instinct or simply and naively ignores the radical contingency and unpredictability of things (the fate of all "good intentions"). This is a position that, with very few exceptions, has been broadly reproduced and extended by many of the best contemporary philosophers, many of whom seem to implicitly prop up Sartre's old distinction between the spontaneity of the group in fusion and bad institutional inertia. Badiou (2005), Rancière (2010), Agamben (2000), Hardt and Negri (2000), etc. all err on the side of a politics of spontaneity and rupture, one less interested in the concrete proposition of new institutions than in the existential and material openness convoked by the failure of old ones. I wonder how you envision your own political philosophy fitting into this conjuncture. Can or should we envision an immanently democratic "plan" today? What residues or possibilities continue to adhere in the concept of planning today?

Bifo: *Neoliberalism has been able to interrupt the disrupting potency of networked culture and networked society. The identification of a planned economy with totalitarian statism has certainly been an abuse and a mystification, but one cannot deny that the Invisible Hand of the neoliberal ideologues has been much better able to cope with the Networked Global Mind (see Kevin Kelly's 1994* Out of Control*) than the socialist's attempts to regulate complexity. In fact, Thatcher's and Reagan's de-regulation—far from being a libertarian dissolution of the rules—has seen the imposition of a violent order of purely economic regulation of daily life. This is described very nicely by Michel Foucault in* The Birth of Biopolitics *(2008), where he speaks of the construction of homo economicus and the reduction of life to the conceptual frame of enterprise.*

But the violent self-implementation of the economic rule has been much more efficient than the political planning of the social-democratic model. Therefore I don't think that we should blame those authors who have tried to start from the point of view of spontaneity rather than from the point of view of centralization and political planning.

That said, it is useless to insist on the rhizomatic and multitudinarian side of the process, as capitalism has become totally rhizomatic: the explosion of racism and populist barbarianism is exposing the dark side of the multitude. However, we cannot either go back to the old good ideas of a rational centralized government of the economy. We have to run along the line of catastrophe. What is important is to abandon any illusion about the possibility of a continuation of modern civilization and of democracy, and to start a process of autonomization of the general intellect.

Pendakis: The sudden appearance within popular discourse of America's growing inequality has been something of a surprise for many on the Left. This is not because the numbers were equivocal—Marxist and heterodox economist have been documenting these changes for the last quarter century—but because of the abruptness with which the tenor of the 90s made contact with economic and ideological coordinates broadly suppressed by its dominant self-understanding. Post-Thatcherite associations of equality with totalitarian sameness and monotony, rapid growth in the "emerging economies," as well as the re-codification of risk as individualist adventure and experimentation all worked to drain distributions of wealth of any useable political leverage. It would appear that the Occupy Protests have dramatically altered this situation. If "equality" was in some sense the keyword par excellence of oppositional politics in the age stretched out between Rousseau's status anxiety and Keynesian welfare consensus, how do you see this notion faring as a lightning rod for political praxis and imagination in the twenty-first century? If not equality, what other master concepts do you see mediating the political struggles to come?

Bifo: *The real problem today is not equality, but the actual survival of the majority of the Western population, a dramatic reversal of the promise of prosperity that has long been the foundation of political consensus. I don't see a socialist project of egalitarianism in the movements that are spreading all over the Western world, nor do I see such a perspective in the Arab upheaval. I see the despair produced by the breakdown of the framework of expectations that has constituted the common ground of civil society. As an effect I see two possible outcomes. The first is the growing barbarization of society, the dissolution of political consensus, ethno-civil war, racism and violence, and—as an answer—violent riots of the unemployed and precarious workers. The second is the secession of a part of society and the creation of an autonomous sphere of production, distribution, and cultural life. A necessary premise for a conscious and organized shift towards this process of autonomization is the explicit abandonment of the illusion of democracy, the declaration of non-collaboration, non-participation, and a refusal to pay the symbolic and economic debt that is implied by the notion of being "part of society." This will involve massive insolvency, the re-appropriation of what is needed by the seceding community, but also occupation and armed defense of the spaces of autonomy.*

Frugality will be the defining feature of this secession in the field of consumption, just as self-organization of the general intellect will be its defining feature in the field of production.

References

#OWS. 2011. "Occupy Wall Street: The Worldwide Revolution Continues!" *Occupy Wall Street*.http://occupywallst.org/; accessed 4 December 2012.

Abbott, Stacy. 2007. *Celluloid Vampires: Life After Death in the Modern World*. Austin: University of Texas Press.

Adorno, Theodor, and Max Horkheimer. 2002. *Dialectic of Enlightenment*. Translated by Edmund Jephcott. Stanford University Press: Stanford CA.

Agamben, Giorgio. 2000. *Means Without Ends: Notes On Politics*. Minneapolis: University of Minnesota Press.

Agger, Ben. 2004. *Speeding Up Fast Capitalism: Cultures, Jobs, Families, Schools, Bodies*. Boulder, CO: Paradigm Publishers.

Akerlof, George A., and Robert J. Shiller. 2009. *Animal Spirits: How Human Psychology Drives the Economy*. Princeton, NJ: Princeton University Press.

Albo, Gregory, Sam Ginden, and Leo Panich. 2010. *In and Out of Crisis: The Global Financial Meltdown and Left Alternatives*. Oakland, CA: PM Press.

Althusser, Louis. 2009. *Reading Capital*. London: Verso.

—1971. "Ideology and Ideological State Apparatuses: Notes Toward an Investigation." In *Lenin and Philosophy and Other Essays*. Translated by Ben Brewster. New York and London: Monthly Review Press: 127–88.

Anderson, Benedict, R. 1983. *Imagined Communities: Reflections on the Origin and Spread of Nationalism*. London: Verso.

Appadurai, Arjun. 1996. *Modernity at Large: Cultural Dimensions of Globalization*. Minneapolis: University of Minnesota Press.

—1992. "Global Ethnoscapes: Notes and Queries for a Transnational Anthropology." In *Recapturing Anthropology: Working in the Present*, edited by Richard Fox, 191–210. Santa Fe: School of American Research.

Appleby, Joyce. 2011. "The Cultural Roots of Capitalism." *Historically Speaking* 12(5): 9–10.

Arendt, Hannah. 2008. *The Human Condition* [1958]. Chicago: University of Chicago Press.

Aries, Philippe. 1980. "Two Successive Motivations for the Declining Birth Rate in the West." *Population and Development Review* 6(4): 645–50.

Aronowitz, Stanley, and William DiFazio. 2010. *The Jobless Future*, 2nd edition. Minneapolis: University of Minnesota Press.

Arrighi, Giovanni. 1994. *The Long Twentieth Century: Money, Power, and the Origins of Our Times*. London: Verso.

Atkinson, Rowland, and Hazel Easthope. 2009. "The Pursuit of Creativity Strategies in Australia's Cities." *International Journal of Urban and Regional Research* 33(1): 64–79.

Badiou, Alain. 2005. *Metapolitics*. London: Verso.

Bagsak, Isang. 2011. "Open Letter to Occupy San Diego." *All Peoples Revolutionary Front.* http://aprfsandiego.wordpress.com/2011/10/26/aprfronts-open-letter-to-occupy-san-diego/; accessed 4 December 2012.

Baker, Nicholson. 1988. *The Mezzanine.* New York: Vintage Books.

Balibar, Étienne. 2007. *The Philosophy of Marx.* Translated by Chris Turner. London: Verso.

Ball, Karyn. 2006. "A Democracy is Being Beaten." *English Studies in Canada* 32.1 (May): 45–76.

Ballard, J. G. 2000. *Super-Cannes.* New York: HarperCollins.

Barbour, Charles, and Thomas M. Kemple. 2005. "Writing the Republic: Politics and Polemics in *The German Ideology*." New York: Telos 130: 9–37.

Barnes, Kendall, Gordon Waitt, Nichlas Gill, and Chris Gibson. 2006. "Community and Nostalgia in Urban Revitalisation: A Critique of Urban Village and Creative Class Strategies as Remedies for Social Problems." *Australian Geographer* 37(3): 335–54.

Barrie, J. M. 1930. As quoted in *The New Dictionary of Thought: A Cyclopedia of Quotations*, edited by Tyron Edwards et al. Champaign, IL: Standard Books..

Bateman, Milford. 2010. *Why Microfinance Doesn't Work: The Destructive Rise of Local Neoliberalism.* London: Zed.

Bateson, Gregory, Don. D. Jackson, Jay, Haley, and John Weakland. 1956. "Towards a Theory of Schizophrenia." *Behavioral Science* 1: 251–64.

Baucom, Ian. 2005. *Specters of the Atlantic: Finance Capital, Slavery, and the Philosophy of History.* Durham, NC: Duke University Press.

Baudrillard, Jean. 1983. *Simulacra and Simulations.* Translated by Paul Foss, Paul Patton, and Philip Beitchman. New York: Semiotext(e).

—1981. "The Ideological Genesis of Needs." In *For a Critique of the Political Economy of the Sign.* Translated by Charles Levin. New York: Telos.

BBC News. 2008. "Ageing Issue: 'Ticking Time Bomb'." *BBC News*, April 16. http://news.bbc.co.uk/2/hi/business/7350130.stm; accessed 20 July 2011.

Bell, Daniel. 1979. *The Cultural Contradictions of Capitalism*, 2nd edition. London: Heinemann.

Beller, Jonathan. 2006. *The Cinematic Mode of Production: Attention Economy and the Society of the Spectacle.* Lebanon, NH: Dartmouth University Press.

Bello, Walden, Nicola Bullard, and Kamal Malhotra, (eds.) 2000. *Global Finance: New Thinking on Regulating Speculative Capital Markets.* London: Zed.

Ben-Yoseph, Miriam and Deborah Nodler Rosen, (eds.) 2009. *Where We Find Ourselves: Jewish Women Around the World Write About Home.* Albany, NY: SUNY Press.

Benjamin, Bret. 2007. *Invested Interests: Capital, Culture and the World Bank.* Minneapolis and London: University of Minnesota Press.

Benjamin, Walter. 2008. *The Work of Art in the Age of Mechanical Reproduction.* Translated by J. Underwood. London: Penguin Books.

Bentham, Jeremy. 1988. *A Fragment on Government* [1776]. Edited by J. H. Burns and H. L. A. Hart. Cambridge: Cambridge University Press.

Berardi, Franco. 2011. *After The Future.* Edinburgh: AK Press.

—2009a. *Precarious Rhapsody: Semiocapitalism and the Pathologies of the Post-Alpha Generation.* London: Autonomedia.

—2009b. *The Soul at Work: From Alienation to Autonomy*. Los Angeles, CA: Semiotext(e).

Berlin, Isaiah. 1980. *Against the Current: Essays in the History of Ideas*. New York: Viking Press.

Berman, Marshall. 1982. *All that is Solid Melts into Air: The Experience of Modernity*. New York: Penguin.

Binnie, Jon, and Beverly Skeggs. 2004. "Cosmopolitan Knowledge and the Production and Consumption of Sexualized Space: Manchester's Gay Village." *Sociological Review* 52(1): 39–61.

Blackburn, Robin. 2007. *Age Shock: How Finance Is Failing Us*. London: Verso.

—2004. *Banking on Death: Or, Investing in Life: The History and Future of Pensions*. London: Verso.

Bloch, Ernst. 1995. *The Principle of Hope, Volume One*. Translated by Neville Plaice, Stephen Plaice, and Paul Knight. Cambridge, MA: MIT Press.

Boehm, Stephen, Christian Gehrke, Heinz D. Kurz, and Richard Sturn, eds. 2002. *Is There Progress in Economics?: Knowledge, Truth, and the History of Economic Thought*. Cheltenham, UK and Northampton, MA: Edward Elgar.

Boltanski, Luc, and Ève Chiapello. 2005. *The New Spirit of Capitalism*. Translated by Gregory Elliott. London: Verso.

Booth, Philip, ed. 2012. *... and the Pursuit of Happiness: Wellbeing and the Role of Government*. London: The Institute of Economic Affairs.

Boschken, H. L. 2003. "Global Cities, Systematic Power, and Upper-Middle Class Influence." *Urban Affairs* 38(6): 808–30.

Botton, Alain de. 2009. *The Pleasures and Sorrows of Work*. New York: Pantheon.

Bourdieu, Pierre. 1998. *Practical Reason: On the Theory of Action*. Stanford, CA: Stanford University Press.

—1986. "The Forms of Capital." In *Handbook of Theory and Research for the Sociology of Education*, edited by John G. Richardson, translated by Richard Nice. New York: Greenwood Press: 240–56.

Brenner, Robert. 2009. *The Economics of Global Turbulence*, 2nd edition. New York: Verso.

Breuer, Josef, and Sigmund Freud. 2000. *Studies in Hysteria* [1895]. New York: Basic Books.

Brown, Wendy. 2005. "Neoliberalism and the End of Liberal Democracy." In *Edgework: Critical Essays on Knowledge and Politics*. Princeton, NJ: Princeton University Press: 37–58.

Buck-Morss, Susan. 1995. "Envisioning Capital: Political Economy on Display." *Critical Inquiry* 21: 434–67.

Caldwell, John C. 1976. "Toward A Restatement of Demographic Transition Theory." *Population and Development Review* 2(3/4): 321–66.

Callon, Michael, Yuval Millo, and Fabian Muniesa. 2007. *Market Devices*. Malden, MA and Oxford: Blackwell.

Carlyle, Thomas. 1969. *Critical and Miscellaneous Essays, volume 6* [1866]. London: Chapman and Hall.

Carver, Terrell. 1998. *The Postmodern Marx*. Pennsylvania: The Pennsylvania State University Press.

Case, Sue-Ellen. 2009. "Tracking the Vampire." In *Feminist and Queer Performances: Critical Strategies*. Palgrave MacMillan: New York: 66–87.

Castells, Manuel. 2010. *The Rise of The Network Society*, 2nd edition. UK: Blackwell Publishing Ltd.

Castiglia, Christopher. 2008. *Interior States: Institutional Consciousness and the Inner Life of Democracy in the Antebellum United States*. Durham, NC: Duke University Press.

Cerni, Paula. 2007. "The Age of Consumer Capitalism." http://clogic.eserver.org/2007/Cerni.pdf; accessed 26 January 2012.

Certeau, Michel de. 1984. *The Practice of Everyday Life*. Berkeley: University of California Press.

Chicchi, Federico. 2010. "On the Threshold of Capital, At the Thresholds of the Common: Sidenotes on the Ambivalences of Biopolitical Capitalism." In *Crisis in the Global Economy: Financial Markets, Social Struggles, and New Political Scenarios*, edited by Andrea Fumagalli and Sandro Mezzadra, translated by Jason Francis McGimsy . Los Angeles: Semiotext(e): 139–52.

Christophers, Brett. 2007. "Enframing Creativity: Power, Geographical Knowledges, and the Media Economy." *Transactions of the Institute of British Geographers* 32(2): 235–47.

Comaroff, Jean, and John L Comaroff. 2001. *Millennial Capitalism and the Culture of Neoliberalism*. Durham, NC and London: Duke University Press.

—2000. "Millennial Capitalism: First Thoughts on a Second Coming." *Public Culture* 12(2): 291–343.

Comunian, Roberta, Alessandra Faggian, and Qian Cher Li. 2010. "Unrewarded Careers in the Creative Class: The Strange Case of Bohemian Graduates." *Papers Regional Science* 89(2): 389–410.

Coté, Mark, and Jennifer Pybus. 2007. "Learning to Immaterial Labour 2.0: MySpace and Social Networks." *Ephemera* 7(1): 88–106.

Coupland, Douglas. 1991. *Generation X: Tales for an Accelerated Culture*. New York: St. Martin's Press.

Coward, Noël. 1963. "Sayings of the Week." *The Observer*, June 21. London.

Cramer, Aron. 2012. "Davos and the Future of Capitalism." http://www.theatlantic.com/business/archive /2012/01/davos-and-the-future-of-capitalism/251991/; accessed 6 February 2012.

Crawford, Matthew. 2009. *Shop Class as Soulcraft: An Inquiry into the Value of Work*. London: Penguin.

Crozier, Michel, Samuel Huntington, and Joji Watanuki. 1975. *The Crisis of Democracy: Report on the Governability of Democracies to the Trilateral Commission*. New York: New York University Press.

De Angelis, Massimo. 2007. *The Beginning of History: Value Struggles and Global Capitalism*. London and Ann Arbor, MI: Pluto.

Dean, Jodi. 2005. "Communicative Capitalism: Circulation and the Foreclosure of Politics." *Cultural Politics* 1(1): 51–74.

Debord, Guy. 1994. *The Society of the Spectacle* [1967]. Translated by Daniel Nicholson-Smith. New York: Zone Books.

—1983. *Society of the Spectacle* [1967]. Translated by Ken Knabb. Detroit: Black and Red.

—1963. "Never Work." http://www.marxists.org/reference/archive/debord/1963/never-work.htm; accessed 15 November 2011.

Dee, Jonathan. 2010. *The Privileges*. New York: Random House.

Deleuze, Gilles. 1995. "Postscript on Control Societies." In *Negotiations 1972–1990*, translated by Marin Joughin. New York: Columbia University Press: 176–82.
—1992. "Postscript on the Societies of Control." *October* 59: 3–7 [reprinted in 1995. *Negotiations*, translated by Martin Joughlin. Columbia University Press].
—and Félix Guattari. 1984. *Anti-Oedipus: Capitalism and Schizophrenia*. Translated by Robert Hurley, Mark Seem, and Helen R. Lane. London: Continuum.
Derrida, Jacques. 2007. "The Retrait of Metaphor." In *Psyche: Inventions of the Other, Volume 1*, edited by Peggy Kamuf and Elizabeth Rottenburg. Stanford, CA: Stanford University Press: 40–8.
—1998. *Resistances of Psychoanalysis*. Translated by Peggy Kamuf, Pascale-Anne Brault, and Michael Naas. Stanford, CA: Stanford University Press.
—1991. "'Eating Well', Or the Calculation of the Subject: An Interview with Jacques Derrida." In *Who Comes After the Subject?*, edited by Eduardo Cadava, Peter Connor, and Jean-Luc Nancy. New York: Routledge: 96–119.
—1982. "White Mythology: Metaphor in the Text of Philosophy." In *The Margins of Philosophy*. Chicago: University of Chicago Press: 207–72.
—1981. *Positions*. Translated and annotated by Alan Bass. Chicago: University of Chicago Press.
Drucker, Peter Ferdinand. 1996. *The Pension Fund Revolution* [1976]. New Brunswick, NJ: Transaction Publisher.
Dufresne, Todd. 2000. *Tales from the Freudian Crypt: The Death Drive in Text and Context*. Stanford CA: Stanford University Press.
Duménil, Gérard, and Dominique Lévy. 2004. *Capital Resurgent: Roots of the Neoliberal Revolution*. Cambridge: Harvard University Press.
Eagleton, Terry. 2003. *Sweet Violence: The Idea of the Tragic*. Oxford: Blackwell Publishing.
Economist, The. 2009a. "Ageing in the Rich World: The End of Retirement." *The Economist*, June 25. http://www.economist.com/node/13900145; accessed 20 July 2011.
Economist, The. 2009b. "A Slow-Burning Fuse." *The Economist*, June 25. http://www.economist.com/node/13888045; accessed 20 July 2011.
Economist, The. 2009c. "A World of Methuselahs." *The Economist*, June 25. http://www.economist.com/node/13888102; accessed 20 July 2011.
Edelman, Lee. 2005. *No Future: Queer Theory and the Death Drive*. Durham, NC: Duke University Press.
Eicholz, Hans, L. 2011. "What's Left for Economics? A Comment on Appleby." *Historically Speaking* 12(5): 11–12.
Elliot, Paul. 2003. "The Origins of the 'Creative Class': Provincial Urban Society, Scientific Culture and Socio-Political Marginality in Britain in the Eighteenth and Nineteenth Centuries." *Social History* 28(3): 361–87.
Eriksen, Thomas, Hylland. 2002. *Ethnicity and Nationalism: Anthropological Perspectives*, 2nd edition. London: Pluto Press.
Faflak, Joel. 2007. *Romantic Psychoanalysis: The Burden of the Mystery*. Albany, NY: State University of New York Press.
Favret, Mary A. 2010. *War at a Distance: Romanticism and the Making of Modern Wartime*. Princeton: Princeton University Press.

Featherstone, Mike. 1991. *Consumer Culture and Postmodernism*. London: Sage.
Ferguson, Niall. 2008. *The Ascent of Money: A Financial History of the World*. New York: Penguin.
Ferris, Joshua. 2007. *Then We Came to the End*. New York: Little, Brown and Company.
Fink, Jonny. 1996. "Douglas Coupland's *Generation X* Neo-logisms." April 29. http://www.scn.org/~jonny/genx.html; accessed 15 November 2012.
Florida, Richard. 2004. *The Rise of the Creative Class*. New York: Basic Books.
Food and Agriculture Organization of the United Nations. 2010. "Global Hunger Declining, But Still Unacceptably High." *Economic and Social Development Department*, September 2010. http://www.fao.org/docrep/012/al390e/al390e00.pdf; accessed 20 June 2011.
Foster, John Bellamy, and Fred Magdoff. 2009. *The Great Financial Crisis: Causes and Consequences*. New York: Monthly Review Press.
Foucault, Michel. 2008. *The Birth of Biopolitics: Lectures at the Collège de France, 1978–79*. Basingstoke: Palgrave Macmillan.
—2007. "The Meshes of Power." In *Space, Knowledge and Power: Foucault and Geography*, edited by Jeremy W. Crampton and Stuart Elden. Burlington, VT and Aldershot, UK: Ashgate Publishing: 153–62.
—1990. *The History of Sexuality* [1978]. Translated by Robert Hurley. New York: Vintage Books.
—1983a. "On the Genealogy of Ethics: An Overview of Work in Progress." In *Michel Foucault: Beyond Structuralism and Hermeneutics*, edited by Hubert L. Dreyfus and Paul Rabinow, 2nd edition. Chicago, IL: University of Chicago Press: 229–52.
—1983b. "The Subject and Power." In *Michel Foucault: Beyond Structuralism and Hermeneutics*, edited by Hubert L. Dreyfus and Paul Rabinow, 2nd edition. Chicago, IL: University of Chicago Press: 208–26.
—1978. *The History of Sexuality, Volume 1: An Introduction*. New York: Vintage.
—1977. *Discipline and Punish: The Birth of the Modern Prison* [1975]. Translated by David Hurley. New York: Vintage Books.
Frankfurt, Harry. 2005. *On Bullshit*. Princeton, New Jersey: Princeton University Press.
—1988. *The Importance of What We Care About: Philosophical Essays*. Cambridge: Cambridge University Press.
Frey, Bruno S. 2008. *Happiness: A Revolution in Economics*. Cambridge, MA: MIT Press.
Fukuyama, Francis. 1993. *The End of History and the Last Man*. New York: Perennial.
Galbraith, John Kenneth. 1958. *The Affluent Society*. Boston, MA: Houghton Mifflin.
Galor, Oded, and David N. Weil. 2000. "Population, Technology, and Growth: From Malthusian Stagnation to the Demographic Transition and Beyond." *The American Economic Review* 90(4): 806–28.
Gane, Nicholas, and David Beer. 2008. *New Media: The Key Concepts*. Oxford and New York: Berg.
Gee, Ellen, and Gloria Gutman, eds. 2000. *The Overselling of Population Aging:*

Apocalyptic Demography, Intergenerational Challenges, and Social Policy. Oxford: Oxford University Press.

Gelder, Ken. 1994. *Reading the Vampire.* Abingdon, UK: Routledge.

Gellner, Ernest. 1983. *Nations and Nationalism.* Ithaca, NY: Cornell University Press.

Gevisser, Mark. 2007. *Thabo Mbeki: The Dream Deferred.* Johannesburg: Jonathan Ball.

Gibson, Chris, and Natascha Klocker. 2005. "The 'Cultural Turn' in Australian Regional Economic Development Discourse: Neoliberalising Creativity?" *Geographical Research* 43(1): 93–102.

—2004. "Academic Publishing as 'Creative' Industry, and Recent Discourses of 'Creative Economies': Some Critical Reflections." *Area* 36(4): 423–34.

Gibson-Graham, J. K. 2006. *The End of Capitalism (As We Knew It): A Feminist Critique of Political Economy.* Minneapolis: University of Minnesota Press.

Giddens, Anthony. 1971. *Capitalism and Modern Social Theory: An Analysis of the Writings of Marx, Durkheim, and Max Weber.* Cambridge, UK: Cambridge University Press.

Giroux, Henry A. 2008. *Against the Terror of Neoliberalism: Politics Beyond the Age of Greed.* Boulder, CO: Paradigm.

Gladwell, Malcolm. 2005. *Blink: The Power of Thinking without Thinking.* New York: Back Bay Books.

Glaeser, E. L. 2000. "The New Economics of Urban and Regional Growth." In *The Oxford Handbook of Economic Geography,* edited by G.S. Clark, M.P. Feldman, and M.S. Gertler. Oxford: Oxford University Press, 83–98.

Glenn, Diana, Eric Bouvet, and Sonia Floriani (eds) 2011. *Imagining Home: Migrants and the Search for a New Belonging.* Adelaide, Australia: Wakefield Press.

Goffman, Erving. 1967. "On Face-Work: An Analysis of Ritual Elements in Social Interaction." In *Interaction Ritual: Essays on Face-to-Face Behavior.* New York: Anchor Books: 5–45.

Goonewardena, Kanishka, and Stefan Kipper. 2005. "Spaces of Difference: Reflections from Toronto on Multiculturalism, Bourgeois Urbanism, and the Possibility of Radical Urban Politics." *International Journal of Urban and Regional Research* 29(3): 670–78.

Gottlieb, Evan. 2007. *Feeling British: Sympathy and National Identity in Scottish and English Writing, 1707–1832.* Lewisburg, PA: Bucknell University Press.

Greenberg, Gary. 2010. "The War on Unhappiness: Goodbye Freud, Hello Positive Thinking." *Harper's Magazine* 321.1924 (September): 27–35.

Gupta, Akhil, and James Ferguson, eds. 1997. *Culture, Politics, Place: Explorations in Cultural Anthropology.* Durham, NC: Duke University Press.

Haiven, Max. 2011. "Finance as Capital's Imagination?: Reimagining Value and Culture in an Age of Fictitious Capital and Crisis." *Social Text* 108: 93–124.

—, and Alex Khasnabish. 2011. "What is the Radical Imagination: A Special Issue." *Affinities* 4(2): i–xxxvii.

Hall, Stuart. 1979. "The Great Moving Right Show." *Marxism Today* (January): 14–20.

Hanieh, Adam. 2011. "Egypt's 'Orderly Transition'? International Aid and the Rush to Structural Adjustment." *Jadaliyya.* http://www.jadaliyya.com/pages/index/

1711/egypt%E2%80%99s-%E2%80%98orderly-transition%E2%80%99-international-aid-and (accessed May 29 2011).
Hannerz, Ulf. 1989. "Notes on the Global Ecumene." *Public Culture* 1(2): 66–75.
Hansen, Høgni Kalsø, and Thomas Niedomysl. 2009. Migration of the Creative Class: Evidence from Sweden." *Journal of Economic Geography* 9(2): 191–206.
Haraway, Donna. 1997. "Race: Universal Donors in a Vampire Culture." In *Modest_Witness@Second_Millenium.FemaleMan_Meets_OncoMouse: Feminism and Technoscience*. New York: Routledge: 213–66.
—1991. *Simians, Cyborgs, and Women: The Reinvention of Nature*. New York: Routledge.
Hardt, Michael, and Antonio Negri. 2009. *Commonwealth*. Massachusetts: Belknap Press.
—2000. *Empire*. Cambridge, MA: Harvard University Press.
Harvey, David. 2007. *A Brief History of Neoliberalism*. Oxford: Oxford University Press.
—2006. *The Limits to Capital*, 2nd edition. London and New York: Verso.
—2003. *The New Imperialism*. Oxford: Oxford University Press.
—1992. "From Space to Place and Back Again: Reflections on the Condition of Postmodernity." In *Mapping the Futures: Local Cultures, Global Change*, edited by Jon Bird, Barry Curtis, Tim Putnam, George Robertson, and Lisa Tickner, 3–29. New York: Routledge.
—1991. *The Condition of Postmodernity: An Enquiry into the Origins of Cultural Change*. New York: Wiley-Blackwell.
—1990. *The Condition of Postmodernity*. Massachusetts: Blackwell Publishing.
Haug, Wolfgang, Fritz. 1986. *Critique of Commodity Aesthetics: Appearance, Sexuality and Advertising in Capitalist Society*. Translated by Robert Beck. Cambridge, UK: Polity Press.
Hayek, Friedrich von. 2006. *The Road to Serfdom* [1944]. London: Routledge.
Hayles, N. Katherine. 1999. *How We Became Posthuman: Virtual Bodies in Cybernetics, Literature, and Informatics*. Chicago: University of Chicago Press.
Healy, Teresa (ed.) 2010. *The Harper Record*. Ottawa, ON: The Canadian Centre for Policy Alternatives.
Hegel, G. W. F. 1977. *The Phenomenology of Spirit* [1807]. Translated by A. V. Miller. Oxford: Oxford University Press.
—1969. *The Science of Logic* [1812–16]. Translated by A. V. Miller. London: G. Allen & Unwin.
Heller, Agnes. 1976. *The Theory of Need in Marx*. New York: Allison and Busby.
Henwood, Doug. 2003. *After the New Economy*. New York: New Press.
Hilferding, Rudolph. 2006. *Finance Capital: A Study in the Latest Phase of Capitalist Development*. London, New York: Routledge.
Hodge, Roger D. 2010. *The Mendacity of Hope*. New York: HarperCollins.
Holiday. DVD. Directed by George Cukor. 1938. Culver City, California: Columbia/Tristar, 2006.
Holmes, Brian. 2009. "Is it Written in the Stars?" *Continental Drift*. November 6, 2009. http://brianholmes.wordpress.com/2009/11/06/is-it-written-in-the-stars/; accessed 14 November 2011.
Invisible Committee, The. 2009. *The Coming Insurrection*. Los Angeles: Semiotext(e).

Jameson, Fredric. 2003. "The End of Temporality." *Critical Inquiry* 29(4): 695–718.
—1997. "Culture and Finance Capital." *Critical Inquiry* 24 (1): 246–65.
—1992. *The Geopolitical Aesthetic: Cinema and Space in the World System.* Bloomington: Indiana University Press.
—1991. *Postmodernism, or, The Cultural Logic of Late Capitalism.* London and New York: Verso.
—1991. *Postmodernism: or, The Cultural Logic of Late Capitalism.* Durham, NC: Duke University Press.
—1984. "Postmodernism, or The Cultural Logic of Late Capitalism." *New Left Review* (146): 53–92.
—1983. "Postmodernism and Consumer Society." In *The Anti-Aesthetic: Essays on Postmodern Culture*, edited by Hal Foster, 111–25. Port Townsend, WA: Bay Press.
—1981. *The Political Unconscious.* Ithaca, NY: Cornell University Press.
—1976. "Introduction/Prospectus: To Reconsider the Relationship of Marxism to Utopian Thought." *The Minnesota Review* 6: 53–8.
Jankelevitch, Vladimir. 1964. *L'ironie.* Flammarion: Paris.
Kapferer, Judith. 2010. "Twilight of the Enlightenment: The Art Fair, the Culture Industry, and the 'Creative Class.'" *Social Analysis* 54(2) 2: 9–27.
Kelley, Robin D. G. 2002. *Freedom Dreams: The Black Radical Imagination.* Boston: Beacon.
Kelly, Kevin. 1994. *Out of Control: The New Biology of Machines, Social Systems, and the Economic World.* Boston: Addison-Wesley.
Kemple, Thomas M. 2000. "Post-Marx: Temporal Rhetoric and Textual Action in 'The Communist Manifesto.'" *Rethinking Marxism* 12(2): 44–60.
—1995. *Reading Marx Writing: Melodrama, the Market, and the "Grundrisse."* Stanford, CA: Stanford University Press.
Kingfisher, Catherine, and Jeff Maskovsky. 2008. "Introduction: The Limits of Neoliberalism." *Critique of Anthropology* 28(2): 115–26.
Kingwell, Mark. 2008. "Idling Toward Heaven: The Last Defense You Will Ever Need." *Queen's Quarterly* 115(4): 569–85.
—, and Joshua Glenn. 2008. *The Idler's Glossary.* Emeryville, ON: Biblioasis.
Kittler, Friedrich. 2010. *Optical Media: Berlin Lectures 1999.* Translated by Anthony Enns. London: Polity Press.
Klein, Naomi. 2000. "New Branded World." *No Logo.* London: Flamingo: 3–26.
Kollewe, Julia, and Philip Inman. 2011. "Value of Global Pension Funds Hits Record High." *The Guardian*, February 7, 2011. http://www.guardian.co.uk/business/2011/feb/07/pension-funds-assets-liabilities; accessed 20 July 2011.
Krätke, Stefan. 2010. "'Creative Cities' and the Rise of the Dealer Class: A Critique of Richard Florida's Approach to Urban Theory." *International Journal of Urban and Regional Research* 34(4): 835–53.
Kroker, Arthur. 1992. *The Possessed Individual: Technology and the French Postmodern.* New York: St. Martin's Press.
Krugman, Paul. 2003. *The Return of Depression Economics.* New York: W. W. Norton & Company.
Kuhn, T. S. 1962. *The Structure of Scientific Revolutions.* Chicago: University of Chicago Press.
Laclau, Ernesto. 2007. *On Populist Reason.* New York: Verso.

—1996. *Emancipation(s)*. London: Verso.
Lakoff, George, and Mark Johnson. 1980. *Metaphors We Live By*. Chicago: University of Chicago Press.
Langley, Paul. 2008. *The Everyday Life of Global Finance: Saving and Borrowing in Anglo-America*. Oxford and New York: Oxford University Press.
Lash, Scott. 2010. *Intensive Culture: Social Theory, Religion and Contemporary Capitalism*. Los Angeles: SAGE
—and John Urry. 1987. *The End of Organized Capitalism*. Cambridge: Polity.
Latour, Bruno. 1983. "Visualization and Cognition: Drawing Things Together." http://www.bruno-latour.fr/sites/default/files/21-DRAWING-THINGS-TOGETHER-GB.pdf; accessed 13 November 2011.
Layard, Richard. 2005. *Happiness: Lessons from a New Science*. London: Penguin.
Lazzarato, Maurizio. 2002. "From Biopower to Biopolitics." Translated by Ivan A. Ramirez. http://www.generation-online.org/c/fcbiopolitics.htm; accessed 7 July 2011.
—1996. "Immaterial Labour." Translated by Paul Colilli and Ed Emery. http://www.generation-online.org/c/fcimmateriallabour3.htm
Lehmann, Chris. 2010. *Rich People Stuff*. New York: OR Books.
Lesthaeghe, Ron. 2007. "Second Demographic Transition." *Encyclopedia of Sociology*, edited by George Ritzer. London: Wiley-Blackwell.
Levinson, Mark. 2011. "The Politics of Inequality." *Dissent* 58(2): 92–5.
Lipietz, Alan. 1987. *Mirages and Miracles: The Crisis of Global Fordism*. London: Verso.
LiPuma, Edward, and Benjamin Lee. 2004. *Financial Derivatives and the Globalization of Risk*. Durham, NC and London: Duke University Press.
Locke, John. 2002. *Second Treatise on Government* [1690]. Edited by Tom Crawford. London: Dover.
—1988. *Two Treatises of Government* [1689]. Edited by Peter Laslett. Cambridge: Cambridge University Press.
—1975. *An Essay Concerning Human Understanding* [1690]. Edited by Peter H. Nidditch. Oxford: Clarendon Press.
Longman, Philip. 2011. "Think Again: Global Aging." *Foreign Policy*, November. http://www.foreignpolicy.com/articles/2010/10/11/think_again_global_aging; accessed 20 July 2011.
—2004. *The Empty Cradle: How Falling Birthrates Threaten World Prosperity and What To Do About It*. New York: Basic Books.
Lotringer, Sylvère. 2004. "Foreword: We the Multitude." In *A Grammar of the Multitude: For an Analysis of Contemporary Forms of Life*, by Paulo Virno, translated by Isabella Bertoletti, James Cascaito, and Andrea Casson. Los Angeles: Semiotext(e): 7–19.
Lucarelli, Stefano. 2010. "Financialization as Biopower." In *Crisis in the Global Economy: Financial Markets, Social Struggles, and New Political Scenarios*, edited by Andrea Fumagalli and Sandro Mezzadra, translated by Jason Francis McGimsy. Los Angeles: Semiotext(e): 119–38.
Lukács, Georg. 1971. *History and Class Consciousness: Studies in Marxist Dialectics*. Translated by Rodney Livingstone. Massachusetts, MIT Press.
MacKenzie, Donald. 2006. *An Engine, Not a Camera: How Financial Models Shape Markets*. Cambridge, MA: MIT Press.

—, Fabian Muniesa, and Lucia Siu, eds. 2007. *Do Economists Make Markets?: On the Performativity of Economics*. Princeton NJ: Princeton University Press.

Maier, Corinne. 2005. *Bonjour Laziness*. Translated by Greg Mosse. Sussex, UK: Orion.

Mamdani, Mahmood. 2009. *Saviors and Survivors: Darfur, Politics, and the War on Terror*. New York: Pantheon.

Mandel, Ernest. 1998. *Late Capitalism*. London: Verso.

Marazzi, Christian. 2010. "The Violence of Financial Capitalism." In *Crisis in the Global Economy: Financial Markets, Social Struggles, and New Political Scenarios*, edited by Andrea Fumagalli and Sandro Mezzadra, translated by Jason Francis McGimsy.– Los Angeles: Semiotext(e): 17–59.

—2008. *Capital and Language: From the New Economy to the War Economy*. Translated by Gregory Conti. Los Angeles: Semiotext(e).

Marcuse, Herbert. 1964. *One-Dimensional Man*. Translated by Andy Blunden. London: Ark Paperbacks.

—1964. *One-Dimensional Man*. Boston: Beacon Press.

Markusen, Ann. 2006. "Urban Development and the Politics of a Creative Class: Evidence from the Study of Artists." *Environment and Planning* 38(10): 1921–40.

Marshall, David. 1988. *The Surprising Effects of Sympathy: Marivau, Diderot, Rousseau, and Mary Shelley*. Chicago: University of Chicago Press.

Martin, Randy. 2007. *An Empire of Indifference: American War and the Financial Logic of Risk Management*. Durham NC and London: Duke University Press.

—2002. *Financialization of Daily Life*. Philadelphia, PA: Temple University Press.

Marx, Karl. 1993. *Grundrisse: Foundations of the Critique of Political Economy*. Translated by Martin Nicolaus. London, New York: Penguin Books/New Left Review.

—1991. "Excerpts from James Mill's 'Elements of Political Economy'" in *Early Writings* [1844]. Translated by R. Livingstone and G. Benton. Harmondsworth: Penguin: 259–78.

—1990. *Capital, Volume I*. Translated by Ben Fowkes. New York: Penguin.

—1982. *Capital, Volume III*. Translated by David Fernbach. New York: Penguin.

—1978a. "The Class Struggles in France" [1850]. In *The Marx-Engels Reader*, edited by Robert C. Tucker. New York: W. W. Norton & Company: 586–93.

—1978b. "Manifesto of the Communist Party" [1848]. In *The Marx–Engels Reader*, edited by Robert C. Tucker. New York: W. W. Norton & Company: 469–500.

—1978c. "Inaugural Address of the Working Men's International Association" [1864]. In *The Marx–Engels Reader*, edited by Robert C. Tucker. New York: W. W. Norton & Company: 512–19.

—1978d. "The Eighteenth Brumaire of Louis Bonaparte" [1852]. In *The Marx–Engels Reader*, edited by Robert C. Tucker. New York: W. W. Norton & Company: 594–617.

—1977. *Capital: A Critique of Political Economy, Volume I* [1867/1871]. Translated by Ben Fowkes. New York: Vintage Books.

—1973. *Grundrisse: Foundations of the Critique of Political Economy* [1857–8]. Translated by Martin Nicolaus. New York: Vintage Books.

—1973. *Grundrisse: Foundations of the Critique of Political Economy* [1857–8]. Translated by Martin Nicolaus. New York: Random House.
—1972. *Theories of Surplus Value*. Vol. II. Progress Publishers, Moscow.
—1964. *The Economic and Philosophical Manuscripts of 1844*. Edited by Drik Struik, translated by Martin Milligan. New York: International Publishers.
—1959. *Economic and Philosophical Manuscripts of 1844* [1932]. Translated by Martin Mulligan. Moscow: Progress Publishers.
—1933. *The German Ideology* [1845–6]. Translated by R. Pascal. New York: International Publishers.
—and Frederic Engels. 2002. *The Communist Manifesto* [1848]. New York: Penguin.
—1983. *Die Deutsche Ideologie*. In *Marx-Engels Werke, Band 3*. Berlin: Dietz Verlag.
—1975. *The German Ideology* [1845–7]. In *Karl Marx–Friedrich Engels Collected Works*, volume 5. Translated by Clemens Dutt et al. London: Lawrence and Wishart.
—1968. "Manifest der Komunistischen Partei." In *Marx–Engels Werke, Band 4*. Berlin: Dietz Verlag.
Maslow, Abraham. 1987. *Motivation and Personality* [1954], 3rd edition. New York: Harper and Row.
McCann, Eugene. 2007. "Inequality and Politics in the Creative City Region: Questions of Livability and State Strategy." *International Journal of Urban and Regional Research* 31(7): 188–96.
McCloskey, Dierdre. 1995. "Metaphors Economists Live By." *Social Research* 62(2): 215–37.
McGoun, Elton G. 2003. "Finance Models as Metaphors." *International Review of Financial Analysis* 12(4): 421–33.
McGranahan, David, and Timothy Wojan. 2007. "Recasting the Creative Class to Examine Growth Processes in Rural and Urban Counties." *Regional Studies* 41(2): 197–216.
McGuigan, Jim. 2005. "Neoliberalism, Culture, and Policy." *International Journal of Cultural Policy* 11(3): 229–41.
McLuhan, Marshal. 1969. "Playboy Interview." *Playboy Magazine* March: 53–74, 158.
McMahon, Darrin. 2006. *Happiness: A History*. New York: Atlantic Monthly Press.
McNally, David. 2011. *Global Slump: The Economics and Politics of Crisis and Resistance*. Oakland, CA: PM Press.
McRobbie, Angela. 2002. "Fashion Culture: Creative Work, Female Individualization." *Feminist Review* 71: 52–62.
Mee, Jon. 2003. *Romanticism, Enthusiasm, and Regulation: Poetics and the Policing of Culture in the Romantic Period*. Oxford: Oxford University Press.
Michels, Robert. 1915. *Political Parties: A Sociological Study of the Oligarchical Tendencies of Modern Democracy* [1911]. New York: Hearst International.
Milewski, Terry. 2012. "Occupy Davos?" http://www.cbc.ca/news/politics/story/2012/01/25/pol-vp-milewski-davos-harper.html; accessed 6 February 2012.
Minns, Richard. 2001. *The Cold War in Welfare*. London, New York: Verso.
Mitchell, W. J. T. 2005. *What Do Pictures Want?: The Lives and Loves of Images*. Chicago: University of Chicago Press.

Moore, John. 2000. "Moore's Laws of Bureaucracy." *Useful Fools*, October 15. http://www.tinyvital.com/Misc/Lawsburo.htm; accessed 15 November 2011.

Moretti, Franco. 1983. "Dialectic of Fear." In *Signs Taken for Wonders*. Translated by Susan Fischer, David Forgcas, and David Miller. London: Verso: 83–208.

Morgensen, Scott Lauria. 2011. "The Biopolitics of Settler Colonialism: Right Here, Right Now." *Settler Colonial Studies* 1(1): 52–76.

Mullan Phil. 2000. *The Imaginary Time Bomb: Why an Ageing Population is not a Social Problem*. London: IB Tauris and Company.

National Council of Elders. 2011. "Statement of Solidarity." *The National Council of Elders*. http://nationalcouncilofelders.com/statement.html; accessed 5 January 2012.

Nealon, Jeffrey Thomas. 2008. *Foucault Beyond Foucault: Power and its Intensifications since 1984*. Stanford, CA: Stanford University Press.

Neilson, Brett. 2009. "Ageing and Globalisation in a Moment of So-Called Crisis." *Health Sociology Review* 18(4): 349–63.

—2003. "Globalization and the Biopolitics of Aging." *The Centennial Review* 3(2): 161–86.

Neocleous, Mark. 2003. "The Political Economy of the Dead: Marx's Vampires." *History of Political Thought* 24(4): 668–84.

Niedzviecki, Hal. 2004. *Hello, I'm Special: How Individuality became the New Conformity*. Toronto: Penguin.

Nietzsche, Friedrich. 1977. "Truth and Lie in an Extra-Moral Sense [1873]," In *The Portable Nietzsche*, translated and edited by Walter Kaufmann. New York: Penguin Books: 42–7.

Nkrumah, Kwame. 1980. *Neo-Colonialism: The Last Stage of Imperialism*. New York: International.

Oakley, Kate. 2004. "Not So Cool Britannia." *International Journal of Cultural Studies* 7(7): 67–77.

Obama, Barack. 2012. "State of the Future." http://www.nytimes.com/interactive/2012/01/24/us/politics/state-of-the-union-2012-video-transcript.html; accessed 6 February 2012.

O'Hagan, Ellie Mae. 2011. "Topshop's Sloganeering T-shirts are a Bad Sign for Students." *The Guardian*, 8 July 2011. http://www.guardian.co.uk/commentisfree/2011/jul/08/topshop-tshirts-student-protest; accessed 8 July 2011.

O'Neill, John. 2004. *Civic Capitalism: The State of Childhood*. Toronto: University of Toronto Press.

—2002. "Televideo Ergo Sum: Some Hypotheses on the Specular Functions of the Media." In *Plato's Cave: Television and its Discontents*. Cresskill, NJ: Hampton Press Inc: 169–92.

Ortner, Sherry. 2011. "On Neoliberalism." *Anthropology of This Century* 1. http://aotcpress.com/articles/neoliberalism/; accessed 30 January 2012.

Palsgrave, Jehan (John). 2003. *L'éclaircissement de la langue française* [1530]. Paris: Champion.

Park, Ed. 2008. *Personal Days*. New York: Random House.

Parkinson, C. Northcote. 1955. "Parkinson's Law." *The Economist*, November 19.

Peck, Jamie. 2011. "Creative Moments: Working Culture through Municipal Socialism and Neoliberal Urbanism." In *Mobile Urbanism: Cities and Policy*

Making in the Global Age, edited by Eugene McCann and Kevin Ward, 41–70. Minneapolis and London: University of Minnesota Press.

—2010. *Constructions of Neoliberal Reason*. Oxford: Oxford University Press.

—2005. "Struggling with the Creative Class." *International Journal of Urban and Regional Research* 29(4): 740–70.

Perelman, Michael. 2011. *The Invisible Handcuffs of Capitalism: How Market Tyranny Stifles the Economy by Stunting Workers*. New York: Monthly Review Press.

Peterson, Peter G. 1999. "Gray Dawn: The Global Aging Crisis." *Foreign Affairs*, January/February 1999: 42–55.

Pfau, Thomas. 2006. *Romantic Moods: Trauma, Paranoia, Melancholy, 1790–1840*. Baltimore: Johns Hopkins University Press.

Phillips, Peter J. 2010. "Financial Crisis of Metaphor." *The Review of Austrian Economics* 23(3): 223–42.

Pink, Daniel. 2004. "The MFA Is The New MBA." *The Harvard Business Review*, February 1: 21–2.

Pinsof, William. 2002. "The Death of 'Till Death Us Do Part': The Transformation of Pair-Bonding in the 20th Century." *Family Process* 41(2): 135–57.

Plato. 1997. "Republic." In *Plato: Complete Works*, edited by John M. Cooper. Indianapolis and Cambridge: Hackett Publishing: 971–1223.

Play Time. DVD. Directed by Jacques Tati. 1967. New York: Criterion, 2001.

Plunkett, Daniel. 2011. "On Place Attachments in Virtual Worlds." *World Leisure Journal* 53(3): 168–78.

Poovey, Mary. 2009. *Genres of the Credit Economy: Mediating Value in Eighteenth- and Nineteenth-Century Britain*. Chicago: University of Chicago Press.

Porter, M. E., 2000. "Location, Clusters, and Company Strategy." In *The Oxford Handbook of Economic Geography*, edited by Gordon L. Clark, Maryann P. Feldman and Meric S. Gertler. Oxford: Oxford University Press, 253–74.

Porter, Roy. 2001. *Enlightenment: Britain and the Creation of the Modern World*. London: Allen Lane.

Pournelle, Jerry. 2005. "The Iron Law of Bureaucracy." *Chaos Manor*, December 14. http://www.jerrypournelle.com/archives2/archives2mail/mail392.html#iron; accessed 15 November 2011.

Prashad, Vijay. 2008. *The Darker Nations: A People's History of the Third World*. New York and London: New Press.

Putnam, Robert. 2000. *Bowling Alone: The Collapse and Revival of American Community*. New York: Simon and Schuster.

Rampage, Cheryl. 2002. "Marriage in the 20th Century: A Feminist Perspective." *Family Process* 41(2): 261–8.

Rancière, Jacques. 2010. *Dissensus: On Politics and Aesthetics*. London: Continuum.

—2004a. *The Politics of Aesthetics*. Translated by Gabriel Rockhill. London: Continuum.

—2004b. *The Philosopher and His Poor*. Translated by John Drury et al. Durham, NC: Duke University Press.

—1989. *The Nights of Labor: The Worker's Dream in Nineteenth-Century France*. Translated by John Drury. Philadelphia: Temple University Press.

Rausch, Stephen and Cynthia Negrey. 2006. "Does the Creative Engine Run?: A Consideration of the Effect of Creative Class on Economic Strength and Growth." *Journal of Urban Affairs* 28(5): 473–89.
Reinsborough, Patrick. 2011. "Giant Whispers: Narrative Power, Radical Imagination and a Future Worth Fighting For ..." *Affinities: A Journal of Radical Theory, Culture and Action* 4(2): 66–78.
Ricoeur, Paul. 1978. *The Rule of Metaphor: Multi-Disciplinary Studies in the Creation of Meaning in Language.* London: Routledge.
Rorty, Richard. 1995. "The End of Leninism and History as Comic Frame." In *History and the Idea of Progress*, edited by Arthur Melzer. Ithaca, NY: Cornell University Press: 211–26.
Ross, Andrew. 2009. *Nice Work If You Can Get It: Life and Labor in Precarious Times.* New York: New York University Press.
—2009. "Love Thy Labor." *Bookforum*, Fall.
Ross, Kristin. 1995. *Fast Cars, Clean Bodies: Decolonization and the Reordering of French Culture.* Cambridge MA: MIT Press.
Rothbard, Murray N. 1995. "Bureaucracy and the Civil Service in the United States." *Journal of Libertarian Studies* 11(2): 3–75.
Russell, Bertrand. 2004. *In Praise of Idleness: And Other Essays* [1932]. London: Routledge.
Sauvé, Roger. 2011. "The Current State of Canadian Family Finances 2010 Report." *The Vanier Institute of the Family.*http://www.vifamily.ca/node/783; accessed 14 November 2011.
Scott, Allen. 2006. "Creative Cities: Conceptual Issues and Policy Questions." *Journal of Urban Affairs* 28(1): 1–17.
Scull, Andrew. 1991. "Psychiatry and Social Control in the Nineteenth and Twentieth Centuries." *History of Psychiatry* 2: 149–69.
Seccombe, Wally. 1983. "Marxism and Demography." *New Left Review* I/137: 22–47. Thinking Ahead Group. 2011. "Global Pension Assets Study: 2011." *Tower Watson*, February, 2011.http://www.towerswatson.com/assets/pdf/3761/Global-Pensions-Asset-Study-2011.pdf; accessed 20 July 2011.
Shorter, Edward. 1997. *A History of Psychiatry: From the Era of the Asylum to the Age of Prozac.* New York: Wiley.
Simmel, Georg. 2009. *Sociology: Inquiries into the Construction of Social Forms* [1908]. Translated by A. J. Blasi, A. K. Jacobs, and M. Kanjiranthinkal. Leiden and Boston: Brill.
—1992. *Soziologie: Untersuchungen über die Formen der Vergesellschaftung.* Frankfurt am Main: Suhrkamp.
—1971. "The Metropolis and Mental Life" [1903]. In *On Individuality and Social Forms*, edited by Donald N. Levine. Chicago: University of Chicago: 324–39.
Slater, Tom. 2006. "The Eviction of Critical Perspectives from Gentrification Research." *International Journal of Urban and Regional Research* 30(4): 737–57.
Sloterdijk, Peter. 1987. *Critique of Cynical Reason.* Minneapolis: University of Minnesota Press.
Smith, Dorothy. 1999. "The Ruling Relations." In *Writing the Social: Critique, Theory, and Investigations.* Toronto: University of Toronto Press: 73–95.
Soja, Edward. 1989. *Postmodern Geographies: The Reassertion of Space in Critical Social Theory.* London and New York: Verso.

Soni, Vivavsan. 2010. *Mourning Happiness: Narrative and the Politics of Modernity.* Ithaca, NY: Cornell University Press.
Soper, Kate. 1993. "A Theory of Human Need." *New Left Review* I 197 (January–February): 113–28.
Soto, Hernando de, and Francis Cheneval. 2006. *Realizing Property Rights.* New York: Ruffer and Rub.
Sovereign Wealth Fund Institute. "Sovereign Wealth Fund Ranking: February, 2012." Revision. www.swfinstitute.org/fund-rankings/; accessed 29 November 2011.
Stanford, Jim. 2008. *Economics for Everyone: A Short Guide to the Economics of Capitalism.* Halifax, NS: Fernwood Publishing.
Strange, Susan. 1997. *Casino Capitalism*, 2nd edition. Manchester: Manchester University Press.
Sullivan's Travels. DVD. Directed by Preston Sturges. 1942. New York: Criterion, 2001.
Targ, Harry. 2006. *Challenging Late Capitalism, Neo-Liberal Globalization, and Militarism: Building a Progressive Majority.* Lulu.com. www.lulu.com/content/315778; accessed 30 January 2012.
Tepper, Steven. 2002. "Creative Assets and the Creative Economy." *Journal of Arts Management, Law, and Society* 32(2): 159–68.
The Social Network. DVD. Directed by David Fincher. 2010. Los Angeles, California: Columbia Pictures, 2010.
Thinking Ahead Group. 2011. "Global Pension Assets Study: 2011." *Tower Watson*, February, 2011. http://www.towerswatson.com/assets/pdf/3761/Global-Pensions-Asset-Study-2011.pdf; accessed 11 February 2012.
Thomas, June M. and Julia Darnton. 2006. "Social Diversity and Economic Development in the Metropolis." *Journal of Planning Literature* 21(2): 153–68.
Thrift, Nigel. 2005. *Knowing Capitalism.* London: SAGE.
—2000. "It's the Little Things." In *Geopolitical Traditions: A Century of Geopolitical Thought*, edited by K. Dodds and D. Atkinson. London: Routledge: 380–87.
Trotter, Thomas. 1976. *A View of the Nervous Temperament* [1807]. New York: Arno.
Turbayne, Colin. 1962. *The Myth of Metaphor.* Columbia, SC: University of South Carolina Press.
United Nations Population Division. 2002. "World Population Ageing: 1950–2050." *United Nations Department of Economic and Social Affairs.* https://www.un.org/esa/population/publications/worldageing19502050/; accessed 20 July 2011.
(un)Occupy Albuquerque. "Why (un)?" *(un)Occupy Abuquerque.* http://www.unoccupyabq.org/why-un/; accessed 15 July 2011.
Verdery, Katherine. 2003. The Vanishing Hectare: Property and Value in Postsocialist Transylvania. Ithaca, NY: Cornell University Press.
Virno, Paolo. 2004. *A Grammar of the Multitude: For an Analysis of Contemporary Forms of Life.* Translated by Isabella Bertoletti, James Cascaito, and Andrea Casson. Los Angeles: Semiotext(e).
—2001. "Labour and Language." Translated by Arianna Bove.http://www.generation-online.org/t/labourlanguage.htm; accessed 1 December 2011.
Walia, Harsha. 2011. "Letter to Occupy Together Movement." *Rabble.ca*, 14

October 2011. http://rabble.ca/news/2011/10/acknowledgement-occupations-occupied-land-essential; accessed 14 October 2011.
Weber, Max. 2002. *The Protestant Ethic and the Spirit of Capitalism* [1903–5]. Translated by Stephen Kalberg. Los Angeles: Roxbury Publishing.
—1958. *The Protestant Ethic and the Spirit of Capitalism*. Translated by Talcott Parsons. New York: Scribners.
—1920. *Gesammelte Aufsätze zur Religionssoziologie Band I* [1920–21]. Edited by Marianne Weber and Johannes Winkelmann. Tübingen: J. C. B. Mohr (Paul Siebeck).
Williams, Billy. 2011. "'A Nightmare on the Minds of the Living': Capitalism is Still the Keyword in Cultural Studies." *Culture Critique* 2(1). http://ccjournal.cgu.edu; accessed 30 January 2012.
Williams, Jeffrey. 2009. "The Pedagogy of Debt." In *Towards a Global Autonomous University*, edited by the Edu-factory Collective. Brooklyn, NY: Autonomedia: 89–96.
Wills, Garry. 1978. *Inventing America: Jefferson's Declaration of Independence*. Garden City, NY: Doubleday.
Wilson, H. T. 2002. *Capitalism after Postmodernism: Neo-conservatism, Legitimacy, and the Theory of Public Capital*. Leiden, The Netherlands: Brill.
Wolff, Richard and Stephen Resnick. 1987. *Economics: Marxian versus Neoclassical*. Baltimore: Johns Hopkins University Press.
World Bank. 1994. "Averting the Old Age Crisis: Policies to Protect the Old and Promote Growth." http://go.worldbank.org/OEU6RWFNI0; accessed 20 July 2011.
Yee, Jessica. 2011. "Occupy Wall Street: The Game of Colonialism and the Left." *Rabble.ca*, October 1, 2011. http://rabble.ca/columnists/2011/10/occupy-wall-street-game-colonialism-and-left; accessed 4 December 2011.
Zelizer, Viviana. 2011. *Economic Lives: How Culture Shapes the Economy*. Princeton, NJ: Princeton University Press
Žižek, Slavoj. 2009. *The Essential Žižek*. London: Verso.
—2008. *In Defence of Lost Causes*. New York: Verso.
—2007. *How to Read Lacan*. New York: W. W. Norton and Company.
—2006a. "Against the Populist Temptation." *Critical Inquiry* 32 (Spring): 551–75.
—2006b. "Freud Lives!" *The London Review of Books* 28(10) (May 25): 34.

Index